Women in
Eternity
Women of
Zion

Women in *Eternity* Women of *Zion*

by

Alma Don Sorensen
and
Valerie Hudson Cassler

CFI
Springville, Utah

ISBN: 1-55517-743-3
e.1

Published by Cedar Fort Inc.
www.cedarfort.com

Distributed by:

Cover design © 2003 by Lyle Mortimer
Cover and insert art © 2003 by David E. Cassler

Printed in the United States of America
10 9 8 7 6 5 4 3 2 1

Printed on acid-free paper

Library of Congress Control Number: 2004100279

We dedicate this book to the women we love . . .

☙ Necia, Ada, Kathryn, Cynthia, Ruth, and Peggy
☙ Ariel, Marion, and Roberta

Facing page:

"The New and Everlasting Covenant of Marriage"
Oil on panel, by David E. Cassler

Prints are available from the artist
(801-226-5508, or 592 East 200 North, Orem, Utah 84097)

Table of Contents

Preface

Our labors on this book began in 1993. That time seems far distant now, for we have been through several drafts of what came to be the volume you hold in your hands today. In this preface, we would like to introduce you to the book, as well as thank the many people who have helped make it better.

Valerie spent the year of 1992 and part of 1993 in great pain over the issue of equality between men and women in the gospel. She had never really felt this pain before and the intensity and suddenness with which it hit astounded her. For almost a year and a half she walked around as if the skin of her body had been rubbed raw by sandpaper. Things she never noticed before—even little things—caused her agony of soul. As she looks back on that time, she sees now the intervention of God in that pain. She feels God gave her that pain as a gift so that she would be motivated to begin this book project, and so that she would know when what we had written had achieved the power to heal such pain. She would like you to know that God's gift of pain accomplished the purposes for which it was given, and that now she is free of it entirely.

In her time of pain, she turned to Don for assistance. Don was a colleague in her department, but more than that, he had been a powerful force in her life twenty years earlier as her professor. The student-teacher relationship thus formed the basis for a meaningful collegial relationship. Don had for many years made issues of equality and Zion a matter of personal study, including scriptural study. These issues also arose in the classes he taught on law and morality. Beginning with a first paper in 1978, he has written much in this area. Finally, as a Latter-day Saint man he feels especially concerned about equality, Zion, and gender issues as they affect Latter-day Saint society. For several years, Don and Valerie also lived two blocks away from each other and attended the same ward.

As we met in Don's office, surrounded by piles of books on political philosophy and ethics, Don began to explicate how the ideas he had been developing on equality applied to the questions with which Valerie struggled. Valerie added her own insights and understandings. After we did a lot of pondering and a lot of searching, answers began to come, some more slowly and some more quickly.

We were asked to present a talk at the 1994 Women's Conference held at BYU, where the response was overwhelmingly positive. Though our session was targeted towards what was thought would be a small audience—faithful women who had some difficulty understanding the equality of men and women in the gospel—the attendees wound up filling a good-sized concert hall. It became clear to us that these ideas had healing power not only for a few, but for many. Some women attending even asked us to go further and apply our insights to issues we had not mentioned, such as polygamy.

It was after this experience that we began to think about writing a book manuscript. We suppose we approached this rather innocently. We decided to write the book to our satisfaction, obtain feedback from good and faithful members of the Church, revise it, and then attempt to get it published. We had no desire to make a profit on the book, and we resolved to self-publish it if no publisher of good reputation would take it on. If you hold in your hand a bound volume, then know that somehow a way was made for us.

Now that you understand the origins of the book, let us tell you something about it. Many have asked us who the audience is for the book. It is primarily for the women we met in 1994, and all those like them: good, faithful Latter-day Saint women who have at some point felt a certain amount of pain because they are not always able to articulate a coherent vision of how they stand as equals with men in the Church and in the eternities. Of course, all men and women would profit from such an articulation, and we invite all to read it. But we especially aim our writing towards those who need to feel a healing touch on these issues.

We would like to introduce two caveats to our readership, however. Neither Don nor Valerie speak from ecclesiastical authority on these issues. We have no authority to "write by way of commandment," but rather we write "by wisdom" alone (D&C 28:5). Any errors or misinterpretations about gospel doctrine in our writings are ours alone, and are no reflection upon the Church of Jesus Christ of Latter-day Saints. Please reconcile everything we say with your own reading of the scriptures and modern revelation and teachings by those called by God to speak to the Church. Discard anything we write that cannot be so reconciled.

Our second caveat has reference to our backgrounds as academics. Understand that the authors of this work are two professors of political science. Indeed, one is a professor of political philosophy. Our style is a bit less conversational than that to which our readers may be accustomed. We have endeavored to write a full and in-depth explication of these matters, and we have done so in the way that we know how. We wanted to write such a detailed and in-depth treatment of these issues because we know there are those who hunger for just such a treatment. Their experience of the controversy surrounding these issues creates the need for depth in order to find satisfying answers. We understand there will be others who will find that such a detailed treatment taxes their patience. We only hope that you will bear with us for the sake of the ideas that you will find within these pages. In our experience thus far, those who have had serious questions or who have felt pain about these issues have been sufficiently motivated to make it through the entire volume. Perhaps those who follow after us, writing in the future when the ideas discussed in this work may be more commonly understood and practiced, will be able to write about them more succinctly and simply, and we look forward to that day.

The style of the book is also unusual. We each wrote half of the book: Don wrote Chapters Two, Three, Four, and Eight, and Valerie wrote Chapters One, Five, Six, and Seven. We have made no attempt to homogenize the chapters so that the voices became indistinguishable. Rather, we want you to hear both voices—the voice of a man and the voice of a woman, speaking separately but also unitedly on these issues. In a sense, the style of this book is symbolic of what we envision for men and women as equal partners in the great works of God.

Finally, we are overjoyed that many persons took the time to read all or part of our manuscript and make useful comments. Despite doing so, the manuscript may still contain errors—and we want you to know that the errors are ours alone and no fault of those who gave us feedback. Indeed, in one or two cases, our reviewers may actually have disagreed with us, so the appearance of a name on this list does not mean that the person necessarily endorses what we have written. Nevertheless, we are grateful to them all. Specifically, we would like to thank Richard Holzapfel, Allison Ellsworth, Dan Belnap, Regina Ellis, Natalie Harris, Mae Blanch, Kathleen Bahr, Howard Bahr, Kristie Seawright, Jill Mulvay Derr, Karen Hyer, Tom Pearcy, Shauna Pearcy, Don Norton, Richard Andrew Young, Ronald Hinckley, Thomas Rogers, Eugene England, Stephen Ricks, Shirley Ricks, John Sorenson, Helen Christianson, James Gordon, Ida Smith, Diane Spangler, Ron Esplin, Cheri Loveless, Becky Schulthies, C.K. Edwards, Beverly Campbell, Doris Dant, Don Parry, Robert Millet, Larry Dahl, Paul Hoskisson, Richard Davis, Mark Wrathall, William Hamblin, Christie Manwaring, and Erika Whitmer. David B. Magleby, as chair of the department of political science at BYU, generously supplied photocopy money during the focus group stage of manuscript preparation. Two special readers, whose insights were very important to our work and to whom we express great gratitude, shall remain anonymous. A special thank you for unflagging emotional support when we were flagging goes to Bonnie Ballif-Spanvill and B. Kent Harrison, who also gave us detailed and useful suggestions for improvement. April Isbell Fife cheerfully and diligently tracked down sources for us at a moment's notice, and her sunny spirit infected us all, for which we are grateful. Stacie Long helped put the manuscript in final form.

Andrea den Boer deserves a paragraph all her own. Andrea has been our ministering angel in the last stages of manuscript preparation. She lived through countless revisions, meetings, and phone conversations; she battled software glitches and viruses on our behalf; she searched computer databases to find appropriate material for us. But Andrea did more than this. Many times the spirit of a sentence or section of the manuscript was simply not right. Other times, important issues were not given their full due. Andrea alerted us to these and we feel she was guided in this. It is no exaggeration to say that this book would not exist, and certainly would not be what it is today, without Andrea. May God bless her for her efforts.

Last, our families played an extremely important role in the evolution of this manuscript. Valerie's husband, David, and Don's wife, Necia, read the manuscript and gave excellent suggestions. Indeed, without their equal partnership with us as spouses, we could never have outlined the wonderful vision of the relationship between man and woman as it was intended by God. David and Necia gave us the ground in which these ideas could be rooted firmly and without equivocation. We know this wonderful and equal partnership between man and woman about which the scriptures and modern revelation speak is true because we live it in our lives every day with our beloved eternal companions. Furthermore, they gave us emotional support, as well as time and space to write. Their sacrifices on our behalf burn brightly within our hearts. And finally, Valerie would like to thank her daughter, Ariel. If Valerie did not have such a wonderful, precocious, and intelligent young female spirit as a daughter, where would all the "Ariel's Questions" that are sprinkled throughout this book and guided the writing of it, have come from? Thank you, "little grandma," for teaching your mother so many things by your excellent questions.

Valerie Hudson Cassler
A. Don Sorensen
February, 2002
Provo, Utah

Addendum, September 2003

We are grateful to Lee Nelson and Cedar Fort Inc. for their vision in offering to publish this manuscript.

We also wish to recognize those individuals and entities that made the publication of this book possible; we are indebted to you, and you are forever in our hearts:

The Women's Research Institute, Brigham Young University
Michele Welch
Allan and Kristie Garber
Roger and Colleen Thompson
Diane Spangler
Bonnie Ballif-Spanvill
April and Stephen Fife
Kelly Patterson
Donna Lee Bowen
Richard McClendon
Rachel and Jonathan Ellis
B. Kent Harrison
June and Mel Mabey
Bill and Brecken Swartz
Suzanne Hendrix and family
Regina Ellis
Allison and Kevin Ellsworth
Jerry Kurtz
Howard and Kathleen Bahr
John Pendlebury
Ken Hulet
Natalie Harris

Prefatory Note on Word Usage

In the United States, there is much confusion over several terms which are central to our thesis. The most important of these is "equality" and its adjective "equal." Given the litigious nature of our society, it is particularly in the legal arena that the word "equality" has come to be defined as "identical" or "same."

This type of definition, we believe, harms women. We do not believe that women are identical to men. (However, we also do not believe that women and men are opposites; in our view men and women are in many ways alike, and in a few respects very different.[1]) If women are treated identically to men, they are often treated inequitably.

By resorting to the adjective "equal," we can begin to recapture a more satisfactory definition for "equality." Though women and men are not identical, think of all they are equal in:

- equal in blessings
- equal partners
- equal in power
- equal in intelligence
- equal in wisdom
- equal in dignity
- equal in respect
- equal in counsel
- equal in consent
- equal in agency
- equal in value
- equal in potential
- equal in fullness when exalted
- equal in virtue
- equal in spirituality
- equal in spiritual gifts

> ❧ equal in temporal things
> ❧ equal heirs with Christ

With this perspective, we can more properly comprehend that two individuals need not be identical to be equal, especially in the things that matter most. Can we not, then, reconfigure the noun that comes from the adjective? Can we not insist that the definition of "equality" is "to be equal even though there exist eternal differences"? Ultimately, it is satanic to insist equality can only exist in the context of "sameness." It is divine to envision equality even in the context of differences. In the second case, differences can be celebrated and valued, whereas in the first case, any differences become obstacles that must be erased. Therefore, throughout this book, when we speak of "equality," we are speaking of this more satisfactory definition of the term.

Second, the word "gender" often causes confusion. Lately, the word has been used to refer to a purely social and changeable construction based primarily, but not entirely, on biology. However, this clearly cannot be the definition of the term most useful to Church members. When the First Presidency says that gender is eternal, we feel confident that they are not asserting that society's contemporary ideas about what is proper male and female behavior are eternal. Indeed, those social constructions may be so off base that one must discard them before coming to an adequate understanding of how men and women are to relate to one another. Therefore, throughout this book, when we speak of "gender," it might be useful for certain readers to translate the word as "sex." However, we also embrace the view that what biological sex differences mean here and in eternity is larger than just the biology itself. We believe that God has a "construction" of sex, and so we might say that God is the author of "gender." If there were some way for readers to disassociate "gender" as a construct created and changed over time and place by mortals, and "gender" as a construct upheld and never changed by God, then the First Presidency's statement on the eternal nature of gender can be more accurately understood. If readers can accomplish this disassociation, the term "gender" as used throughout this book should be understood to mean this God-authored, unchangeable construction of "gender."

When we speak, then, of "gender equality," the reader should translate this as "a state of equality (defined as above) between the sexes in the context of eternal differences between them."

The reader may notice that we did not attempt to develop an overall, coherent theory of equality based on scripture which might satisfy the philosophical or legal mind. We are not opposed to such an effort, but we decided it would not be appropriate in this book. Hopefully, we have remained faithful, at least for the most part, to what some scriptures say about gender equality by not elaborating overly much as we went along.

Notes

1. As Sheri L. Dew, former member of the Relief Society Presidency has put it, "[Satan] would have us believe men and women are so alike that our unique gifts are not necessary, or so different we can never hope to understand each other. Neither is true." "It is Not Good for Man or Woman to Be Alone," Sheri L. Dew, *Ensign*, November 2001: 12-14.

"The New and Everlasting Covenant of Marriage" by David E. Cassler

CHAPTER 1

Ariel's Question

by
Valerie Hudson Cassler

*In the effort to give good and comforting answers to
the young questioners whom we love, we very often
arrive at good and comforting answers for ourselves.*
— *Ruth Goode*

I remember well the day I knew I would have to write something about women and the gospel for my daughter's sake. I was on sabbatical in New Zealand, pregnant and ill with my third child. A colleague had given me a news clipping, which I had taken home and just finished reading. It told the story of Samira, a four-year-old Bosnian girl who had been gang-raped by Chetniks (Bosnian Serb soldiers). I was weeping and my then six-year-old daughter, Ariel, came to find out why. In the anguish of my soul, and not knowing precisely why, I felt I should read her the article. When I finished, Ariel, with tears dripping down her cheeks, asked me in a voice of innocent and overwhelming pain, "Mommy, why did God make men stronger than women?"

As I have pondered her question, I see more and more why it is the essential question for those women who struggle to understand the fullness of Christ's gospel, whether they are in or out of the Church. There are many women who experience no struggle in this regard, but there are also many who do. We rejoice for the first group and we are moved by the situation of the second. This chapter, and Ariel's question, are relevant to the concerns of our sisters who have wrestled in their hearts over gender issues. As Elder Jeffrey R. Holland expressed it, "One day, and we pray sooner rather than later, we will enjoy the perfect peace that surpasseth understanding—in gender

2 — Women in Eternity, Women of Zion
issues as well as every other matter troubled by human inade-
quacy."[1] We hope that this book, prompted by the innocent
question of a six-year-old Latter-day Saint girl, will in some
small measure help speed the coming of that day.

What Ariel was asking is why differences between men and
women are such that men are able to usurp power over women,
against their wills, in a way that cannot be considered "fair" or
reflective of "equality." These differences—especially those
concerning the biology of childbearing—have led, in a
predictable and even natural fashion, to male dominance over
women in the fallen world.

If the proverbial martian were to arrive on this planet, one
of the first things that would strike it would be the clear assignment of power to men. The alien would note that very few
rulers, legislators, judges, and ecclesiastical leaders are
women; and that women "comprise half the population,
perform two-thirds of the world's work, receive one-tenth of
the world's wages, and own one-hundredth of the world's property."[2] The alien would note the prevalence of physical and
sexual abuse of women by men, even in nations where ideology
decrees men and women to be equals. It would note how, for
most women, men determine where they will live, whether they
can leave the house, what they must wear, when they will have
sexual intercourse, whether they will receive health care, whom
they will marry, and in some cultures, whether a woman will
live or die. These things, which we so take for granted that we
almost can no longer see them, would be clear and striking to
the alien.

If the enlargement of male power over females has
proceeded from differences between the sexes, and if God is the
author of such differences, then one could easily wonder, as did
little Ariel, why God appears to have purposely dealt men a
better hand. Indeed, some cultures do believe that men are
favored creatures in the sight of God, and that to be born a
woman is testimony that one was not especially righteous or
valiant in a former life. Being born a woman is seen as a curse
from God, justified on the basis of one's spiritual inferiority.

If one's soul rejects this conclusion—if one's soul cries out that "the one being is as precious in His sight as the other" (Jacob 2:21)—then one is left with these questions Ariel essentially asked: How can God be no respecter of persons and yet seemingly be the author of such inequity? How can He be "the source of all fairness"[3] if He set in motion a system that appears to naturally breed oppression of one gender by the other? Is God a respecter of gender? Did he intend for men and women to be unequal? These questions cannot be hidden any longer. Questions about the inequality between men's and women's lives are increasingly being raised in the world, and they will increasingly be raised within the Church, especially among the bright young spirits who come to our families as our daughters. We must address these questions, not run from them or ignore them.

Within the community of Saints the problem of inequality, perceived or real, is greatly ameliorated because of the gospel of Jesus Christ. Indeed, we feel that the gospel of Jesus Christ is the only way whereby true equality between men and women can be fully manifested. The remaining chapters of this book testify of this truth and explain in great detail why it is true. Nevertheless, the problem of inequality is not yet fully resolved in our community even though we have the doctrine to resolve it. This situation has not come about because of lack of concern or comment by our ecclesiastical leaders. The General Authorities of our Church have been quite blunt and plain in their assertions that women and men are equal before the Lord, and that any man who views a woman as anything less is in a state of spiritual suffering.

For example, let us look at three recent statements, out of a multitude of quotations on the same subject, made by our prophet, President Gordon B. Hinckley. In a regional conference in Mexico, the prophet reminded husbands:

Your wives are indispensable to your eternal progress. I hope you will never forget that. There are a few men in this Church—I'm glad there are not very many, but there are a few—who think they are superior to their wives. They had better realize that they will not be able to achieve the highest degree of glory in the celestial kingdom without their wives standing at their side equally beside them. Brethren, they are daughters of God. Treat them as such.[4]

Similarly, at a July 1996 meeting in Kansas City, Missouri, President Hinckley addressed the youth, saying, "I hope there is not a young woman who does not feel she cannot stand equal with her male friends."[5] And in July 1997, the prophet stated, "[E]very man ought to regard his wife as a daughter of God, a daughter who is his equal, with whom he walks side by side. Marvelous is that concept that does not place a woman in an inferior position."[6]

Despite the plainness of these teachings by our prophet and our leaders, practices and beliefs are found in our communities that are not easily reconciled with the doctrine that God is no respecter of persons or of gender. Critics of our church see a sham of gender equality and assert that our religion discriminates against women. However, believers strongly oppose this criticism, trusting the prophet when he proclaims the equality of men and women before God. Yet the unbelievers ask questions that believers may find difficult to answer: How can one reconcile gender equality in the gospel with the impression that men appear to have more power than women because of their ordination to the priesthood? How can one reconcile the early Church practice of polygamy with equal valuation of men and women? Why do scriptures seem to be about men only, with little or no reference to women? Why are we asked to live a patriarchal order, and what does this mean for those eternal beings who, because of gender, will never be patriarchs? Will the inequality experienced here in fallen mortality continue on into eternity? What is the role of women in Zion and in the celestial kingdom? How do men and women stand before God?

Though these are not the same questions the world asks, the root of these questions is the same as that posed by Ariel:

the perceived inequality between men and women. As one mother put it, "I know the Church is true. I also know through personal prayer and study that I am the equal of a man. I just don't know how to explain to my nonmember friends why I can say this, when appearances may sometimes make it look like I am not a man's equal."

Through reason and the Spirit, we must attempt to reconcile our beliefs about gender equality in the gospel and the perceived inequality that a good number of women (and men) in the Church cannot explain to their own satisfaction or to that of their daughters. First, we have faith that such a reconciliation is possible. God is not the author of confusion—the devil is. It is Lucifer who rejoices when the women of Zion are confused about their standing in the kingdom. God holds the understanding that will release us from this confusion and we believe He desires to impart this understanding, if we will only seek to receive it.

Second, we feel that such a reconciliation is imperative. The secret pain of some orthodox and believing Latter-day Saint women, only recently beginning to emerge, must not be allowed to fester without the rest of the Church community actively striving to receive and impart the divine balm of understanding that will bind up these wounds. We are commanded to "mourn with those who mourn; and comfort those who stand in need of comfort" (Mosiah 18:9). To deny that any orthodox and believing Latter-day Saint woman could also feel some pain and confusion about these matters, or to refuse to succor those who do feel pain and confusion, is to refuse to love our neighbor as Christ would wish us to love her.

Last, this reconciliation is a prerequisite to building up and establishing Zion. If establishing Zion is our covenanted mission, then we will fail in that mission if we neglect to address the issue that disturbs the relationship that is the heart of Zion and of the celestial kingdom: the bond between husband and wife in the new and everlasting covenant of marriage.

Unless the community of Saints answers Ariel's questions to the satisfaction of women, then the world and the god of this world, Lucifer, will try to convince them that God is either a liar or fiction. God declares procreation is sacred, but the act of procreation is often used to oppress women in the fallen world and in many cases, sex is presented as a commodity for the pleasure of males. God says that all things should be had in common, but in the fallen world, men typically control material resources, and women and children comprise a disproportionate percentage of the poor. God proclaims the equality of men and women—even the equality of their power—but it may be difficult to experience or perceive equal power in the fallen world.

But God is neither the liar nor the fictional being Satan hopes to convince us He is. Because of this, and because God loves His daughters as much as He loves His sons, we write this book as an offering to our community—an offering of peace, hope, and understanding.

To reach an understanding we must probe more deeply into the sources of women's pain in the world and in the Church. We do so only in cursory fashion in the introduction because our focus is not women's pain, but the balm of Christ's gospel and its power to heal. A fuller exposé of the situation of women in the fallen world is given in Appendix A. Nevertheless, without a prefatory exploration of the malady, the significance of the cure and the sense of urgency we feel about that cure may not be clear.

The Pain of Women in the Fallen World

There is plenty of pain in the fallen world that surrounds us, for men, women, and children alike. Regardless of gender, people suffer because of poverty, racism, language barriers, religious persecution, and so forth. Here, however, we wish to discuss a particular type of pain: the suffering women undergo simply because they are women, and not because they are poor or of a despised ethnic group. This suffering crosses all other divisions between people, because it is countenanced within the most nuclear unit of every society: the family circle. This suffering, found within the very unit that God has ordained for our eternal happiness, provides the rationale for our specific examination of women's pain. To wit, the degree of righteousness found at the very core of society—the family—will be the foundation of every blessing and every curse God gives us (Jacob 3:7-8). Thus the answer to women's suffering is important to men, as well, for if the women are suffering, the men will suffer, too.

Women's pain in the fallen world derives from inequality with men due to differences in power and status between men and women that permeate the cultures of the natural man. This will become apparent in the detailed overview of women's situation in the world that is given in Appendix A. This overview is not pleasant. I have wrestled with how to present the unlovely side of some women's existence in the fallen world to my children and my students. My answer came while reading the ninth chapter of Moroni in the Book of Mormon, specifically Mormon's epistle to his son Moroni. This passage provided an exemplar to me of how such a presentation may be made. Mormon does not shrink from giving his son a graphic catalogue of the atrocities being perpetrated on Nephite and Lamanite women and children by Nephite and Lamanite men in those days (torture, rape, murder, cannibalism). When I was a teenage convert to the Church, I could barely stand to read that chapter because it was so disturbing to me. Why did Mormon include those descriptions? I feel the answer to that question lies in verse 25, where Mormon tells his son:

> *My son, be faithful in Christ; and may not the things which I have written grieve thee, to weigh thee down unto death; but may Christ lift thee up, and may his sufferings and death, and the showing his body unto our fathers, and his mercy and long-suffering, and the hope of his glory and of eternal life, rest in your mind forever.*

It is to Christ, not to the fallen world, where we need to look for our salvation and hope. Though we should strive to make conditions better, as Elder M. Russell Ballard has said, God is the only source of all "fairness,"[7] and Christ is the only source of all hope. Even in the best of lives there would be deadly despair without hope in Christ, and if Christ lives, there cannot be deadly despair even in the worst of lives—even in the worst lives of women. The gospel of Jesus Christ is the only plan that will overcome the Fall and all its tragic consequences, including those that directly and negatively affect the lives of women. The gospel is the strongest and most progressive force for women, period. There can never be true equality for women and men outside of the restored gospel of Jesus Christ.

A Bewildering Chorus of Secular Voices

Numerous men and women in the fallen world have attempted to come to terms with the situation and pain of women. Indeed, there are so many voices on the "feminist question" that the chorus is no longer harmonious. Some of the voices openly clash with respect to aims and prescriptions.[8] Finding an effective antidote to women's pain among the plethora of voices can be a daunting, even bewildering, task. Each analysis of the problem and each set of solutions has its own adherents and detractors, even within the feminist community of scholars.

Most puzzling of all is how women and men are to relate to one another. Should women become more like men to achieve their goals of equality? Should women view marriage and motherhood with happiness or dread? Is it possible to live in harmony and equality with men, or is it only possible for women to live in harmony and equality with other women? Is heterosexuality itself suspect as a source of exploitation? Are men now expendable, given advanced reproductive technologies?

At its best, feminist literature is useful, enlightening, and enriching, as it clearly points out instances of inequity in the fallen world and brings to light women's experiences that have long been invisible. However, at its worst, feminist literature can leave one permanently angry and bitter, without hope that men and women can live together without oppression and enmity. At its worst, it brings one to the conclusion that love between a man and a woman is inevitably a lie and invariably exploitative of the woman. And, if maleness and God are associated within a particular culture, it brings one to the conclusion that the love God bears for women is similarly false and oppressive.

The Pain of Women in the Community of Saints

When we take upon ourselves the name of Christ and enter into sacred covenants with God, we enter a world higher than the fallen world: the community of Saints. Though many Saints in fact live celestial lives, most live somewhere between the fallen and celestial worlds. We would expect to find that the situation of women in the community of Saints is far superior to that of women in the fallen world, and indeed it is. The gospel of Jesus Christ proclaims that the true and living God is "no respecter of persons," be they "bond or free, black or white, male or female" (D&C 38:16; 2 Nephi 26:33). Christ had female disciples and many important events in the New Testament involve women.

The teachings of the restored Church reinforce this positive vision of women. President Gordon B. Hinckley has been outspoken on the equality of men and women, as previously noted, and the First Presidency of the Church has called motherhood "the highest, holiest service to be assumed by mankind."[9] Physical, verbal, and emotional abuse of wives by husbands has been excoriated by our current leaders, and the pitfalls of unrighteous dominion have been a frequent topic of articles in Church publications.[10] Elder Dallin H. Oaks has taught us that Eve was not a sinner in the Garden of Eden, but that she made a necessary and courageous transgression of the law so that we might all receive our second estate.[11] President Howard W. Hunter encouraged husbands to consider their wives as full partners in the leadership of the home, with full knowledge of and counsel in all decisionmaking.[12] Boyd K. Packer has proclaimed that men should help their wives in household tasks and childcare.[13] The Prophet Joseph Smith revealed that women and children have claim upon their husbands and fathers for support (D&C 83:2), and he taught that the man who shirked such a duty was worse than an infidel. We are taught that men should love their wives as Christ loved the Church, for which He gave His life (Ephesians 5:25). Truly, the lot of women in the community of Saints is brighter than the lot of those in the fallen world as the moon is brighter than the stars.

Yet, can we note the corrupting influence of earthly traditions in the celestial culture we are trying to create in the community of Saints? Lamentably, yes. These traditions are probably not the fault of anyone living in the kingdom. They come from outside the kingdom and are not a part of it. Yet we find their traces, as we find the traces of termites in the joists of our homes. We find unrighteous dominion propped up by holy scripture in certain families. For example, do women offend God if they do not "submit" to the will of their husbands? In other cases, some women feel pain over polygamy, priesthood, or the patriarchal order, seeing in these a reflection of the inequality between men and women that exists in the fallen world. Some women wonder if they will be required to practice polygamy in the hereafter, and they wonder whether heaven is really where they wish to be if that is the case. If all power is priesthood power, and women are not ordained to the priesthood, some women wonder whether this means they are but powerless womb appendages to a priesthood holder in the plan of salvation and exaltation. Are they but biological vessels designed to increase a man's patriarchal priesthood kingdom and to spare him the messy and painful chore of childbearing? Others do not understand how, if they are equal to men, women could be so "hidden" in the scriptures and in discussions of the celestial realm. If the scriptures are the word of God, does this mean that God is uninterested in women and their lives? In some broken families, laws pertaining to sealing are viewed as operating inequitably and to the detriment of women. Must women and their children choose between loved ones in the hereafter when a family is broken? How can heaven be heaven if a righteous mother is ever to be separated from her righteous children?

One woman expressed her deep spiritual confusion this way:

I don't see how they can say men and women are equal in the Church. Men have all the power and authority. My 12-year-old son gets the priesthood and all of a sudden he's got more power and authority than me! And how many women do you see on the stand in general conference? But you see row after row of men. God is all concerned about men, not about women. Just think about the scriptures: hardly any women show up. God is always talking about his sons. We're all supposed to be like the Father, like Jesus. But the Father and Jesus are men; I'm a woman! I can't be a son of God; I can't be a Father or an Elder Brother.

They say we have a Mother in Heaven, but she's top secret. No one knows anything about her and it's subversive to even mention her. So who's supposed to be my role model? How can I be like a person I know nothing about? I don't know. Maybe they don't tell us about her because there's nothing much to tell. You know, my son will be anointed to be a king and priest to the most high God, to rule and reign in the house of Israel forever. I get to be a queen and priestess to my husband. So is my husband my God, then? I don't get to serve God; only his sons do? The patriarchal order— doesn't that just mean "men rule forever"? Doesn't God love me, too? If I had a daughter, I wouldn't make her feel like such a second-class citizen. I wouldn't make her feel like I feel right now.

The problems in the community of Saints are not about flaming radical feminism; they are not about abortion rights; they are not about discarding heterosexuality; they are not about renouncing motherhood. One of the tough problems for women in the community of Saints is that which faces many a good Latter-day Saint woman as she lives her life within the bounds the Lord has set: How does she explain to herself how she is an equal within these bounds? How can she explain to herself and her daughters why certain appearances might appear inequitable to fallen sensibilities but are not truly inequitable when one fully understands the teachings of the gospel? Many Latter-day Saint women have no difficulty answering these questions to their own satisfaction, and we rejoice for them. But there are also many, such as the painfully confused woman quoted above, who struggle to find the answers to these questions.

This pain and confusion has long been secret among many good and faithful orthodox Latter-day Saint women: to openly express it was to invite a rebuke from uncharitable brothers and sisters that one did not have enough faith or that one's heart was not yet righteous enough to accept divine will. I dismiss these rebukes as un-Christlike. The pain being felt is innocent pain felt by clearly righteous women (though this pain is occasionally used and exploited by others who are neither innocent nor righteous and who have harmful political agendas aimed against the Church). If Christ were here and met the good but confused woman quoted above, would He really say, "Stop feeling sorry for yourself and get on with the program; yours is not to understand"? Or would He strive with all His power to give her the light and knowledge she needs to dispel the feeling that she is worth less in the sight of God than her brethren? Would He banish the influence and trace of those earthly traditions? Would He reveal unto her why it was a wonderful and glorious thing to be a woman—as equally wonderful and glorious as it is to be a man? I believe with my whole heart that Christ would offer healing and understanding to her, and not chastisement. I believe God cries when this confused woman cries. I believe His bowels are full of compassion for her.

And so we begin our journey to find the balm that only He can give us. The bewildering voices of the world and those disloyal to the Church cannot show us the way; we must find the right way with the help of God. Along with prayer, contemplation, and revelation, the holy scriptures are a primary source of light on all things. Therefore, using the scriptures, we will start at the beginning, with the nature of God and of eternal life. We will explore how the scriptures say men and women are to relate to one another in the celestial kingdom and in Zion. We will unfold a partial vision of the stewardship of women, so often hidden, in the plan of salvation and in the eternities. We will take this vision and use it to address the concerns of those women in the Church who wrestle with Ariel's question in pain and confusion. And we will expand that vision outward to address not only the concerns of the community of Saints but the problems of the fallen world, as well. Finally, we will discuss women and the future of Zion. In the end we will find, with Elder Jeffrey R. and Sister Patricia T. Holland, that the strongest course of action is to "hold fast to our beliefs until . . . we realize the exalted ideal of women and men crowned with equal majesty."[14]

To do so, we must first savor the richness of our beliefs and doctrines concerning men, women, and their equality before God—for only if we sincerely understand our beliefs can we become a living testimony to their truthfulness. President Spencer W. Kimball stated, "Much of the major growth that is coming to the Church in the last days will come because many of the good women of the world will be drawn to the Church in large numbers. This will happen to the degree that the women of the Church reflect righteousness and articulateness in their lives and to the degree that they are seen as distinct and different—in happy ways—from the women of the world."[15] Our humble hope is to help develop the "articulateness" of which President Kimball spoke. The profound words of Elder Jeffrey R. and Sister Patricia T. Holland also echo in our minds on this subject:

In times of difficulty and stress ahead, it will be the women of the Church, as well as the men, who will speak persuasively of God's plan, of his eternal government, and of his priesthood assignments. In the years ahead, some of the great defenders of priesthood roles for men will be women speaking to other women. A woman can speak to another woman in language men would not normally use and with a fervor men would not dare invoke. God has a view of women, who they are, what they do incomparably, and what eter - nally they will be. Women must seize that vision and embrace it, or they—and the human family with it— will perish.[16]

Come with us now on a journey through the scriptures, and see clearly (if you have not been able to do so before) the equality of men and women in the gospel of Jesus Christ and a vision of their glorious roles now and in eternity. As we have been counselled, let us seize that wonderful vision and embrace it and make it our own! Should we fail, promised destructions will come; but should we succeed, we will pass on to future generations a legacy of peace and joy that will be to them a wellspring of life, even life everlasting.

Notes

1   Jeffrey R. Holland and Patricia T. Holland, "Considering Covenants: Women, Men, Perspective, Promises," in S. F. Green and D. H. Anderson, eds. *To Rejoice As Women: Talks from the 1994 Women's Conference* [Salt Lake City: Deseret Book Company, 1995], 110.

2   Barber Conable, former president of the World Bank.

3   M. Russell Ballard, "Equality Through Diversity," *Ensign* 23 (November 1993): 89-91.

4   The prophet's remarks were made at the Veracruz, Mexico Regional Conference, priesthood leadership meeting, 27 January 1996 and were reprinted in *Ensign* 26 (October 1996): 73.

5   Noted in *Ensign* 26 (October 1996): 76.

6   See *Ensign* 27 (July 1997): 72. For President Hinckley, this theme of the equality of men and women is longstanding. For example, in 1984 he stated, "God our Eternal Father ordained that [men and women] should be companions. That implies equality . . . It is commonplace with us to say that we are sons and daughters of God. There is no basis in the gospel for inferiority or superiority between the husband and wife. Do you think that God our Eternal Father loves his daughters less than he loves his sons? No man can demean or belittle his wife as a daughter of God without giving offense to her Father in Heaven." (From "Cornerstones of a Happy Home," an address given by President Gordon B. Hinckley at a satellite broadcast fireside for husbands and wives on 29 January 1984.)

7   1993 General Relief Society Meeting. See M. Russell Ballard, "Equality Through Diversity," *Ensign* 23 (November 1993): 89-91.

8   See, for example, Christina Hoff Sommers, *Who Stole Feminism? How Women Have Betrayed Women* (New York: Simon and Shuster, 1994).

9   "Motherhood is near to divinity. It is the highest, holiest service to be assumed by mankind. It places her who honors its holy calling and service next to the angels" (Message of the First Presidency, Conference Reports of the Church of Jesus Christ of Latter-day Saints [Salt Lake City: The Church of Jesus Christ of Latter-day Saints, October 1942], 13).

10 See, for example, Anne L. Horton, B. Kent Harrison, and Barry L. Johnson, eds. *Confronting Abuse: An LDS Perspective on Understanding and Healing Emotional, Physical, Sexual, Psychological, and Spiritual Abuse* (Salt Lake City: Deseret Book Company, 1993); H. Burke Peterson, "Unrighteous Dominion," *Ensign* 19 (July 1989): 7; Boyd K. Packer, "The Father and the Family," *Ensign* 24 (May 1994): 20; Howard W. Hunter, "Being a Righteous Husband and Father," *Ensign* 24 (November 1994): 49-51; Richard P. Lindsay, "I Have a Question: What Are the Best Ways to Fight the Horrors of Child Pornography and the Sexual Abuse of Children?" *Ensign* 14 (July 1984): 29-30; Carlfred Broderick, "I Have a Question: So Many Children are Abused, Offended and Abandoned. If Little Children Are Precious to God, What Justification Can There Be for Permitting Some to be Born into Such Circumstances?"*Ensign* 16 (August 1986): 38-39; Boyd K. Packer, "Little Children," *Ensign* 16 (November 1986): 16-18; Gordon B. Hinckley, "Keeping the Temple Holy," *Ensign* 20 (September 1990): 62-66; Gordon B. Hinckley, "Our Solemn Responsibilities," *Ensign* 21 (November 1991): 67-70; "A Refuge for the Oppressed," *Ensign* 22 (January 1992): 62-64; Richard G. Scott, "Healing the Tragic Scars of Abuse," *Ensign* 22 (May 1992): 31-33; Maxine Murdock, "Hope and Healing," *Ensign* 23 (January 1993): 62-67; Anonymous, "I Just Need to Cry," *Ensign* 23 (September 1993): 22; Maxine

Murdock, "I Have a Question: Am I in Error to Avoid All Contact with a Family Member Who Has Seriously Wronged Me and Continues to Emotionally Abuse Me?" *Ensign* 24 (June 1994); 60-61; Judy C. Olsen, "Invisible Heartbreaker," *Ensign* 26 (June 1996): 23-29.

In addition to these *Ensign* articles, which include several general conference addresses, the Church has addressed abuse issues in the *General Handbook of Instructions* (Salt Lake City: The Church of Jesus Christ of Latter-day Saints), 11-15 (for bishops and stake presidents); Child Abuse: Helps for Ecclesiastical Leaders (Salt Lake City: The Church of Jesus Christ of Latter-day Saints, 1985); and priesthood and Relief Society manuals, for instance, "Love One Another — the Prevention of Abuse," in *Seek to Obtain My Word: Melchizedek Priesthood Personal Study Guide*, 1989 (Salt Lake City: The Church of Jesus Christ of Latter-day Saints). In addition, the temple recommend interview, which determines worthiness to go to the temple, includes a question about treatment of family members.

11 "Some Christians condemn Eve for her act, concluding that she and her daughters are somehow flawed by it. Not the Latter-day Saints! Informed by revelation, we celebrate Eve's act and honor her wisdom and courage in the great episode called the Fall" (Dallin H. Oaks, "The Great Plan of Happiness," *Ensign* 23 [November 1993]: 72-75).

12 President Howard W. Hunter, "Being a Righteous Husband and Father," *Ensign* 24 (November 1994): 49-51.

13 "There is no task, however menial, connected with the care of babies, the nurturing of children, or with the maintenance of the home that is not his [the husband's] equal obligation. The tasks which come with parenthood, which many consider to be below other tasks, are simply above them" (Elder Boyd K. Packer, "A Tribute to Women," *Ensign* 19 [July 1989]: 72-75).

14 Jeffrey R. Holland and Patricia T. Holland, "Considering Covenants: Women, Men, Perspective, Promises," in S. F. Green and D. H. Anderson, eds. *To Rejoice As Women: Talks from the 1994 Women's Conference* (Salt Lake City: Deseret Book Company, 1995), 109.

15 Kimball, Spencer W. *My Beloved Sisters* (Salt Lake City: Deseret Book Company, 1979), 44.

16 Jeffrey R. Holland and Patricia T. Holland, "Considering Covenants: Women, Men, Perspective, Promises," in S.F. Green and D. H. Anderson (eds.), *To Rejoice As Women: Talks from the 1994 Women's Conference,* Salt Lake City: Deseret Book Company, 1995, p. 107.

CHAPTER 2

Gender Equality in Eternal Life

by
Alma Don Sorensen

We have observed that in most times and places, women have had and continue to have less status as persons than men and less power to determine the outcome of their lives (see appendix). Too often, as a result of these inequalities, women have lived their lives subordinate to men, been exploited by them and suffered indignities, hardships, physical harm, and lost opportunities. In our time, voices are being raised in protest, and movements are afoot to end wrongful gender inequalities and the sufferings they cause. Inevitably, these protests and movements are having their impact on the Latter-day Saint community, revealing that among Latter-day Saints, all is not always well in relations between the sexes. These movements also raise disturbing questions about what the relations between women and men should be now, and what they will be in eternity. Our purpose in this book is to seek out answers from the scriptures to some of these important questions, for the benefit of believers who desire further light on these matters and to bring understanding to those ignorant or misinformed about us. But the reader should keep firmly in mind that we do not presume or claim that we have the final answers to the issues we address or that our interpretations of scripture are without error.

In this chapter we consider the general status and power of women and men in eternal life. We begin our search for answers here because how women and men live together in eternity, insofar as it has been revealed to us, provides the perspective for understanding what scripture can tell us about how we should live together in this life. Without first knowing what scripture reveals about their eternal relationships, much about how women and men should live together on earth as a people of God to prepare themselves for exaltation will remain hidden or be misunderstood. The status and power enjoyed by women and men in eternity should enlighten and inspire all our relationships and direct all our thoughts and deeds as we prepare ourselves for eternal life.

The Eternal Family

The family of God includes all the offspring of our Heavenly Father and Heavenly Mother, born of their "seed" in the celestial world, and to us they are without number and their "increase" will never end (Moses 1:35-39; D&C 132:16-17, 19-24; 131:1-4).[1] But there is a family within God's family. It consists of those among our Heavenly Parents' children who are just and true in mortality and through His grace and their faithfulness receive exaltation in the highest degree of celestial glory (D&C 76:53-58). We refer to them as God's eternal family because they enjoy eternal life with Him and with Him engage in the great work of love peculiar to exaltation, that of "eternal increase." The eternal family is God's ruling family. Its members are "gods" who have "all power" over "all things" and are "rulers over many kingdoms" (D&C 52:13; 76:54-59; 78:15; 132:19-20). They are as God is.[2] Their reign includes dominion over the lower degrees of heaven, where members are "not gods," "cannot have an increase," and who act as "ministering servants" of those who are gods (D&C 76:88; 131:1-4; 132:16-17).

The basic organization of the eternal family consists of relations between women and men formed by "the new and everlasting covenant of marriage" (D&C 131:1-3). First, celestial marriage joins together Heavenly Father and Heavenly Mother[3] and unites them forever with their eternal increase in the "many heavens" and "worlds" they have populated (Moses 1:35, 37). Second, that covenant unites in marriage every exalted woman and man and binds them to their own eternal increase.[4] And finally, eternal marriages tie together in one lineage all who pass through mortality together and afterward receive exaltation. In the case of our own world, the genealogical tree begins with Adam and Eve as husband and wife and branches out to connect their exalted posterity as married couples, thereby completing the family of eternal beings. No doubt many kinds of relations exist between exalted persons, enabling them to enjoy heavenly life together, but the relations between them particularly as women and men, united by covenants of celestial marriage, are basic to all others.

What is the status of a woman in the eternal family? What is her position of power in that ruling body? How do women and men share the power they possess as gods? Do exalted men generally have dominion over exalted women? Does the husband rule over the wife? Though scripture does not reveal in detail what the roles of women and men are in the eternal family, certain general principles and concepts have been made known by revelation so we can find answers to these questions and learn to live together in ways that help prepare us for eternal life.

Heavenly Power as Light and Love

Before considering how heavenly power organizes the lives of exalted women and men, let us consider its nature, for the nature of heavenly power discloses how it should be organized so that members of the eternal family can be "gods" with "all power" over things. The power of heaven is the "power" of "light," meaning "the light of Christ." His "light" is "the power of God who sitteth upon his throne, who is in the bosom of eternity, who is in the midst of all things." That light "proceeds forth from the presence of God to fill the immensity of space." It is "in all things," gives "life to all things," and "is the law by which all things are governed" (D&C 88:7-13). These characteristics of heavenly power as light, though beyond our present comprehension, hint at how it can be that exalted persons have "all power" so that "all things" are subject to them.

But however unexplainable some properties of the light as power might be to us now, scripture indicates plainly what its basic nature is: the power of light is essentially the ability to know and realize good. In the words of Moroni, the light involves "the power and gifts of God," sent forth by "the power and gifts of Christ," which enables all who fully acquire it to "know" and "lay hold upon every good thing." Without these "gifts" and "power," he says, "none" can "do good, no not one" (Moroni 7:6-21; 10:24-25). Whatever other properties make it possible for the light to fill the immensity of space and govern and give life to every thing, as the power of heaven it always takes as its form the capacity to know and lay hold upon good.

The light of Christ involves love as well as power. As mortals, we know that love and power are not always found together on earth. But in the light, they are inseparable, with a life of perfect love impossible without power, and power impossible without love. Let us see how this is so. Whereas "the power" of "the light" (D&C 88:13) enables persons to lay hold upon every good thing, "the love of the light" (John 3:19; D&C 29:45), or "pure love of Christ" (Moroni 7:47-48) makes them alive to and eager to embrace every good thing. The "every good thing" the light comprehends (Moroni 7:16, 20) naturally becomes the object of the light's pure love. So, on the one hand, the power of the light enables persons to live the life of love and the full power of the light helps make possible the perfect life of love. God Himself could not live the *perfect* life of love, the love that comprehends and wills the existence of all good things, if He were not omnipotent (see 1 Nephi 9:6; Alma 26:35; Ether 3:4; Moses 2:31). Likewise, no exalted woman or man could realize fully the life of love without the full power of the light.

On the other hand, persons can possess the power of the light only if they embody the light itself. And they receive the light and "the light groweth brighter and brighter" only as they keep God's commandments and he fills them with his love (D&C 50:24; D&C 95:12; 1 John 2:5-10). The power of the light is the power to do good and only good, and one must be good, a person of pure love, to possess and enjoy fully that power. Only a "good tree" can "bring forth good fruit" (3 Nephi 14:16-18). God cannot be the omnipotent being he is if he were not wholly good, if he were not a perfect being of love (Alma 42:13, 22-23, 25; 1 John 4:8). What is true of him is true of all his exalted daughters and sons. To receive all power from him, they must be perfect even as he is perfect (3 Nephi 12:48) They must be love just as he is love (1 John 4:8, 16).

The love of the light comprehends all that is good in relations between persons, and between them and God, as well as between them and all else. That explains the saying that by loving God and by loving all others as neighbors—by realizing all that is good in our relations with them—we fulfill the whole law (Matthew 22:36-40; Galatians 5:14). Of course, God himself is the perfect embodiment of the pure love of the light (1 John 1:5, 4:8), and he wants us to love one another as he loves us (John 15:9-12).

Equal in Heavenly Things

In the eyes of the Father's love, every daughter and son has "great worth" (D&C 18:10) and one is "as precious" as another (1 Nephi 17:35; Alma 31:24,35). The great and equal worth of each child is the fundamental good among all the good things his perfect love comprehends and brings to pass. That is why the foremost purpose of his existence, his "work and glory," is to make possible "eternal life" for all his children (Moses 1:39). In making attainable that "greatest of all his gifts" (D&C 6:13), he assures us that he "esteems all flesh as one" (1 Nephi 17:3) and is "no respecter of persons" (D&C 38:16). He "inviteth all to come unto him and partake of his goodness; and he denieth none to come unto him" (2 Nephi 26:33). They who prove themselves willing to come unto him and embody his goodness, become members of his exalted family and live together as one in his love.

Consequently, a certain equality exists among members of the Father's eternal family. The Lord introduces us to that heavenly equality by asking us to respond to the message of a parable about a father who has "twelve" children and "who is no respecter of them." He asks us if that father would be "just" if all his children "serve[d] him obediently, and he saith to one:

Be thou clothed in robes and sit thou here; and to the other: Be thou clothed in rags and sit thou there." As God's people, we are expected to know the answer: every one who is faithful to the Father of us all will be fully and equally well clothed and dwell in his presence. They will be "one" with him, because each will "esteem" and "respect" every other as herself or as he esteems them all (D&C 38:16, 24-27). Humility

The Lord expands on the teaching of the parable in further revelations when he says that every person who is "just and true" receives "all the Father has," or "all things," as members of his eternal family (D&C 76:54-55; 84:38).[5] Needless to say, the "just and true" include women as well as men (D&C 93:22). The Father does not say to his obedient sons: Be thou clothed in robes and sit thou here; and to his equally obedient daughters: Be thou clothed in rags and sit thou there. Every exalted daughter receives all the Father has and lives in his presence, just as every exalted son does. The Father himself finds it necessary to proclaim to a fallen world through his prophet that he "invites" both "male and female" to "partake of his goodness." Both, he insists, are "alike" unto him (2 Nephi 26:33).[6]

Though each exalted woman and man receives all the Father has, she or he does not possess all things separately from other exalted persons. Exalted persons are bound together as a family by everlasting covenants of marriage, and so each receives all things from the Father only as a wife or husband, and each couple possesses all the Father has only as "joint heirs with Christ," and hence with all other members of the Father's eternal family (Romans 8:17, 32). In other words, members of the eternal family have all things common among them. Referring to them in their governing capacity as "the church of the Firstborn," the Lord says, "They are they into whose hands the Father hath given all things" (D&C 76:54-55). But the fact remains that one exalted person does not possess that which is above another. As joint heirs with Christ, the women and men of the eternal family are "equal with him" and hence with each other (D&C 88:107).

When the Father bestows all he has on his exalted daughters and sons, "all things" become "subject" unto them (D&C 50:27; 132:20). In other words, by virtue of possessing all things from the Father, members of the eternal family have "all power" over those things (D&C 132:20). But here again, just as they possess all things only as married couples and members of the larger eternal family, exalted persons have "all power" over things only as husband and wife and as members of that family (D&C 132:20; 76:55-56). And since they possess all the Father has jointly and equally, one person not having that which is above another, so they possess all power jointly and equally, one person not having more than another. In the words of modern revelation, "the Father" bestows "all things" on members of the eternal family in their capacity as "the church of the Firstborn," and "makes them equal in power, and in might, and in dominion" over those things (D&C 76:54-55, 94-96). So it is that in the eternal family women and men in perfect cooperation manage all things held in common by means of an order of equal power.

The Patriarchal Order of Heaven

We now have before us a bare sketch, albeit an incomplete one, of how the love of the light constitutes and organizes the power of the light among exalted beings. We have observed that each exalted person's power to lay hold upon every good thing, his or her "all power" as "a god," depends on being a member of the eternal family as a perfect community of love. The full power of the individual is the overall power of the community in which he or she shares. Having as they do all things common, members of the eternal family have the power to realize all things good because they labor together without inferiority or subordination in the great work of eternal love. In other words, to be all power, the power of the light must be equal power, as the scriptures reviewed above indicate. This is the true order of power, an order fitting a perfect commandment of love, and within that order women and men are equal in power, might, and dominion (D&C 132:20; 76:94-95).

That much said, we turn to what may be a source of serious misunderstanding about the relations between women and men in the eternal family. We have in mind the patriarchal order of heaven. In the fallen world, whose alluring influence encircles us and where in most places and times many men exercise dominion over women, the idea of patriarchy entails the rule of men over women. But that is not the term's meaning when it refers to the order of heaven. In modern revelation, the patriarchal order is described as the order of family government formed by the new and everlasting covenant of marriage.[7]

We observed earlier that celestial marriages unite in one lineage all who pass through mortality together and afterward receive exaltation. Among the peoples of the earth, that lineage begins with Adam and Eve as husband and wife and branches out to connect their exalted posterity as married couples, thereby forming the eternal family, sometimes referred to as the patriarchal order. These ties of lineage spring from the relation each member and each couple have with Jesus Christ. Latter-day Saint scripture teaches that Adam and Eve rule together as the head of the eternal family under the Savior (D&C 78:16; 107:55-56).

The mortal descendants of Eve and Adam become their eternal posterity only by first becoming "the children of Christ." They becomes Christ's children, "his sons and his daughters," by being spiritually "born of him," and by "abounding in good works" until he "may *seal* you his" and "ye may have everlasting salvation and eternal life" (Mosiah 5:7-15, emphasis added). Let us underscore our point here: <u>the relationship of lineage that helps order the celestial family and make it a patriarchal order arises out of the relationship exalted beings have with one another as sons and daughters of Christ.</u> And what is the nature of this fundamental relationship between Christ as Father and exalted beings as his spiritually begotten sons and daughters? It is one of equality. When persons become perfected as his children, he makes them "joint heirs" and "equal with him" and therefore joint heirs and equals with one another (Romans 8:17, 32; D&C 88:107).[8] Both exalted women and exalted men possess equally all things and all power (D&C 76:54-55, 94-95; 132:20), one not having that which is above another.

As far as power is concerned, the eternal family is as much matriarchal as it is patriarchal,[9] because it involves the rule of women and men in equal partnership.[10] Even though exalted men have particular stewardships to perform as patriarchs in the great work of eternity, they must do so within an order of equal power and dominion in which women as matriarchs perform their own equally important stewardships. Not only are the stewardships equal in importance, but the power wielded by exalted women in performing matriarchal steward-ships is equal to the power of exalted men in performing patriarchal stewardships. In the eternal family, patriarchy does not mean the rule of men over women.

Heavenly Mother

We have a Heavenly Mother[11] who is united with our Heavenly Father in celestial marriage. This must be true given what has been revealed about the life of exalted beings and the nature of the eternal family. The marriage between Heavenly Father and Heavenly Mother represents the prototype of the unions that must exist between all immortal beings in order for them to be gods who themselves have eternal increase. Only they who live in the lower degrees of heaven "remain separately and singly" without "exaltation" and "are not gods" (D&C 132:16-17). Heavenly Father through his Son tells us that to know this about him—to know that we must be united as couples by everlasting covenants of marriage in order to be like him and enjoy his fullness and our own eternal increase—is "to know the only wise and true God" (D&C 132:6, 16-24).

The fact that our Heavenly Mother is the eternal partner of our Heavenly Father means that she possesses all that he possesses just as every one of her exalted daughters possesses all things in relationship with her exalted husband. It means that our Father has all power only in his marriage relationship with our Mother as his equal in power, just as every other exalted man has all power only in equal partnership with his wife (D&C 132:20; 76:94-95). Heavenly Father's omnipotence depends on Heavenly Mother's omnipotence. We find ourselves wondering if the term "God" in the most sacred name of the holy priesthood—the "priesthood" after the "holy order of God" (Alma 4:20)—may have a plural meaning.[12] If this is so—if the holy name of the priesthood refers to our Heavenly Mother as well as our Heavenly Father—its very name signifies one of the great truths revealed by the restoration of all things (D&C 86:10; 132:45) in the latter days: the full equality of exalted woman and man in eternal life. This deepens our understanding of the teaching that perfected women and men, united by the everlasting covenants of marriage, are "gods" who share equally "all things" and "all power" (D&C 132:19-20; 76:94-95).

The Fullness of Eternal Life

There remains a dimension of eternal life we have not yet considered in our scriptural account of the standing of women in eternity. It is a dimension that makes eternal life the "greatest gift" God offers humankind (D&C 14:7) and gives endless meaning and happiness to the lives of exalted beings. The scripture refers to this dimension as "fullness"—flourishing or abounding (John 10:10)—in the highest "celestial" degree. Just as there are many degrees of heaven (D&C 131:1; 76:71-79, 98), so there are many degrees of "fullness" (D&C 88:29-31), the greatest being the fullness of eternal life. Our discussion of women in eternity would be incomplete if we failed to observe how their equality with men helps make possible the fullness of life enjoyed by all exalted beings.

The reason exalted persons enjoy the fullness of life they do can be simply put: love is life. Like the love of light and its perfect fulfillment, the fullness of eternal life consists of being alive to all that is good with the power to lay hold upon every good thing. That is why in scripture "the tree of life" represents both "the love of God" (1 Nephi 11:21-23) and "everlasting life" (Alma 32:40-41), and why both of them can be God's "greatest gift[s]" to us (D&C 14:7; 1 Nephi 15:36). It explains why God himself is "love" and "life" (1 John 4:8, 16; 5:20; 1:2, 5; John 1:4). Relatedly, "eternal death," the polar opposite of eternal life, consists in having "perish[ed] from that which is good," or "die[d] as to things pertaining to the things of righteousness" (2 Nephi 2:5; Alma 5:42; Alma 40:26). Eternal death is being filled with the love of darkness and obsessed by its power to destroy all that gives fullness to life (D&C 29:45; Alma 40:13; Moroni 9).

We cannot now imagine what fullness of life involves for perfected beings of love who are alive to and can lay hold upon every good thing by means of the power that fills the immensity of space (D&C 88:12-13; Moroni 7:16-19). Even the "telestial" fullness, which is the lowest degree of flourishing in eternity, "surpasses all understanding" (D&C 88:31; 76:89).

What is true of God is true of all his exalted daughters and sons: love is life (Ephesians 3:19). The love of the light, when fully operative, is a form of human community (Ephesians 4:13-16), and each exalted person can be a perfect being of love and live fully the life of love only as a member of that community. The relations of love forming that community help constitute the very nature of exalted persons, without which they could not enjoy the fullness they do. Their aliveness to good in their relations to one another provides the foundation for their aliveness to good in their relations to all else. Their fullness is rooted in their life as a community of pure love, which flowers out to comprehend and lay hold upon all other things good.

The core good in the love of the light and the fullness it makes possible is the absolute and equal worth of every human life (D&C 18:10; Romans 8:35, 38-39; 2 Nephi 26:33). If exalted persons did not fully live that core value, for example, if among themselves they did not possess equally all things and all power, their fullness would not be celestial fullness in the highest degree. To be fully alive to good, to be perfect in their love, they must be equal in heavenly things (D&C 38:25-27; 78:5-7, 21-22). God himself would not be perfect in his love and his fullness would be wanting if he did not desire to empower his faithful daughters and sons so they might become perfect even as he is perfect (3 Nephi 12:48; D&C 76:69 (53-70)) and receive from him all he has (D&C 84:38).

What we have said about the love of the light's core value explains why the foremost purpose of exalted existence is the work of eternal increase. More than anything else, that work distinguishes eternal life from all other degrees of immortal life and helps account for its greater fullness. To the gods, intelligent life is something profoundly precious, to be eternally increased and perfected. That this is so is reflected in the very meaning of "god" and "eternal life": by definition, being a god and enjoying eternal life involves having a "continuation of the seeds forever and ever" (D&C 132:19-24). One of the names of God himself is "Eternal" (Moses 7:35), signifying among other things his endless Fatherhood. The reason life in the highest heaven is called "the fullness of the Father" (D&C 76:20, 56, 71, 72) is because God's foremost purpose in everything he does, in bringing forth all the good and beautiful things he creates, includes bringing to pass the eternal life of his daughters and sons so that they might be all he is and possess all he has (Moses 1:31-39; 2:31). That purpose is the primary good in his aliveness to everything good as the creator of all that is good. It is the central part of his "fullness" as the Perfect Being of Love.

We are fully persuaded that God the Father would not be the perfect being of love and enjoy the fullness he does without our Heavenly Mother as his eternal companion, equal in perfection and fullness to him. Their love for one another is at the very center of their aliveness to all things good. Without her as his wife, he would be much like those in the lower degrees of immortal life who live "separately and singly without exaltation" (D&C 132:16-17), who "cannot have an increase" (D&C 131:1-4), and hence, who enjoy a lesser "fullness" (D&C 76:75-77). And without her being equal to him in heavenly things, God himself would be less than perfect as a being of love and his fullness would be diminished.

What is true of our Heavenly Father and Mother is true of their exalted daughters and sons who, by realizing their Parents' "likeness" (D&C 20:18), become gods with eternal increase and enjoy the highest degree of fullness forever (D&C 132:6, 19-24). Every exalted woman and man would be less than perfect as beings of love and would achieve a lower degree of fullness if they were not united in the eternal bond of marriage as equals in heavenly things.

Conclusion

The fullness of life enjoyed by exalted women is equal to the fullness exalted men enjoy. The highest degree of celestial perfection and fullness does not have a higher degree for men and a lower degree for women. Woman possesses all the Father has just as man does. Her power to be a creator of things good and beautiful is all power just as his is. She is no less a god than he.

Notes

1. The Prophet Joseph Smith said, "Here, then, is eternal life—to know the only wise and true God; and you have got to learn to be gods yourselves, and to be kings and priests to God, the same as all gods have done before you" (*Teachings of the Prophet Joseph Smith*, ed. Joseph Fielding Smith, Section Six 1843-44 [Salt Lake City: Deseret Book Press, 1938], 346). Elder Bruce R. McConkie stated: "We are members of the family of the Eternal Father. He is a glorified and exalted and eternal Being, having a resurrected body of flesh and bones. His name is God, and the kind of life he lives is God's life. His name is also Eternal, and the name of the kind of life he lives is eternal life. Eternal life is God's life, and God's life is eternal life. We are commended to be perfect as he is prefect and to advance and progress until we become like him, or in other words, until we gain eternal life" (*The Mortal Messiah, The Messiah Series,* vol. 1 [Salt Lake City: Deseret Book, 1979-82], 23).

2. President Lorenzo Snow bore powerful testimony that we ourselves may becomes gods or as God is: "The Spirit of God rested powerfully upon me and showed me more clearly that I can now see in your faces a certain principle and its glory, and it came to me summarized in this brief sentence: As man is now, God once was; as God is now, man may be. The Spirit of God was on me in a marvelous

manner all that day, and I stored that great truth away in my mind. I felt that I had learned something that I ought not communicate to others" (Lorenzo Snow, *Deseret News*, 15 June 1901, p.1). President Joseph F. Smith bore much the same testimony: "In other words, we must become like Him; peradventure to sit upon thrones, to have dominion, power, and eternal increase. God designed this in the beginning" (Joseph F. Smith, *Journal of Discourses*, 26 volumes, London: Latter-day Saints Book Depot, 1855-86, 25:58).

3. See footnote 11 below.

4. The Prophet Joseph Smith taught: "Except a man and his wife enter into an everlasting covenant and be married for eternity, while in this probation, by the power and authority of the Holy Priesthood, they will cease to increase when they die; that is, they will not have any children after the resurrection. But those who are married by power and authority of the priesthood in this life, and continue without committing the sin against the Holy Ghost, will continue to increase and have children in the celestial glory" (*Teachings of the Prophet Joseph Smith,* ed. Joseph Fielding Smith, Section Six 1843-44 [Salt Lake City: Deseret Book Press, 1938], 300).

5. The Prophet Joseph Smith taught that the people of God, if faithful to the end, "shall be heirs of God and joint heirs with Christ. What is it? To inherit the same power, the same glory and the same exaltations, until they arrive at the station of God, and ascend the throne of eternal power the same as those who have gone before" (Joseph Smith, *History of the Church*, Vol. IV, (Salt Lake City: Deseret Book Company, 1949, p. 306).

6. President Brigham Young indicated that in the celestial kingdom both men and women would be heirs to all that the Father hath: "When we get home to our Father and God, will we not wish to be in the family? Will it not be our highest ambition and desire to be reckoned as the sons of the living God, as the daughters of the Almighty, with a right to the household, and the faith that belongs to the household, heirs of the Father, his goods, his wealth, his power, his excellency, his knowledge and wisdom?" (*Discourses of Brigham Young*, comp. John A. Widtsoe [Salt Lake City: Deseret Book, 1978], 179).

7. President Ezra Taft Benson explained, "The order of priesthood spoken of in scriptures is sometimes referred to as the patriarchal order because it came down from father to son. But this order is otherwise described in modern revelation as an order of family government, where a man and woman enter into a covenant with God—just as did Adam and Eve—to be sealed for eternity, to have posterity, and to do the will and work of God throughout their mortality." (Ezra Taft Benson, "What I Hope You Will Teach Your Children About the Temple," *Ensign* 15 [August 1985]: 9).

8. Elder Bruce R. McConkie describes a "joint heir" as "one who inherits equally with all other heirs including the Chief Heir who is the Son. Each joint heir has an equal and undivided portion of the whole of everything. If one knows all things, so do all others. If one has all power, so do all those who inherit jointly with him. If the universe belongs to one, so it does equally to the total of all upon whom the joint inheritances are bestowed" (Bruce R. McConkie, *Mormon Doctrine*, second edition (Salt Lake City, Utah: Bookcraft, 1966, p. 395).

9. In a recent *Ensign* article, Robert L. Millet teaches that the patriarchal order is an order of the Melchizedek Priesthood presided over by both the husband and wife: "The patriarchal order, established in the days of Adam (see D&C 107:40-42), was and is an order of the Melchizedek Priesthood. It is, in fact, what we know as the new and everlasting covenant of marriage . . . . God established the patriarchal order, a system of family government presided over by a father and mother, patterned after what exists in heaven" ("The Ancient Covenant Restored," *Ensign* 28 [March 1998]: 38).

10. President Spencer W. Kimball stated the same thought in this manner, "When we speak of marriage as a partnership, let us speak of marriage as a full partnership. We do not want our Latter-day Saint women to be silent partners or limited partners in that eternal assignment! Please be a contributing and full partner!" (*My Beloved Sisters* [Salt Lake City: Deseret Book Company, 1979], 31: emphasis added). James E. Faust added that "every father is to his family a patriarch and every mother a matriarch as coequals in their distinctive parental roles" ("The Prophetic Voice," *Ensign* 26 [May 1996]: 6). Elder Russell M. Nelson taught that many lessons can be learned from studying the lives of Adam and Eve, the first of which is that Adam and Eve labored side by side and that "Eve served in matriarchal partnership with the patriarchal priesthood." In speaking on how we can learn from their example, he added that "the complete contribution of one partner to the other is essential to exaltation" and that "any sense of competition for place or position is not appropriate for either partner" ("Lessons from Eve," *Ensign* 17 [November 1987]:87).

11. Although the concept of a Heavenly Mother is not spoken of often in the Latter-day Saint Church, it is nevertheless accepted that we do have a mother in heaven, as the Latter-day Saint hymn "O, My Father," originally a poem written by Eliza R. Snow, indicates. President Wilford Woodruff stated, "That hymn is a revelation, though it was given unto us by a woman" (*The Discourses of Wilford Woodruff*, comp. G. Homer Durham [Salt Lake City: Bookcraft, 1946], 61-62). Regarding the principle of a mother in heaven as expressed in Eliza's poem and hymn, President Joseph F. Smith added, "God revealed that principle to Joseph Smith; Joseph Smith

revealed it to Eliza Snow Smith, his wife; and Eliza Snow was inspired, being a poet, to put it into verse" (*Collected Discourses*, ed. Brian H. Stuy, vol. 4, January 20, 1895 [Burbank, California, and Woodland Hills, Utah: B.H.S. Publishing, 1987-1992]). See also Linda P. Wilcox, "The Mormon Concept of a Mother in Heaven," in *Sisters in Spirit: Mormon Women in Historical and Cultural Perspective,* ed. Maureen Ursenbach Beecher and Lavina Fielding Anderson (Urbana and Chicago: University of Illinois Press, 1987), 64-77. That this is true was revealed in 1909 by the First Presidency of the Church, then composed of Joseph F. Smith, John R. Winder, and Anthon H. Lund. The First Presidency composed the statement "The Origin of Men," in which they stated that "man, as a spirit, was begotten and born of heavenly parents, and reared to maturity in the eternal mansions of the Father," and that "all men and women are in the similitude of the universal Father and Mother, and are literally the sons and daughters of Deity" (James R. Clark, ed., *Messages of the First Presidency of The Church of Jesus Christ of Latter-day Saints* 1833-1951, vol. 4 [Salt Lake City: Bookcraft, 1965-1975], 200-206). More recent latter-day prophets also speak of our Mother in Heaven. In an address to women, President Spencer W. Kimball told them that they were "made in the image of our Heavenly Mother" (*Teachings of Spencer W. Kimball,* comp. Edward L. Kimball [Salt Lake City: Bookcraft, 1982], 25); he further stated that both God "and our mother in heaven value us beyond any measure. They gave our eternal intelligences spirit form just as our earthly mothers and fathers have given us mortal bodies" (*My Beloved Sisters* [Salt Lake City: Deseret Book, 1979], 25). The First Presidency under the leadership of President Heber J. Grant taught that "man is the child of God, formed in the divine image and endowed with divine attributes, and even as the infant son of an earthly father and mother is capable in due time of becoming a man, so the undeveloped offspring of celestial parentage is capable, by experience through ages and eons, of evolving into a God" (Heber J. Grant, *Improvement Era*, Vol. 28: 1090-91, September 1925). President Gordon B. Hinckley recently stated that "logic and reason would certainly suggest that if we have a Father in Heaven, we have a Mother in Heaven. That doctrine rests well with me" ("Daughters of God," *Ensign* 21 [November 1991]: 100). Elder Bruce R. McConkie wrote that "implicit in the Christian verity that all men are the spirit children of an Eternal Father is the usually unspoken truth that they are also the offspring of an Eternal Mother. An exalted and glorified Man of Holiness (Moses 6:57) could not be a Father unless a Woman of like glory, perfection, and holiness was associated with him as a Mother" (*Mormon Doctrine*, 2d ed., rev. [Salt Lake City: Bookcraft, 1966], 516).

12.   The Hebrew word for God in the singular is *El* or *Elowahh*. The plural or honorific form takes the ending "im" as in Elohim, a term

commonly used in the Hebrew bible which means "divine ones" or "gods" (male and female inclusive) in the plural form, or "god," "goddess," and "the true god" in the honorific form. See Francis Brown, S. R. Driver, and Charles A. Briggs, eds. *A Hebrew and English Lexicon of the Old Testament With an Appendix Containing the Biblical Aramaic, Based on the Lexicon of William Gesenius as Translated by Edward Robinson* (Oxford: Clarendon Press, 1977), 43.

CHAPTER 3

Gender Equality in Zion

by
Alma Don Sorensen

Eternal life is "the greatest of all the gifts of God" (D&C 14:7). The foremost purpose of mortal existence and the primary purpose of the gospel of Jesus Christ is to gather a people from among the family of the earth and prepare them to receive that gift. The idea underlying this preparation is straightforward enough: in order to be received into the highest heaven, we must become a people "pure in heart" and learn to live and serve on earth much as exalted persons do in the eternal family, being "united" here by the same "union" that unites them there, the union "required by the law of the celestial kingdom" (D&C 97:21; 105:4-5).[1] In other words, they must become a people of Zion. The term "Zion" currently has various uses among Church members, but precisely speaking, it refers to a people pure in heart who live by celestial law in preparation for life in the highest heaven.[2]

The celestial world is a community of perfect love whose members enjoy the highest degree of never-ending fullness of life. In this community, women and men have all things common and manage those things by means of an order of equal power. The exalted man does not possess that which is above the exalted woman nor does he rule over her in the eternal family. Much the same is true in Zion, modeled as it is after the celestial world and designed as it is to prepare a people to live in that world. Women and men, living and laboring together in a community of love, possess equally all things and manage those things by means of an order of equal power. So in contrast to much of the fallen world, where men typically are the dominant gender, in Zion women and men dwell together equal in dominion (see D&C 76:94-95). Zion represents a revolution in the relations between women and men; it liberates women and in doing so, liberates men.[3]

Zion as a Community of Love

Zion is "the pure in heart" (D&C 97:21), a people filled with the love of the light or pure love of Christ. They are a people alive only to that which is good in their relations to one another. In the words of scripture, those whose "hearts" have been "purified" have "no disposition to do evil but to do good continually" (Mosiah 5:2). Filled as they are with the light's pure love, the women and men of Zion live together in the union required by celestial law (D&C 105:4-5; John 15:10-12; 1 John 4:7). The core value in divine love, and hence in celestial law and the union it entails, is the full and equal worth of every citizen of Zion, and indeed of every human soul. In the eyes of pure love, every soul is "precious" beyond price, and so one soul is as precious as any other (Jacob 2:21; D&C 18:10). Among a people of Zion, each esteems every other as herself or himself and there is no respecter of persons among them (D&C 38:16, 24-27; 2 Nephi 26:28, 33).

Recall once more how the eternal family, whose members have equal esteem for one another and who are no respecter of persons, live together as a community of love. What is true of the eternal family is true of a people of Zion united as they are according to the same union: the Father bestows all things upon his daughters and sons and they live together as joint heirs, equal in earthly things.[4] In words familiar to any student of Zion, "they," women as well as men, "have all things common among them" (3 Nephi 26:19), "all things" are "subject" unto them, and "one" does not "possess that which is above another" (D&C 49:20).

Having blessed them with "all things," the Father commands the people of Zion to dedicate all he gives them, all they are and have, to the great work of eternal love on earth (D&C 59:5). This commandment is the law of consecration for which Zion is well known. It is a celestial law that also governs the labors of the eternal family.[5] The Father fulfills the conditions he gives to us in that law as he devotes himself and all he has to bringing to pass the immortality and eternal life of his children (Moses 1:39; D&C 76:54-56).

A people of God cannot dedicate themselves and all they have to His work as required by the law of consecration as long as they believe or behave as though their lives and possessions are their own. Bear in mind that the law of consecration is a celestial law, designed to operate as an integral part of the overall celestial order, and when a people live according to that order and obey that law, they always have all things common among them.

Put differently, a people of God on earth can live the law of consecration only as His stewards, not as private owners, over all the Father gives them. As the Lord tells us, if we accept and live the truth that all things are the Father's, "then ye are stewards; otherwise ye are no stewards" (D&C 104:56). Just as a people of God cannot obey fully the law of consecration until they have all things common among them, so they cannot join together in their labors as stewards over all with which God has blessed them unless they have those things in common. The idea that a people can live the law of consecration only as stewards who possess commonly all the Father gives them, explains why in the Church we often speak of "the law of consecration" and of "stewardship" in the same breath.

Having all things common organizes how a people of Zion live together in accord with the law of consecration in two principal ways. One is that they provide for the welfare of all members without respect for persons so that all "receive alike" (D&C 38:16, 24-27; 51:9). As modern revelation teaches, if God's people want to receive a "place in the celestial world," then they must become "equal in earthly things" so they can prepare to "be equal in obtaining heavenly things" (D&C 78:5-7; 84:38; 70:14; 49:20).[6] This is not to say that each person in Zion receives the same amount of the same things. That, of course, would make no sense. Rather, it means that the "people" are "appoint[ed]" their "portions," "every" person "equal according to [their] family" and "according to [their] circumstances and [their] wants and needs" (D&C 51:3). Nevertheless, this principle of equal distribution, being a precept of divine love and applied by a people who have all things common, operates so that in Zion the people live together as "one" and there are "not rich and poor" among them (D&C 51:9; 38:27 (24-27); 4 Nephi 1:3).

We have come to expect that in the first days of Zion there will still be poor among God's people because until that time they have not loved one another as they should; they have not loved each other as their Father loves them all. To remedy this neglect, equal consideration of the wants and needs of all the people requires that special efforts be made to raise up the poor (D&C 104:14-18). That this be done is one requirement of the law of consecration when it operates as a celestial law among a people who hold everything in common (D&C 42:30-31). So the time soon arrives when there will be no poor in Zion. Indeed, "the Lord" calls "his people Zion" precisely because (among other things) there are "no poor among them" (Moses 7:18).

In Zion, unlike in many places and times in the fallen world, including the United States to this day, women and men will be "equal" in "temporal things" (D&C 70:14) in preparation for being "equal in obtaining heavenly things" (D&C 78:5-7). The equality of women and men in temporal things will appear extraordinary and revolutionary to those who are not of Zion, but will seem right and proper to those of Zion.

The second way that having all things common organizes how a people of Zion live together as one is that possessing equally all things includes having equal power over those things. This is in accord with the order of the celestial world after which Zion is modeled (D&C 105:4-5). Recall that when the Father bestows all things on his exalted daughters and sons, so that they have all things common among them, he thereby confers on them all power over those things. Modern revelation tells us that they are "given all things" by the Father and are "made equal in power, and in might, and in dominion" over those things (D&C 76:54-55, 94-95). So it is among a people of Zion: by means of the heavenly order of equal power they labor together cooperatively in a community of love and devote all they are and have to the work of Zion in fulfillment of the law of consecration. Again, this aspect of Zion will be perceived by many outsiders as truly remarkable: a society wherein not only are women and men equal in temporal things, but women and men are equal in power!

We may summarize briefly what we have observed so far about gender equality in Zion by saying that in Zion women and men "are of one heart and one mind" (Moses 7:18). Their oneness originates in their equal esteem and respect for one another in the Lord (D&C 38:16, 24-25, 28). Hence, they receive all things alike or as one (D&C 51:9; 38:26) and they manage all things cooperatively by united consent or as one (see, for example, D&C 26:2; 104:21). They dwell together as one on earth in order to prepare themselves to dwell together as one in the highest heaven (John 17:21, 23).

The Power of Men in Zion

We noted in the previous chapter that though the general concepts of gender equality in eternal life can be found in Latter-day Saint scripture, the details of how these concepts actually operate in the daily lives of exalted women and men have not yet been revealed. Consequently, based on these revelations alone, we cannot describe in detail how women and men should serve together in Zion as equals in power. The most we can say is what we have already said—that in the highest heaven and in Zion they possess equally all the Father gives them, including the power over those things.

However, the scriptures do contain some important details about how the order of equal power should operate in Zion on earth when it is organized according to celestial law. By examining these details in light of the general premise that in eternity women and men receive equally all the Father has, we can draw some tentative conclusions about how they should share power in Zion to prepare themselves for life together in the eternal family. In what follows, we will first consider the power of men in Zion and then apply what we have learned to understanding the power of women in Zion.

In considering the power of men in Zion, we must evaluate certain general features of the Melchizedek Priesthood. We do this because that priesthood, when fully organized, constitutes the highest authority in Zion as it does in heaven and comprehends all other priesthoods and powers.[7] To understand the priesthood as a system of power, we must keep in mind its basic design and its foremost purpose in mortality. Its principal purpose includes gathering a people of God from among the inhabitants of the earth and preparing them for life in the eternal family by establishing Zion among them (D&C 14:6-7; 133:8-9).[8] Since this preparation requires that the people learn to live and serve together united by the union prescribed by celestial law (D&C 105:4-5), the purpose of the priesthood includes instituting that heavenly order on earth (D&C 113:7-8).

So, as we might expect, the design of the priesthood is itself an embodiment of the celestial order. In the words of modern revelation, "the order of Melchizedek" is "after the order of Enoch" (the order of Zion) which is "after the order of the Only Begotten Son" (the order of the highest heaven) (D&C 76:57).[9] The primary reason that here on earth the priesthood is not called "the Holy Priesthood after the Order of the Son of God" is to show "reverence for the name of the Supreme Being" and "to avoid the too frequent repetition of his name" (D&C 107:1-4).

The system of power after the order of the Only Begotten is a system of equal power (D&C 76:95), which is to say that the order of Enoch (the order of Zion) and the order of Melchizedek are also systems of equal power, since they are all after the same order. Accordingly, all who hold the Melchizedek Priesthood are equal in power. Though their offices and callings differ, the elder does not have more or less power than the seventy, nor the seventy than the high priest. Indeed, every elder has as much priesthood power as the Prophet and President of the Church himself.[10]

We cannot consider in detail all that has been revealed about how the priesthood should operate as a celestial order of equal power. Suffice it to say, the power of the priesthood (the power of the light) and the love of the light are inseparable: the light's pure love organizes and gives direction to priesthood power and that power enables those who possess it to live the life of love. That love must infuse and inform all uses of that power so that all who possess it can learn to labor together as one (D&C 121:41-46).[11]

When examining the priesthood, one must consider two of the priesthood's most general features as an order of equal power. One feature concerns the highly decentralized nature of the organization of the priesthood and the other is its highly centralized nature.[12] Both are essential and integral parts of the priesthood as an order of equal power. On the one hand, so that all holders of the priesthood can exercise its powers as equals in power, (1) the duties of the priesthood are given by revelation from the Lord Himself and defined in a general way and (2) the organization for carrying out these duties is highly localized. Accordingly, when well established, Zion is organized into relatively small territorial communities called "stakes" (D&C 133:9) and within each stake, members of the priesthood are divided into units called "quorums." Each quorum conducts its affairs and carries out its God-given duties according to the counsel and united consent of its members, each member having an equal right to offer counsel and give consent in conformity with the principle of equal power (see, for example, D&C 28:13; 107:27-28).[13]

Modern revelation tells us, "Of necessity there are presidents, or presiding officers," called from among the members of the priesthood (D&C 107:21-26, 60-66). The "necessity" noted here arises, at least in part, from the nature of the priesthood as an order of equal power. Because those who hold the priesthood possess equally its power and because (among other things) that power must be highly decentralized so that all members can participate fully in its exercise, a central authority must exist to set in order that system of power and oversee it so that it operates according to its design and purpose. The authority to institute the priesthood order of equal power are appropriately called "keys of the kingdom" (D&C 124:143), and those who hold them are called presidents or presiding officers. These presiding officers are organized in a highly centralized way, beginning with the prophet who serves as "the Presiding High Priest over the High Priesthood" (D&C 107:91-92), he being the only one who can both possess and exercise all keys of the kingdom at any one time on earth (D&C 107:65-66, 91-92), and continuing out from him through the administrative levels that include the presidencies of stakes and ending with those who preside over the various local quorums mentioned earlier (D&C 107).

Though the organization of keys gives the order of the priesthood a hierarchical appearance, it is not a hierarchy like any typically found in the world. For one thing, keys, as an integral part of the priesthood order of equal power, are not a means by which some rule over others, but a means by which some enable all to serve together cooperatively as equals in power in carrying out their God-given duties. Accordingly, chief among the duties of those on whom "the keys" of "the kingdom" have been "conferred" is to see to it that those over whom they preside, whatever "their several callings and offices," become "perfected in the understanding of their ministry in theory, in principle, and in doctrine, in all things pertaining to the kingdom of God on earth" (D&C 97:13-14). The idea underlying this teaching reflects the main thesis of this chapter: since "Zion is in very deed the kingdom of our God" on earth (D&C 105:32), it being after the order of the highest heaven when "built up" as it should be (D&C 105:4-5), a principal duty of priesthood presidents and presidencies includes making it possible for fellow members to learn how to serve together cooperatively as equals in power in Zion, much as exalted persons do in heaven.

In carrying out this principal duty, the relations between levels of presiding officers themselves and between them and fellow priesthood holders remain relations of equal power.[14] This equality is not superseded or overridden by the organization of keys—that would hinder the purpose of preparing priesthood holders for godhood in the eternal family. Keys are not a scepter; keys are gifts that are to be shared. The exercise of keys is not a ruling over, but an empowering of others.

Since those who preside and those over whom they preside remain equal in power, all things are to be done by common consent. Common consent means nothing less than united or unanimous consent (see, for example, D&C 26:2; 28:13; 38:34; 104:21; 107:27). Accordingly, when any person is called to be a presiding officer in the priesthood, it must be done with the common consent of those over whom he will preside (see, for example D&C 20:63). Even God's chosen prophet over his people can become and continue to be "the Presiding High Priest" in all of Zion only by "the voice" of the people (D&C 102:9). Also, in the general quorums of the presiding officers in Zion (the Quorum of the First Presidency, the Quorum of the Twelve Apostles, and the Quorums of the Seventy), "every decision" must be "by the unanimous consent of the same," meaning that "every member in each quorum must be agreed to its decisions" (see, for example, D&C 107:27). Likewise, as indicated earlier, the presidents and other members of local quorums of the priesthood spread throughout the stakes of Zion conduct their business by united consent, each member having an equal voice. [15]

What, then, does presiding mean? Presiding does not mean ruling over others. Rather, it means empowering others to rule with you over all things, not over others who are your equals. It is a means for serving together cooperatively, without inferiority or subordination.[16]

Let us conclude our brief discussion of the priesthood as an order of equal power with the example Jesus himself sets for all who exercise authority among his people. He declares that he does not "exercise dominion over" or "authority over" his people the way "the princes" of the world do over their subjects (Matthew 20:25-26).[17] Unlike worldly princes, he acts as a "minister" or "servant" of this people (ibid.) by enabling them to become perfect even as the Father is perfect (3 Nephi 12:48) and be equal with him in power and all else the Father has (D&C 76:54-55, 94-95). So even though he is indeed our "king and lawgiver" (D&C 45:59) to whom "all power" is given (D&C 84:28; 93:17), he wants those who follow him to become "equal with him" (D&C 88:107) and "kings" themselves with "all power" (D&C 76:54-55, 94-95; 132:20). The "law" he lays down organizes and directs his people to that end. In this and all other things, the Savior's desire is that of our Father, who wants to bestow nothing less than all he has on every daughter and son willing to become like him and thereby receive it (D&C 84:38).

The Power of Women in Zion

Since very little has been explicitly revealed about the power of women in Zion and since the priesthood is the source of all power in Zion, it might appear that men are meant to be the dominant gender in that society, as they possess its primary source of power. In the final analysis it may seem as if women should live lives ruled over by men, albeit in a benevolent way. However, a closer look at revelations regarding the order of power in Zion discloses that women serve with men as equals in power. The order of power in Zion is the same as the order of power in the highest heaven, wherein every exalted individual enjoys all the Father has and is made equal in power and in might and in dominion.[18]

If our understanding of gender equality in eternity and in Zion is correct, then the work of women in Zion will be organized after the order of Enoch, which is after the order of the Only Begotten Son (D&C 76:57), in much the same way that the work of men in the priesthood will be organized. The same principles of celestial law and precepts of equal power apply to both.

Accordingly, the stewardships of women will be defined in a general fashion and organized in a highly decentralized way so that all can participate fully in them. Of necessity, a centralized authority will exist to set in order and oversee the operation of that organization. Presumably, if the power women have to perform their stewardships in Zion is equal to the power men have to carry out theirs, then the immediate positions of centralized authority needed to set in motion women's work will be filled by women themselves. In conducting their affairs, at whatever level, all things will be done by the counsel and united consent of all involved, each woman having an equal voice.

Of course, the labors of Zion cannot be neatly and exhaustively divided between women and men. Indeed, it is difficult to imagine that any major part of Zion's work would not concern and require the attention or cooperation of both.[19] Consequently, we expect that much of the work of Zion will be organized so that women and men sit in council together at all levels of administration and make decisions by united consent. We believe this is as it should be in any society or community modeled after the eternal family as a perfect community of love where women and men serve together, being equal in dominion and power.

In saying this, we do not overlook the fact that mothers in Zion—especially mothers with young children—may find themselves shouldering heavy responsibilities to care for the needs of their own immediate families. But in Zion, fathers, too, will fully share in the responsibilities of the home, doing so in equal partnership with their wives.[20] Surely in the nuclear family itself, and when the local communities of Zion serve as extended families as they should, arrangements can be made so that women can participate in the common councils of Zion.

The power relations between women and men in Zion are mirrored in the power relationship between the woman and man joined together in that "order of the priesthood" called "the new and everlasting covenant of marriage" (D&C 131:2): that relationship is one of equal power. Bear in mind that this order of the priesthood occupies center place in the overall order of the Holy Priesthood and is the foundation of the eternal family itself. It is principally within the order of eternal marriages, and only within it, that exalted persons live as "gods" and together possess equally "all things" and "all power" (D&C 132:19-20; 76:54-55, 94-95). What is true of the eternal family is true in Zion: couples joined in eternal marriage live together equal in possession and power as required by the celestial law that governs their union.

We face now the difficult question of whether women in Zion will hold the same priesthood keys and power as men. We know that in eternity all power of the light, which both women and men somehow possess equally, is after the order of the Only Begotten Son, meaning that all heavenly power is priesthood power. Presumably in Zion as well, when it is fully organized according to celestial law, all power is priesthood power and somehow women share it equally with men. But still we cannot conclude that women will receive the same rights of the priesthood and occupy the same offices (e.g., elder, seventy, high priest, apostle) as men now do. For example, perhaps the women of Zion will have conferred on them the same general priesthood as men, the power of the light after the order of Enoch and the Only Begotten, but their rights and offices will differ, reflecting their particular callings as women. Or, perhaps in Zion only men will hold the priesthood, much as they do now, but the details of how women are empowered so they can serve with men in equal partnership will be made clearer. Or, perhaps as we approach Zion we will begin to better understand that women have held a priestesshood with its own special rights and powers all along.

We do not know whether women will hold the priesthood in Zion which only men now hold. It goes without saying that we are not in any position of authority to settle this question. But as we await the answer, let us bear in mind that "the rights of the priesthood are inseparably connected with the powers of heaven, and the powers of heaven cannot be controlled nor handled only upon the principles of righteousness" (D&C

121:36). And what are "the principles of righteousness" that must always govern "the powers of heaven" both in Zion and in heaven? They include "the principles of the law of the celestial kingdom" (D&C 105:4-5) which require that women and men learn to dwell and serve together as one, possessing equally all the Father gives them, including all power (D&C 96:94-95; 132:20). In order to live and labor together in equal partnership and as one, "no power or influence can or ought to be maintained by virtue of the priesthood, only by persuasion, by longsuffering, by gentleness and meekness, and by love unfeigned" (D&C 121:41).

The Lord promises that when the principles of heaven govern the rights of the priesthood, "the doctrine of the priesthood shall distill upon thy soul as the dews from heaven," "thy scepter" shall be "an unchanging scepter of righteousness" and "thy dominion shall be an everlasting dominion, and without compulsory means will flow unto thee forever and ever" (D&C 121:45-46). According to "the doctrine of the priesthood" as we have presented it, the only "everlasting dominion," the only "scepter" that is an "unchanging scepter of righteousness," is one wherein God makes women and men "equal in dominion" (D&C 76:94-95).

If our interpretation of gender equality in eternity and in Zion is substantially correct, then we can exclude any relation of unequal power in which men rule over women by having the final authority to say how women will conduct their lives or perform their stewardships. However benevolent such rule may seem to be, typically it will be a form of "unrighteous dominion" (D&C 121:39). However benevolent in appearance, in the end, such rule thwarts the preparation women and men must undergo to prove themselves ready for life in the eternal family.

Equal Power and United Orders

A principal purpose of the women and men who serve within the priesthood order as equal partners is to establish Zion among God's people.[21] Among other things, this involves instituting the order of equal possession and power throughout Zion. The same celestial principles that form the order of the priesthood and make it an order of equality underlie the overall order of Zion itself. Zion as an order of power reflects the priesthood as an order of power.

Much of what has been revealed about how the order of equal possession and power should be introduced generally in Zion under the direction of the priesthood concerns united orders set up for the purpose of managing temporal affairs. United orders exemplify many of the general features of a Zion society and were designed to enable the early saints to take a major step toward becoming a people of Zion.

Like Zion in general, the purpose of united orders is to help enable God's people to work out their "salvation" and prepare themselves to receive "a crown of glory at [the Lord's] right hand"—in other words, to help prepare people for godhood and membership in the eternal family (D&C 104:1, 7). As in Zion and the eternal family, united orders are founded on the truth that all things initially belong to the Lord and ultimately to the Father himself. In the words of scripture, concerning united orders: "I, the Lord, stretched out the heavens, and built the earth, my very handiwork; and all things therein are mine" (D&C 104:14).[22] Once that truth is embraced, the Lord can then bestow "all things" on members of each order to become "the properties of the order" (D&C 104:1-19; 82:17-18). In other words, members of an united order have all things common among them. Inasmuch as united orders together are after the order of Zion, we can see how a people of Zion possess all things common: they do so by means of a system of decentral-ized communities or groups organized in much the same way as united orders.

The Lord, then, requires members of each order to manage their properties held in common as his "stewards" in obedience to the law of consecration (D&C 4:2; 104:55-56). One of the first requirements of the law of consecration is that united orders provide for the needs and wants of all God's people so that, as in Zion, they are equal in temporal things (D&C 70:14) and there is no poor among them (Moses 7:18).[23] Concerning a principal purpose of united orders, the Lord says: "[B]ehold, this is the way that I, the Lord, have decreed to provide for my saints, that the poor shall be exalted in that the rich are made low" (D&C 104:16-18).[24]

In Zion as well as in the eternal family, having all things common includes having common or equal power over those things. Accordingly, in Zion, and we presume in the eternal family as well, all things are done by the counsel and united consent of the citizens (see D&C 26:2; 28:13). They labor together cooperatively by means of an order of equal power. And so it is in each united order: "[A]ll things [are to] be done by the united consent or voice of the order," each member having equal voice in offering counsel and equal vote in giving consent (D&C 104:21). Power in a united order has much the same general purpose and is organized according to some of the same celestial principles as the priesthood itself, both being after the same heavenly order.

So far in our discussion of power in Zion, first in the priesthood and now in united orders, we have focused almost entirely on how members conduct their affairs as a group or community. So it might seem that the power of the individual is confined to his or her role in group decisionmaking. That raises a question about the extent to which the individual woman or man is subject to collective power in Zion. It is true that the requirement that decisions be made by unanimous, rather than majority, consent means that each individual woman and man enjoys a central position of power in any group or community. Making decisions by united consent puts a premium on the views and vote of every member, helping to assure that none is marginalized, that each receives full respect as a person and citizen of Zion, so that each has an equal opportunity to learn the ways of heaven. Still, the fact that all things must be done by common consent might seem to make the individual subject to the power of the group in all he or she does.

But this is not the case. As scripture on united orders reveal, the power of every individual to manage their particular stewardship in a self-directed way is maximized when celestial law governs how people labor together in the service of the Lord. We should expect this in a society aimed at preparing each member to become a god who possesses all things and all power over those things. Once a god, a person's power as an individual cannot be greater.

The Lord tells his people that "you shall organize yourselves and appoint every man his stewardship" so that "every man may give an account unto me of the stewardship which is appointed unto him" (D&C 104:11-13). In order to serve the Lord as stewards accountable to him, members must be in a position to act as "agents unto themselves" in managing their appointed stewardships (D&C 104:11-17).[25] The Lord explains in another revelation that because "the power is in them, wherein they are agents unto themselves," his stewards should "bring to pass much righteousness" by doing "many things of their own free will." Inasmuch as they do this, "they shall in no wise lose their reward" (D&C 58:27-28). And what is "their reward"? We are told that if the stewards are "faithful over a few things" in this world, the Father will make them "rulers over many things" in the world to come (D&C 52:13; Matthew 25:21).

The commandment that united orders should be organized so that members can be accountable to the Lord by serving him as agents unto themselves in managing their individual stewardships both limits and defines the purpose of an order's collective power. The order must use its power, the power to "do all things" by "counsel" and "the united consent" of its members, in accord with this commandment. To illustrate, consider the power an order has over its own treasury on which members depend to manage their particular stewardships as agents unto themselves. According to revelation, "all moneys" members of an order receive from their "stewardships" by "improving upon their properties . . . shall be cast into the treasury as fast as [they] receive moneys;" and these funds "shall be" taken out of the "treasury" for use by individual stewards "only by the voice and common consent of the order" (D&C 104:67-71). Typically, the power of the purse is a formidable power in any organization, and whoever controls the treasury can impose their will on how funds will be used and by whom— but not in the united orders of Zion.

The Lord explains a purpose and limit of any order's power over its treasury in distributing funds to individual members. "And this," he says, "shall be the voice and common consent of the order." Continuing, he says, "If any man among you says to the treasurer: I have need of this to help me in my stewardship [and if it is not] manifest before the council of the order plainly that he is an unfaithful and an unwise steward, [then] this shall be his token to the treasurer that the treasurer shall not withhold" (D&C 104:72-75). So it is a wise and faithful steward's decision about how to manage his stewardship, not the common view of its order, that ultimately determines the money he should receive to perform his labors. The common power of the order over the treasury is limited so that each steward might serve as an agent unto herself or himself accountable to the Lord.

To better see how these instructions limit the common power of an order over individual members, think of what it means to be a faithful and wise steward. A faithful steward is one who conducts her stewardship in accord with the principles of celestial law that govern a united order. Furthermore, a faithful steward is a wise steward, one who demonstrates the practical know-how and good judgment that enables and makes him willing to perform well his stewardship as a member of the order.

When all members of an order willingly abide the heavenly principles and laws that have been set forth, each member enjoys maximum power to perform her stewardship in a self-directed way compatible with all having the same power. But when any member is unfaithful and unwise, then he behaves in a way inconsistent with everyone enjoying maximum individual power. It stands to reason that only stewards obedient to the laws and principles of the order should receive funds from the order.

In short, by denying treasury money only to a member that all members of the order decide is clearly unfaithful and unwise, an order attends to one of its main purposes for existing, namely, to enable every member to serve the Lord as an accountable steward acting in a self-directed way without at the same time imposing its collective will on how members manage their particular stewardships.

We should mention that the degree of autonomy enjoyed by stewards in performing individual stewardships is equal autonomy. This is in accord with the celestial precept of equal power. By way of illustration, consider how this precept of equality governs the consideration wise and faithful stewards must receive when they make claims on the properties of a united order for the purpose of conducting their particular stewardships. "And you are to be equal, or in other words, you are to have equal claims on the properties, for the benefit of managing the concerns of your stewardships, every man according to his wants and needs, inasmuch as his wants are just" (D&C 82:17).

We should guard against presenting too narrow a view of the scope of a united order's collective power. We do not want to leave the impression that individual stewardships are carried out only as separate enterprises by members acting entirely on their own, and that the order's power is limited to securing that possibility. No doubt a united order can undertake projects requiring that collective decisions be made about how those projects will be carried out. In such cases it would be necessary to divide and allocate tasks to individual members by the common consent of all involved. But the precept of equal power and the principle of individual accountability would still operate, both in making collective decisions and executing them by means of individual assignments. Each member would serve as an equal to every other member and would enjoy an equal opportunity to act in a self-directed way.

The revelations on united orders indicate how they should operate by focusing on the management of certain kinds of economic properties and the moneys generated from them. But the idea of united orders has wider application than that. The essence of united orders is in the combination of the celestial principles that govern them, not in the particular implementations of those principles. The purpose of those general principles, which includes preparing a people for life in the highest heaven, requires that all temporal labors in Zion be arranged so that those labors can be conducted by various groups and organizations according to the counsel and consent of the members and so that individual members can perform their particular stewardships as self-directed agents accountable to the Lord.

We feel it necessary to repeat that in Zion the same celestial principles that govern the temporal work of men govern the temporal work of women as well.[26] Some may think it satirical to mention once more that, after all, Zion's purpose and design include preparing women as well as men to receive all things and all power from the Father in the world to come. Accordingly, in Zion, women are self-directed agents accountable to the Lord. Women's counsel and consent as individuals are as necessary as that of men's when any group or community desires to act. Women are the center of initiative and decision-making in their own individual stewardships. Women's wants and needs as stewards are given equal consideration with men's. Women have equal claim on the common properties and moneys generated from the properties in order to live their lives and fulfill their stewardships. In a word, women are equal in power and possession to men in any united order, and in Zion, and in the highest heaven.

Preparing for Eternal Life as One People

The celestial principles and laws that define and organize a Zion society spring ultimately from the love of the light which comprehends all good in relations between persons. So to become a people of Zion, the people of God must be filled with that love and live together as a community of love. One underlying idea here is that a people cannot prepare for eternal life together simply as single individuals or even as separate couples. Eternal life is a common life lived as an exalted family, and a people must prepare for it together as one people. As we continue to observe, they must become a people pure in heart and live together according to celestial law in preparation for eternal life. That is a major reason why God establishes his church among his people: so they can serve together as one on earth in order to purify and ready themselves to live and labor as one in eternity. About this, scripture seems perfectly clear: the people of the Lord on earth must become united according to the union required by celestial law or he cannot receive them unto himself (D&C105:4-5); to receive a place in the celestial world, they must prepare themselves to be equal in heavenly things by being equal in earthly things (D&C 78:5-7); to become gods in eternity and labor together in the great work of creation as equals in power, they must learn to labor together cooperatively in Zion as equals in power (D&C 88:107; 76:94-95).

The love of the light cannot begin filling the lives of a people so that Zion can be established among them until they take into their hearts two simple truths (among others) implicit in their Father's perfect love for them; namely, that all good things come from and belong to him and that he wants to bestow all things on them equally. As a people let into their hearts these rudimentary truths, they become eager to forsake worldly inequalities that exist among them and live together in heavenly equality. In particular, they willingly cast off carnal inequalities rooted in gender and as women and men begin new lives without the one being inferior or subordinate to the other. In order to put off worldly inequalities and become a community of love, a people of God must demonstrate a united willingness to live together by celestial law and exercise mighty faith in the saving power of Christ and allow into their hearts the healing power of the Holy Spirit.

Consider the conversion of King Benjamin's people, recorded in the Book of Mormon, when they finally opened their hearts to God's love for them. King Benjamin labored many years as a prophet in the hope that his people might become a people pure in heart and live by celestial law in preparation for eternal life (Words of Mormon 1:17-18). His ministry was not without success, for just three years before he died, Benjamin described his people as "a diligent people in keeping the commandments of the Lord" and "a highly favored people of the Lord" (Mosiah 1:11-13). Yet, Benjamin knew that his people still clung to carnal ways which were preventing them from having their hearts purified and becoming a people of Zion. The record tells us that despite their diligent obedience, they were still in "a carnal state" which, as they themselves would soon acknowledge, was "worth less than the dust of the earth" (Mosiah 4:2). So Benjamin brought his people together in one place to hear a final address from him, hoping that with the help of heaven, he might convince them to forsake their remaining worldly ways and become a people pure in heart.

What did this diligently obedient people still have to repent of as a group? And what did Benjamin say to them, hoping that they would abandon their carnal nature? For some time, the people had refused to take into their lives the elementary gospel truths mentioned earlier, namely, that all good things come from and belong to God and that he wants his children on earth to be alike and receive alike. Basic as they are, the people had been taught these truths many times before. Referring to them and related teachings, Benjamin told his people "that there are not any among you, except it be your little children, that have not been taught concerning these things" (Mosiah 2:34 (9-41)). Nevertheless, he found it necessary to devote a large part of his final address to opening his people's hearts to the fact that all good things do indeed come from and belong to God and that they should possess equally all things.

In language eloquent and powerful, King Benjamin proclaimed to his people once more that it was God who "created them" and "granted" them their very "lives;" that it is he who "keeps" and "preserves" them from "day to day," "lending them breath" so that they can "move and do according to [their] own wills" and "supporting" them "from one moment to another." King Benjamin emphasized that from God do they obtain their "food and raiment," "gold and silver," and "all their riches" of "every kind;" even the "dust" out of which their bodies were made and their very "lives" "belong to him." In a word, all they are and have originate with and belong to God their Father (Mosiah 2:20-25; 4:19-22).

To dispel any notion his people had that God owed them the blessings he bestowed on them because they were a diligent people in keeping his commandments, or that by diligently obeying him they could repay him for his many blessings (Mosiah 1:11), King Benjamin informed them that if they were to "render all thanks and praise" to God that "the whole soul has power to possess" and "serve him with all [their] whole souls," they would "forever and ever" remain "unprofitable servants" and "indebted to him" (Mosiah 2:20-24). Compared to God's "greatness" they are "nothing" and before his "goodness" they are "unworthy" (Mosiah 4:5, 11).

Benjamin's words about the goodness and greatness of God had a two-fold impact on his people. As we can readily imagine, his words completely undermined the rationalizations that the people had conceived in their hearts to justify the carnal inequalities that existed among them. In the awesome presence of God's goodness and greatness, who among them could think himself better or more deserving than another because of his wealth or power or popularity or family name—or gender? In particular, how could he who has plenty say to God about him who is poor and in need "the man has brought upon himself his misery," while I have brought upon myself my riches, and "therefore I will stay my hand, and will not give unto him of my substance that he may not suffer, for his punishments are just" (Mosiah 4:17)? Benjamin asks his people whether any person among them can "boast" or even "say aught of himself"? He replies: "I answer you, Nay. Ye cannot say that ye are even as much as the dust of the earth." To drive home his point, Benjamin says of himself: "And I, even I, whom ye call your king, am no better than ye yourselves are; for I am also of the dust" (Mosiah 2:25-26).

But the deeper message in Benjamin's teachings about God's goodness and greatness and the people's nothingness and unworthiness is that God has unsurpassable love for his people and indeed for all humanity. Clearly, the Father does not want to bestow endless blessings on his children just so he can demonstrate their nothingness in view of his greatness and underscore their unworthiness in light of his goodness. He blesses us because, purely and simply, he loves us and wants us to love as he loves. That this was the message King Benjamin wanted his people to receive into their hearts becomes manifest when he counsels them saying that in order to always "be filled with the love of God" after they "have known of his goodness" and "tasted of his love," they must "always retain in remembrance, the greatness of God, and your own nothingness, and his goodness and longsuffering towards you, unworthy creatures, and humble yourselves even in the depths of humility" (Mosiah 4:11-12).

The greatest of all the gifts of God's love is the gift of eternal life (D&C 14:7). And of all the acts of divine love that make possible that greatest of all gifts, none can compare to the atoning sacrifice of Jesus Christ. In language recognized for its passion, King Benjamin spoke of how the "Lord Omnipotent" himself, "who was from all eternity to all eternity," would dwell "among the children of men" in a "tabernacle of clay," doing much good and performing "great miracles." He told how the perfect Christ would atone for the sins of all humanity by suffering "more than man can suffer" and still live, "blood coming from every pore" because of "his anguish for the wickedness and abominations of his people." He testified that there is "no other name given nor any other way nor means, whereby salvation can come unto the children of men, only in and through the name of Christ, the Lord Omnipotent" (Mosiah 3).

King Benjamin's final address bore the fruit he hoped it would: the people opened their hearts to God's love and they became one in their desire to be purified and be filled with love. The record says "they all cried aloud with one voice, saying: Oh have mercy, and apply the atoning blood of Christ that we may receive forgiveness of our sins and our hearts may be purified; for we believe in Jesus Christ, the Son of God" (Mosiah 4:2). In answer to their prayer uttered in one voice, "The Spirit of the Lord Omnipotent . . . wrought a mighty change [in their] hearts," and they had "no more disposition to do evil, but to do good continually" (Mosiah 5:2). They were filled with the love of God that comprehends all good.

If "Zion" means "the pure in heart," as it does (D&C 97:21), then King Benjamin's people, his people as one community, were well on their way to becoming a people of Zion. Before their rebirth, the people had been diligent in keeping the commandments of God. Now, as a people purified, they entered a new "covenant to be obedient to his commandments in all things" (Mosiah 1:11; 5:5). As we should expect, believing with their hearts as they now did that all things belong to God and that God esteems all his children equally, they began to live by celestial law, specifically the law of consecration.

A major precept of the law of consecration requires that citizens care for and lift up the poor and needy among them so that one might be rich like unto another (see, for example, Jacob 2:17-21). In the words of modern revelation, they "impart" of their "substance unto the poor," so that "every man who has need may be amply supplied and receive according to his wants" (D&C 42:30-31; 104:14-16). In terms much the same as those of modern revelation, King Benjamin instructed his people that they now "should impart of [their] substance to the poor, every man according to that which he hath," so their needs could be fulfilled and they could "receive according to their wants" (Mosiah 4:26). Decades later, many church members lived in obedience to this requirement of the law of consecration hoping, we suppose, that the day would finally arrive when they would be a people among whom there would be no poor (Alma 1:27-31; 4:12-13; 5:55; 34:28). Apparently, King Benjamin's people tried to live together equal in earthly things, for Mormon tells us that about forty years later, a "great inequality" began to exist again in "the church," indicating that it had not existed among them to the same extent before. This growing inequality caused the younger Alma, the prophet and head of the church, to be "very sorrowful" and to give up his governmental position as chief judge so he could devote all his time "preach[ing] the word of God" (Alma 4:12, 15-19).

In the account of the conversion of King Benjamin's people, no mention is made of gender inequality being among the worldly inequalities that initially stood in the way of their spiritual rebirth and purification. To be precise, the record neither confirms nor denies the existence of gender inequality. But we know that among nearly all peoples of the carnal world, men typically are the favored and dominant gender. And when a people of God are still of the world because of carnal inequalities, as King Benjamin's people were, we typically find gender inequalities among them as well. In any case, when gender inequalities do exist among God's people, as they do in the fallen world that surrounds them, those inequalities, because they are deeply set and exist almost universally, constitute what seems to be an almost insurmountable obstacle to their spiritual progress. But like other worldly inequalities, those between women and men melt away before the purifying love of Heavenly Father—a love which invited both male and female to partake of his goodness, a love that wants and requires them to live as one and as equals on earth as they do in heaven.

The message intended for the Latter-day Saints is clear: that they, we, under the leadership of our prophet, should desire to undergo that heart-changing awakening to God's love, an awakening that undermines all worldly inequalities, causing us to cry out, not just as separate individuals, but "with one voice" (Mosiah 4:2) as a people, that the Spirit of the Lord Omnipotent might purify our hearts and that we might live together as a community of love, equal in the bounds of earthly things and heavenly things also.

There are many questions about Zion we have not attempted to answer here. Our purpose has been less ambitious, focusing as we have on gender equality in Zion. But even our coverage of gender equality remains incomplete. There is much that has not yet been revealed or discovered concerning how women and men labor together in Zion. But this much seems clear: in Zion women and men possess and manage all things cooperatively by means of the heavenly order of equal power as required by celestial law.

Now, we might be tempted to put off making needed changes in how we serve together as women and men as we prepare for Zion, thinking perhaps that we can wait until we become a people pure in heart before uniting according to heavenly law. We wish to offer a different view. It is true that a purified people do live together united by the union prescribed by celestial law, but it is also true that a people of God, through the power of His spirit, purify themselves in part by learning to live by celestial law. As has been revealed to the church, "that which is governed by law" is also "perfected and sanctified by the same" (D&C 88:34). Accordingly, to become a purified people through sanctification, the women and men of God perhaps should strive to "abide the law of the celestial kingdom" even now (D&C 105:45). Otherwise, how can they prepare themselves to "abide a celestial glory" (D&C 88:21-22)? In short, we become a people of Zion partly by learning to live by the law of Zion, a law that requires, among other things, that women and men live and labor together as equal partners within an order of equal power.[27]

As we anticipate and prepare for the day when Zion will be fully established among us, we can even now favor ways that provide the greatest opportunity for women and men to live and serve together as equals in earthly and heavenly things. Among the people of God, men and women should be free to rejoice both in their similarities and in their differences. They should not have to fear that their differences will lead to inequality, as gender differences so often do in the fallen world. Neither should they be tempted to abolish gender differences

in a misguided attempt to abolish inequality among them. May
God grant that our understanding of the ways of Zion may
increase along with our desire to see Zion realized in our midst,
so that men and women may live in harmony, peace, and
equality now as well as in the celestial world for which we
strive.

Notes

1. The Prophet Joseph Smith taught that, "They who obtain a glorious
resurrection from the dead are exalted far above principalities,
powers, thrones, dominions, and angels, and are expressly declared
to be heirs of God and joint heirs with Jesus Christ, all having
eternal power" (Joseph Smith, *Teachings of the Prophet Joseph
Smith,* p. 374). President Lorenzo Snow also tells us that "[T]he
system of union . . . Which God has taken so much pains to reveal
and manifest, has been, and is, for the purpose of uniting the Latter-
day Saints . . . And preparing them for exaltations in his celestial
kingdom, and also preparing them on earth to live together as
brethren . . . (*Journal of Discourses* 19:342). George Q. Cannon
said: "The organization of society that exists in the heavens must
exist on earth; the same condition of society, so far as is applicable
to mortal beings, must exist here" (*Journal of Discourses* 13:99).

2. Discourses from prophets in the early days of the Church emphasized
this interpretation of Zion, as evidenced by an address given by
President Lorenzo Snow: "It is high time to establish Zion. Let us try
to build up Zion. Zion is the pure in heart. Zion cannot be built up
except on the principles of union required by the celestial law. It is
high time for us to enter into these things. It is more pleasant and
agreeable for the Latter-day Saints to enter into this work and build
up Zion, than to build up ourselves and have this great competition
which is destroying us" (*Teachings of Lorenzo Snow,* comp. Clyde J.
Williams [Salt Lake City: Bookcraft, 1984], 181). According to
President Brigham Young, the "Lord created you and me for the
purpose of becoming Gods like himself; when we have been proved
in our present capacity, and have been faithful with all things he
puts in our possession." (*Discourses of Brigham Young,* comp. By
John A. Widtsoe, Salt Lake City: Deseret Book Company, 1954, p.
50). President John Taylor also taught, "if ever we build up a Zion
here on this continent, and in case Zion ever comes down to us and
we expect it will, or that ours will go up to meet it, we have got to be
governed by the same principles that they are governed by, or we
cannot be one. And if we ever get into the eternal worlds, we shall
have to be heirs of God and joint heirs with Jesus Christ" (John
Taylor, *The Gospel Kingdom: Selections from the Writings and*

Discourses of John Taylor, ed. by G. Homer Durham, Salt Lake City: Bookcraft, 1987, p. 258.)

3. The Prophet Joseph Smith taught that in order for any person of God to prepare herself or himself to "dwell with Him," she or he "must be instructed in the government and laws of that kingdom by proper degrees, until his [or her] mind is capable in some measure of comprehending the propriety, justice, equality, and consistency of the same." Then, when God finally turns "the kingdom" over to "his son," those who have been properly instructed in the government and laws of that "kingdom," and are obedient to them, will be "made equal with him in the same." Those who are disobedient to these laws and not properly prepared, will "have no portion in his government" (*Scriptural Teachings of the Prophet Joseph Smith*, selected and arranged by Joseph Fielding Smith, Salt Lake City: Deseret Book, 1993, p. 63-65.)

4. Concerning the law of consecration, much of what we know about it was revealed and practiced by some of the early Latter-day Saints for a short while in a larger culture and society in which men were the dominant gender. We should not let that fact mislead us concerning how celestial law operates among a pure-in-heart people who have, as women and men, put off the inequalities of the world through a mighty change of heart. In the early days of the Church, members attempted to practice the law of consecration in united order communities, but their efforts fell short of the mark.

5. President Ezra Taft Benson affirms that "the law of consecration is a celestial law, not an economic experiment. . . . I repeat and emphasize that the law of consecration is a law for an inheritance in the celestial kingdom. God, the Eternal Father, his Son Jesus Christ, and all holy beings abide by this law. It is an eternal law. It is a revelation by God to his Church in this dispensation. Though not in full operation today, it will be mandatory for all Saints to live the law in its fullness to receive celestial inheritance" (Ezra Taft Benson, "A Vision and a Hope for the Youth of Zion," in *1977 Devotional Speeches of the Year*, Provo, Utah: Brigham Young University Press, 1978, p. 74-75).

6. In his imaginary account of the establishment of Zion among Enoch's people, Elder Neal A. Maxwell writes, "We now see clearly, as pertaining to our goods and possessions, that unless we are equal in earthly things we cannot be equal in heavenly things. We have goods in common because we have Christ in common" (Neal A. Maxwell, *Of One Heart*, Salt Lake City: Deseret Book, 1975, p. 39).

7. President Brigham Young taught that "when we talk of the celestial law which is revealed from heaven, that is, the priesthood, we are talking about the principle of salvation, a perfect system of government, of laws and ordinances, by which we can be prepared to pass

from one gate to another, and from sentinel to another until we go into the presence of our Father and God" (*Discourses of Brigham Young*, comp. By John A. Widtsoe, Salt Lake City: Deseret Book Company, 1954, p. 130.)

8. President Brigham Young said that the "Gospel and the priesthood are the means [God] employs to save and exalt his obedient children to the possession with Him of the same glory and power to crown with crowns of glory, immortality, and eternal lives" (*Discourses of Brigham Young*, comp. By John A. Widtsoe, Salt Lake City: Deseret Book Company, 1954, p. 133). President John Taylor also taught that the priesthood must lead the way to Zion, "we read of the Zion that was built up by Enoch, and that this Zion and the people that were united with Enoch, who were subject to the same laws which God is seeking to introduce among us, were caught up into the heavens. We have been expecting all along to build up a similar Zion upon these mountains, and we have talked a great deal about going back to Jackson County. We cannot build up a Zion unless we are in possession of the spirit of Zion, and of the light and intelligence that flow from God, and under the direction of the priesthood, the living oracles of God, to lead us in the paths of life" (John Taylor, *The Gospel Kingdom: Selections from the Writings and Discourses of John Taylor*, ed. by G. Homer Durham, Salt Lake City: Bookcraft, 1987, pp. 258-259).

9. This has always been the case in every gospel dispensation: the order of the Melchizedek Priesthood is after the order of heaven, and because it is, it has the power to sanctify a people so they can be received into the celestial world. Accordingly, when Adam and, we must assume, Eve were "born of the spirit" and "sanctified from all sin," the Lord said that they were "after the order of him who was without beginning of days or end of years, from all eternity to all eternity" (Moses 6:67). They were after the order of the Holy Priesthood or the order of the Only Begotten Son. Similarly, when "the people in the days of Melchizedek" lived and labored together according to "the high priesthood after the order of the Son," they were "sanctified" and "entered into the rest of the Lord of their God" (Alma 13:5-19). Conversely, Moses "sought diligently to sanctify his people" through the "Holy Priesthood," but they "hardened their hearts," and consequently they could "not enter" into God's "rest" while "in the wilderness" (D&C 84:23-24). Therefore, God took "Moses out of their midst, and the Holy Priesthood also," leaving them with only "the lesser priesthood" and "the preparatory gospel" (D&C 84:25-26). Unlike the lesser priesthood and its gospel, the word and the Holy Priesthood themselves are not "preparatory" for living according to the celestial order in this world. They are after the celestial order itself, and because they are, they prepare a people of the Lord during their time of probation for the celestial world and the enjoyment of eternal life.

10. Elder Bruce R. McConkie reminds us that the "priesthood is greater than any of its offices. No office adds any power, dignity, or authority to the priesthood. All offices derive their rights, prerogatives, graces, and powers from the priesthood . . . Further, there is no advancement from one office to another within the Melchizedek Priesthood. Every elder holds as much priesthood as an apostle or as the President of the Church, though these latter officers hold greater administrative assignments in the kingdom." (Bruce R. McConkie, *Mormon Doctrine,* Salt Lake City: Bookcraft, 1966, pp. 595-596.)

11. Elder John A. Widtsoe tells us that, "Since the Gospel plan is founded in love, the priesthood, the power of the Almighty God, must likewise show forth abounding, unselfish love. Unless that is done, priesthood loses its edge and power and becomes a hollow mockery" (John A. Widtsoe, *Priesthood and Church Government,* Salt Lake City: Deseret Book Company, 1962, pp. 49-50).

12. Elder John A. Widtsoe describes the centralized-decentralized nature of the priesthood. He writes, "that although the President of the Church may hold and dispense the powers and administrative responsibilities of that office, the power of the priesthood is decentralized: first, according to offices and the jurisdictions of those respective offices; second, according to individual priesthood-bearers. This means that while the Church as a whole is delicately responsive to central authority for Church-wide purposes, the central-local relationships in the organization do not restrict the full initiative and free development of either territorial divisions of the Church, individual quorums, groups of quorums, or the member as an individual. . . . The priesthood provides a "functional" instrumentality for Church government which is at once efficient and responsive in centralization, but flexible and decentralized in actual administration. As such, the priesthood, if developed properly in each quorum, affords perhaps the only successful means for reconciling without violence the concept of freedom with authority, liberty with equality—a quest as ancient in the realm of social institutions as the search for the "philosopher's stone" in ancient alchemy and its modern variants." (*Priesthood and Church Government,* compiled by John A. Widtsoe, Salt Lake City: Deseret Book Company, 1962, footnote 2 p. 103).

13. We presume that the decentralized nature of the priesthood as a system of equal power in Zion reflects the order of heaven itself. That helps explain how it can be that every member of the eternal family from the many worlds created and populated by our Eternal Parents can be given all they have and possess all power over those things in joint heirship with others.

14. President Joseph F. Smith taught that "in their fullness the keys are held by only one person at a time, the Prophet and President of the

Church. He may delegate any portion of this power to another, in which case that person holds the keys of that particular labor. Thus, the president of a temple, the president of a stake, the bishop of a ward, the president of a mission, the president of a quorum, each holds the keys of the labors performed in that particular body or locality. His priesthood is not increased by this special appointment, for a seventy who presides over a mission has no more priesthood than a seventy who labors under his direction; and the president of an elders quorum, for example, has no more priesthood than any member of that quorum. But he holds the power of directing the official labors performed in the mission or quorum, or in other words, the keys of that division of labor" (*Gospel Doctrine*, fifth edition, p. 136.).

15. "We deny the existence of arbitrary power in the Church; and this because its government is moral government purely, and its forces are applied through kindness and persuasion. Government by consent of the governed is the rule of the Church" (*Priesthood and Church Government*, compiled by John A. Widtsoe, Salt Lake City: Deseret Book, 1962, p. 198).

16. President Joseph F. Smith explained how members of the priesthood labor together cooperatively as one; "The truth will never divide councils of the priesthood. It will never divide Presidents from their Counselors, nor Counselors from their Presidents, nor members of the Church from one another, nor from the Church. The truth will unite us and cement us together. It will make us strong, for it is a foundation that cannot be destroyed. Therefore, when Bishops and their Counselors do not see eye to eye, or when Presidents and their Counselors have any difference whatever in their sentiments or in their policy, it is their duty to get together and humble themselves before Him until they get revelation from the Lord and see the truth alike, that they may go before their people unitedly. It is the duty of the Presidents of Stakes and High Councilors to meet often, to pray together, to counsel together, to learn each other's spirit, to understand each other, and unite together, that there may be no dissension nor division among them. The same with the Bishops and their Counselors. The same may be said of the councils of the priesthood from first to last. Let them get together and become united in their understanding of what is right, just and true, and then go as one man to the accomplishment of the purpose they have in view." (*Priesthood and Church Government*, compiled by John A. Widtsoe, Salt Lake City: Deseret Book, 1962, pp. 96-97).

17. In Elder Neal A. Maxwell's imaginary account of Zion in Enoch's time, he has its main character partially describe the fact that a people of Zion labor together cooperatively without some ruling over others. "I am astonished at the efficiencies of righteousness. By this I mean, Prince Omner, that the great governmental systems

built up in the cities you and I have known are perpetually preoccupied with the pain of obtaining compliance from citizens toward
their government and toward each other. Servants are piled upon
servants and functionaries check on other functionaries. Much
wealth is spent to strive to insure that men deal justly one with
another. This city of the Lord is different wherein we seek not only
that which is better, but that which is best. Filled as our city is with
people who are increasingly of one heart and of one mind and who
are moved by the same basic beliefs, there is need for less and less
in the way of structure to see that people do their duty toward each
other. Here we do not divert people from their own labors into
wasteful secondary tasks; basic love and honesty obtain increasingly
between our people" (Neal A. Maxwell, *Of One Heart*, Salt Lake
City: Deseret Book, 1975, p. 31).

18. For President Gordon B. Hinckley, the theme of the equality of men
    and women is longstanding. For example, in 1984 he stated, "God
    our Eternal Father ordained that [men and women] should be
    companions. That implies equality . . . It is commonplace with us to
    say that we are sons and daughters of God. There is no basis in the
    gospel for inferiority or superiority between the husband and the
    wife. Do you think that God our Eternal Father loves his daughters
    less than he loves his sons? No man can demean or belittle his wife
    as a daughter of God without giving offense to her Father in
    Heaven" (From "Cornerstones of a Happy Home," an address given
    by President Gordon B. Hinckley at a satellite broadcast fireside for
    husbands and wives on 29 January 1984). During the April 1998
    session of general conference, Elder Boyd K. Packer stated, "In the
    home it is a partnership with husband and wife equally yoked
    together, sharing in decisions, always working together. While the
    husband, the father, has responsibility to provide worthy and
    inspired leadership, his wife is neither behind him nor ahead of him
    but at his side" ("The Relief Society," *Ensign* 28 [May 1998]:73).
    President James E. Faust added that "every father is to his family a
    patriarch and every mother a matriarch as coequals in their distinc-
    tive parental roles" ("The Prophetic Voice," *Ensign* 26 [May
    1996]:6).

19. President Brigham Young taught that both men and women came to
    earth endowed with both spiritual and temporal gifts and talents. "If
    they [women] had the privilege of studying, [they] would make just
    as good mathematicians or accountants as any man; and we think
    they ought to have the privilege to study these branches of knowl-
    edge that they may develop the powers with which they are
    endowed" (*Journal of Discourses*, ed. George D. Watt, et al, vol. 13
    [Liverpool: F.D. Richards, et al, 1854-1886], 61). President Young
    encouraged the women to educate themselves, and provided moral
    and sometimes temporal support for many to enter fields of medi-
    cine, journalism, law, physics, business, and any other areas that

would assist in building up Zion (see Jill Mulvay Derr, "Women's Place in Brigham Young's World," BYU Studies 18, no. 3 [1978]: 377-395).

20. In the April 1998 general conference, Elder Boyd K. Packer taught that although women and men can and often do similar work within and without the home, there are distinct male and female natures which must be recognized: "Be careful lest you unknowingly foster influences and activities which tend to erase the masculine and feminine differences nature has established. A man, a father, can do much of what is usually assumed to be woman's work. In turn, a wife and a mother can do much—and in time of need, most things—usually considered the responsibility of the man, without jeopardizing their distinct roles. Even so, leaders, and especially parents, should recognize that there is a distinct masculine nature and a distinct feminine nature essential to the foundation of the home and the family. Whatever disturbs or weakens or tends to erase that difference erodes the family and reduces the probability of happiness for all concerned" ("The Relief Society," *Ensign* 28 [May 1998]: 73). Elder Packer also counselled that: "There is no task, however menial, connected with the care of babies, the nurturing of children, or with the maintenance of the home that is not his [the husband's] equal obligation. The tasks which come with parenthood, which many consider to be below other tasks, are simply above them" (Elder Boyd K. Packer, "A Tribute to Women," *Ensign* 19 [July 1989]: 72-75).

21. President John Taylor asks: "What is this priesthood given us for? That we may be enabled to build up Zion of our God . . . that his will may be done on earth as in heaven" (John Taylor, *The Gospel Kingdom: Selections from the Writings and Discourses of John Taylor*, ed. by G. Homer Durham, Salt Lake City: Bookcraft, 1987, p. 130).

22. According to President Ezra Taft Benson, "the basic principle of the united order is that all things belong to the Lord" (Ezra Taft Benson, "A Vision and a Hope for the Youth of Zion," in *1977 devotional Speeches of the Year*, Provo, Utah: BYU Press, 1978, p. 75).

23. In his imaginary account of Enoch's Zion, Elder Neal A. Maxwell reaffirms "that it is not given that one man should possess that which is above another, wherefore the world lieth in sin" (Neal A. Maxwell, *Of One Heart*, Salt Lake City: Deseret Book Company, 1975, p. 38).

24. President Brigham Young observed that, "the underlying principle of the United Order is that there should be no rich and no poor, that men's talents should be used for the common good and that selfish interests should make way for a more benevolent and generous spirit among the saints" (Quoted in High Nibley, "Approaching

Zion, volume 9 of the *Collected Works of Hugh Nibley*, ed. by Don Norton, Salt Lake City: Deseret Book, 1986, p. 440).

25. President John Taylor recalls the words of Joseph Smith in establishing and preserving a perfect order in which persons govern themselves by true principles. "Some years ago in Nauvoo, a gentleman in my hearing, a member of the Legislature, asked Joseph Smith how it was that he was enabled to govern so many people, and to preserve such perfect order; remarking at the same time that it was impossible for them to do it anywhere else. Mr. Smith remarked that it was very easy to do that. "How?" responded the gentleman: "to us it is very difficult." Mr. Smith replied: "I teach them correct principles, and they govern themselves." (*Priesthood and Church Government*, compiled by John A. Widtsoe, Salt Lake City: Deseret Book, 1962, p. 100).

26. The early Latter-day Saints, who tried to conduct their temporal affairs in united orders according to celestial law, lived in a larger culture and society in which men were the dominant gender, and they failed to achieve equality for men and women. For example, when wages were instituted in one community, men made 22 cents per hour, and women made 14 cents per hour. Also, women's domestic labor did not count as work. Women also did not sit in the councils of the united order. Clearly, the ideal was not achieved with respect to women. Also, the united order as practiced did not live up to a celestial order in other ways. For example, it was designed to promote economic equality so that the Saints would be equal in temporal matters, but it failed in this as well. See L. Dwight Israelson, "An Economic Analysis of the United Order," BYU Studies 18, no. 4 (1978): 536-562.

27. As President Spencer W. Kimball counselled the Latter-day Saints, they "must cooperate completely and work in harmony one with another. There must be unanimity in our decisions and unity in our actions . . . if the Spirit of the Lord is to magnify our labors, then this spirit of oneness and cooperation must be the prevailing spirit in all that we do" (Spencer W. Kimball, "Becoming the Pure in Heart," *Ensign*, Vol. 8, May 1978, pp. 79-81).

CHAPTER 4

The Story of Eve

by
Alma Don Sorensen

In the history of women's subordination to men, powerful rationalizations have been invented to make male domination appear as righteous dominion. In societies and groups whose cultural roots include the Old Testament, no sacred text has been more influential in providing authority for those rationalizations than the story of Adam and Eve. That narration presents with divine authority the prototype of who men and women are, what they can and should become, the foremost purpose of their mortal and eternal existence, and fundamental to all this, who God is and the quality of their relationship to Him. For that reason, the misconstrued story of Adam and Eve has served well to perpetuate wrongful relations between women and men.

In their particulars, the misunderstandings of the account of the first man and woman vary from one group and time to another, some being more humane and benevolent toward women than others, but all rest on familiar texts. According to those texts, man was created first in the image of God, who happens to be male. And then woman was created second in the likeness of God, from a part of man (Genesis 2:7, 21, 22). God declares that it is not good for man to be alone and that he needs a helpmeet for him, thus His reason for creating woman (Genesis 2:18). No mention is made of woman existing in her own right, being alone without man, and needing him as a helpmeet. Furthermore, the burden of blame for the Fall seemingly rests on Eve, because she took the leading part in the Fall that resulted in the loss of innocence and paradise for all humanity. Finally, because she initiated the Fall, God cursed Eve and told her that her desire should be to Adam and he was to rule over her (Genesis 3:16).

It takes little imagination to see how these texts could be interpreted to justify, on the basis of divine authority, a society that favors men and upholds the exercise of dominion by men over women. But all such interpretations are mistaken. What we want to do here is help revive the long-forgotten story of Eve that can now be found in the additional scripture given by the Lord in the latter days. We desire to help restore full dignity to our noble foremother and bring to light her marvelous callings and accomplishments as the first woman on earth. We hope to further illuminate and elevate the lives of women and men in the Church as they prepare themselves for Zion and eternal life together.

We first consider Eve's creation from Adam in the image of God, next we evaluate the significance of her leading role in the Fall, and then we examine the nature of her transgression which resulted in her so-called cursing by God and his giving Adam rule over her.

The Creation of Eve

The story of the life of Adam and Eve on earth begins with the affirmation that "God created man in his own image" as "male and female" (Genesis 1:27). This simple declaration promises to reveal the full identities of the first man and woman—indeed, of all men and women—with their earthly and eternal possibilities. Everything else God has revealed about who men and women are and what they can and should become in relationship to Him is but an elaboration on their having been made in His divine likeness. One might conclude, as many have, that since God formed the first woman as well as the first man in "His" image, that the male is the ideal or prototype human and that the female, though human, is a secondary creature.

This view seems borne out by when, how, and why Eve was created. God first made Adam and then later, after Adam had for some time lived and labored by himself without Eve's companionship or help, God finally created Eve (Genesis 2:7, 15-21). And when He did form Eve, he did not do it from scratch in his own likeness, as he did Adam, but he formed her from a part of the man Adam (Genesis 2:21-22). Furthermore Eve was not only made from Adam sometime after him, but for him as well. The reason God gave for creating her was that it was "not good" for Adam as "man" to be "alone" and he needed a woman to be his "helpmeet" (Genesis 2:18, 20). No mention is made of Eve existing in her own right as woman, about her being alone if she did not have Adam as a male companion, or about her needing him as a helpmeet.

In this light, it might seem that man is indeed the primary and more desirable gender in God's eyes and that woman is a lesser human being who exists for the benefit of man. Though entirely implausible to enlightened humanity, views of this type are nevertheless common in human history. If any such interpretation of the scriptural story of Eve's creation proved correct, that by itself would constitute sufficient reason to refuse to believe the story as being the precise word of God.

Happily, a more plausible interpretation of God forming Eve in the divine image presents a view quite the opposite. When interpreted with the benefit of scripture given in the latter days, the narrative of how, when, and why Eve was created discloses her high calling from her Father as the first woman and Adam's dependency upon her as his equal in the eyes of God. Let us explain, beginning with God forming Eve in the divine likeness.

The Hebrew word for "God" in the Genesis account of creation is *Elohim*, a name sometimes used to indicate the exalted position of God the Eternal Father. Perhaps Eve was formed in the likeness of her Father, who is male. Certainly, she was formed "in the image of the Only Begotten," who is male (Moses 2:26-27). How can woman and man be equal in their humanity if they were both created in the image of creators who are male? Both Eve and Adam do have certain characteristics in common as persons with God the Father and the Only Begotten. According to some accounts of Eve's and Adam's earthly creation, both were made in "the image" of God's "own body" (Moses 6:8-9) and the "image" of the Son's "body" as well (Ether 3:14-16). So it could be said that both were formed in the same image insofar as they are human beings with the same general bodily likeness as the Father and the Son. What is more, as a pattern of creation, the divine image is not only a bodily one, but one of spiritual perfection as well, which all persons can realize, through God's grace and their obedience to him, regardless of gender (3 Nephi 12:48).

But one problem with this interpretation, insofar as it notices only characteristics and possibilities that woman and man have in common with the Father and the Son, both of whom are men, is that it ignores those features that distinguish woman and man. According to all scriptural accounts, Eve and Adam were not only formed in God's image as human beings but as female and male human beings. Indeed, their bodies were created specifically as male and female (Moses 6:9), and their subsequent development as woman and man constitutes a central theme in the story of their creation and their subsequent life together.

Though *Elohim* is sometimes used as the exalted name of God the Father, it is also a plural term whose literal meaning is "Gods."[1] So the Genesis story of the creation of Eve and Adam might be read as saying, "And the Gods said, let us make [the woman and the man] in our image after our likeness" (Genesis 1:26-27). In fact, the story of the creation of Eve and Adam in the Book of Abraham reads precisely that way: "And the Gods took counsel among themselves and said: Let us go down and form man in our own image . . . So the Gods went down to organize man in their own image" as "male and female" (Abraham 4:26-27). The fact that "male and female" were made in the image of the "Gods" leads some to believe that the Creators themselves must have been male and female. In fact, through modern revelation we know that only exalted beings who are joined in eternal marriage can bring forth life in their own image, indicating that Heavenly Father is a co-creator with our

Heavenly Mother (D&C 132:16-20; 131:1-2). Furthermore, since Adam and Eve are the spirit children of Heavenly Mother and Heavenly Father, some conclude that our Heavenly Parents probably formed them in their likeness as male and female in their new environment, just as they brought them forth spiritually in their likeness as male and female in premortal life

This may be true. But we still must take into account that Eve and Adam were also created as "male and female" in "the image" of the "Only Begotten" (Moses 2:26-27), who at the time presumably did not have an eternal mate as co-creator. This leads us to believe that the focus should not be on the plural meaning of "God" in the story of Eve's creation as on the plural meaning of the "image" of God. Whether or not our Heavenly Parents together formed Eve and Adam in their new environment, certainly the pattern followed in that creation includes both male and female.[2]

That this is so becomes apparent as we follow the story of Eve's and Adam's creation to its completion. In forming Eve and Adam, God first made them "in the image of his own body" as "male and female" (Moses 6:9), indicating that God's bodily "image" is relational and includes the bodily image of female as part of it. But forming Adam's and Eve's bodies marked only the beginning, not the end, of their creation in His own likeness. Their bodily natures provided the starting point from which God, through his Only Begotten, could develop their full identities as woman and man after the divine image. A first indication of what their final natures as woman and man could be like is given in the figurative account of Eve being formed in the divine likeness from a part of Adam (Moses 3:21). It seems that without Adam being a part of her, the divine image would not reach fruition in her full identity as woman. Indeed, the text says that she was first called "woman" precisely because, as one formed in the divine likeness, she embodies the presence of man (Moses 3:23).

But making Eve from a part of Adam in the divine image also meant that he would be incomplete without the part of him represented by her. She was created because it was "not good that man should be alone" (Moses 3:18), indicating that without Eve, Adam could not fulfill the image of God. The story of Eve's creation makes clear how each becomes whole through the other: they must become husband and wife.[3] That is precisely what Adam himself was given to know when he realized that, because Eve was made from him, she was "bone of [his] bone" and "flesh of [his] flesh." He concluded that she was to be his "wife," that he should "cleave unto her," meaning that he should love her with all his heart (D&C 42:22), and that they should be "one flesh," indicating, among other things, that they should bring forth children together (Moses 3:21, 24).[4] Notice that Adam himself did not conclude that because Eve was made from him as man—that she became bone of his bone—that woman is a secondary creature or inferior to man.

God joined Eve and Adam together as wife and husband for all eternity as a further step in making them in His image.[5] In order to realize the divine image implicit in their union, they must fulfill the terms and conditions of their marriage covenant, and therefore, it is necessary that they be sanctified together and live as one, according to the law that orders celestial life. In the words of the prophet Alma, they must have "the image of God engraven upon [their] countenances" by being "spiritually born of God" through faith in Christ and by "walk[ing] after the holy order of God" (Alma 5). By and by, they will embody the full likeness of God as an exalted couple and, as gods, live together with Him and Heavenly Mother forever in the highest heaven. Like their Heavenly Parents, Eve and Adam would then bring forth their own children in the spirit and provide them with the opportunity to realize the divine likeness after which they were created.[6] As we observed in Chapter Two, they would live and serve together in the great work of eternal love as equals in perfection and power, one not being subordinate to the other. This important truth—that in the likeness of God women and men are equal in perfection and power[7]—should bound any attempt to understand what it means to say that God formed woman and man to realize His likeness.

Eve as First Steward of the Light and Mother of All Living

If our interpretation of the creation of Eve in God's image is correct, why then was Adam created first and Eve second? Why was it "not good" for "man" to be "alone"? And why did he need a "helpmeet"? (Genesis 2:18, 23). Why is no mention made of Eve existing in her own right, of her being alone without Adam, or of her needing him as a helpmeet? Why were they not created together so that neither would be alone in the Garden without the other as helpmeet, thereby indicating their equality in the likeness of God? We can see why the narration in Genesis might leave the impression that woman was indeed made primarily for man and not each equally for the other.

But it seems apparent to us that creating Eve after Adam for the reasons given sets the stage for introducing her high calling from her Father as the first woman and for bringing to light Adam's and all humanity's dependency on her to fulfill that calling. Let us consider the specific occasion in which Adam's aloneness and immediate need for Eve first becomes apparent.

In all scriptural narratives, God Himself calls attention to Adam's aloneness and need for Eve when he introduces him to the tree of the knowledge of good and evil and forbids him to eat of its fruit. It appears that the two details might be related to form one event in an unfolding series of events (Moses 3:17-18; Abraham 5:13-14; Genesis 2:17-18). In two of the accounts, God first plants a garden in Eden, which conspicuously included the tree of the knowledge of good and evil. Next, he places Adam in the Garden, introduces him to the tree of knowledge of good and evil and commands him not to eat of it, and then immediately notes that he is alone and in need of Eve as helpmeet, all of which seems to constitute another event. Before God actually forms Eve, He brings "every beast of the field and every fowl of the air" before Adam to receive their names, which is an altogether different event; and then God observes once more that Adam requires a woman as helpmeet and he finally forms Eve (Moses 3:8-22; Genesis 3:17-22). In the remaining account, God introduces Adam to the tree of the knowledge of good and evil and tells him not to eat of it, notes his need for a helpmeet, and immediately forms Eve (Abraham 5:13-16).

It seems the stage was deliberately set for Eve to enter the scene and perform her role as the first woman and act as Adam's helpmeet, and that in its commencement her role would have something to do with the tree of knowledge of good and evil. As we know, Eve was the first to eat the fruit of the tree and persuaded Adam to partake also. Let us consider, then, why it fell upon Eve to initiate the Fall and how what she accomplished by doing so was in accord with her God-given role as the first woman and constituted acting as Adam's helpmeet for the first time.

We should bear in mind that Eve was foreordained in premortal life to be "the first of all women," "the mother of all living," and "the wife" of Adam (Moses 3:24; 4:26). She was among the "noble and great ones" whom God called to perform key roles in the plan of salvation for our world (Abraham 3:22-23; Moses 4:26).[8] Furthermore, the Fall itself was an absolutely pivotal and essential part of the plan, which implies that it was in the design of that plan for Adam and Eve to cause the Fall as they did.[9] It stands to reason that Eve's leading part in the Fall was itself not fortuitous. Surely that epochal step in causing the Fall of our first parents and all humanity was also provided for in the plot. We should fully expect that what she did was in accord with her calling as the first woman. And so it was: what she did when she initiated the Fall was to begin enacting her role as the mother of all living and hence as Adam's helpmeet.

Think about what Eve immediately accomplished by being the first to eat of the fruit of the tree of the knowledge of good and evil: her act provided the way into mortality through which all humankind could pass, and, of course, she introduced into that world the knowledge of good and evil with its inherent power to realize good. Since it is the "light of Christ" that enables people to "know good from evil" and "to lay hold upon every good thing" (Moroni 7:12-19), we may say that Eve introduced this attribute of the light into the mortal world by partaking of the fruit. Now, what she did fittingly and dramatically represents the role we should expect the "first of all women" and "the mother of all living" (Moses 4:26) to perform in the plan of God. For it is through the woman that all humankind must enter mortality, and typically it is (or should be) principally through the nurturing love of woman that human beings first awaken to the light as the power to know and realize good.

Before Eve partook of the fruit and convinced Adam to eat also, they themselves had not yet entered mortality. We could say they had not yet been born into mortal life. In the Garden, before the Fall, they were much like little children, inasmuch as they were in a "state of innocence," not knowing good from evil, and incapable of doing good or experiencing joy (2 Nephi 2:23). The light of Christ, as the power to "know good from evil" and "lay hold upon good" (Moroni 7:12-19), had not yet matured in them. Once Eve had eaten of the fruit, entered mortality, and become an agent of light, she immediately began acting as the first steward of the light. She persuaded Adam to do what she had done and become what she had become, acting as his helpmeet as she was foreordained to do. It may be said that Adam was, in an important sense, born of Eve. Of course, he did not enter mortality through her womb. Nevertheless, like all children of the earth, Adam entered the mortal world through the woman.

Furthermore, being born of woman typically involves much more than the purely physiological passage of a child from the uterus. It involves the birth of a human being in the larger sense, which includes the passage form a state of innocence toward accountable personhood by awakening to the light, initially through the love of woman. Within this larger sense, also, Adam was born of Eve. Adam grew in the light's power to know good from evil and realize good, which enabled him to pass form a state of innocence to one of moral agency, all through the love of a woman (2 Nephi 2:23-26; Alma 12:31).[10] Eve, on the other hand, gave birth to herself as a mortal being and an agent of the light by yielding to her desire to become as the gods, knowing good from evil and realizing good. So woman was also born of woman.

Of course, Eve's role in introducing humankind to the light and mortal life did not end with her part in the Fall. She brought forth the first children and nurtured them in the light. She conceived and carried each of them within herself and gave birth to them in sorrow (Moses 5:11-12; 4:22). In doing so, we presume she experienced that special connection to human life of which only woman is capable. Eve was a being of love, and her love enfolded her physical connection to the child within and naturally formed the primary nurturing relationship between herself and the child during the first years after birth. Before the child could know that he or she knows, Eve began awakening within her child the power to distinguish good from evil and to lay hold upon good. Her love opened her child to the light, bringing the child into existence as a self-aware person and making it possible for her or him to realize that which gives fullness to life.

So Eve acted as the mother of all living in two parallel ways: she opened the way for all humankind to enter mortality and grow up in the light by being the first to eat of the fruit, and she made it possible for humankind to enter mortality and awaken to the light by giving birth to and nurturing the first children, becoming the mother from whom all life descends. Eve fulfilled the meaning of her name given to her by her Father (Moses 4:26) by which He foreshadowed that she would be the one through whom all humanity would enter mortality and begin learning the way of the light.[11]

We should underscore here Eve's importance as Adam's "helpmeet" (Moses 3:18), in convincing him to partake of the fruit, helping him to enter mortality, turning him toward the light, and soliciting him to join her in bringing forth new life. Capturing Adam's attention, stimulating his commitment, and enlisting him in the cause of love and family were her divine stewardships as his wife, and as the mother of their future c h i ldren. Eve's persuading Adam to partake is as important to the plan of salvation and exaltation as her partaking of the fruit herself and is a great and sacred accomplishment in its own right. To his credit, Adam humbled himself and hearkened unto his wife, and by partaking of the fruit, committed himself to the future of his and Eve's children, and their children's children even unto the end of the world. When Adam later "blessed" the "name of God" for his "transgression" (Moses 5:10), he also surely must have been grateful to Eve.[12]

To conclude, let us return to where we began, to the scriptural account of Eve being created after Adam to serve him as helpmeet. We have maintained that this sequence of events set the stage for Eve to enter the world to fulfill the need of Adam and their posterity. What emerges from this segment of the story of Eve is the divine nature of her calling as the first woman and the debt of gratitude humanity owes her for what she accomplished. Suppose the places of Eve and Adam in that sequence of events had been reversed. Then the focus would have been on Eve's and humankind's need for Adam to open the way to mortality and introduce the light as the ability to know good and evil into that world. As a consequence, the role she played as the first steward of the light and mother of all presumably would have been performed by him as the father of all, entirely eclipsing her great calling while greatly enlarging his contribution to humankind and the gratitude owed him. How unfitting it would have been for Adam to have done what Eve did, for the man is not the one through whom life enters mortality and typically is not the primary one who first cultivates the light in new life. Suppose Eve and Adam had been created together and eaten of the tree at the very same time. The upshot would have been similar: Eve's sacred calling, inasmuch as it was tied to the critical need for someone to open the way into mortality and introduce the light's moral knowledge into that world, would not have been differentiated. Consequently, the importance of her calling and her accomplishments and the gratitude owed her would have accrued to Adam at least by half.

Eve's Transgression

As scripture makes clear, Eve's action in initiating the Fall was a transgression in disobedience to a commandment of God (1 Timothy 2:14). Traditionally, her act has been thought a great sin—a sin of unrighteous pride—resulting in the loss of innocence and paradise for all humanity. Blame for it has been ascribed mostly to Eve, and many women since have shared in her shame. Satan apparently thought he could not persuade Adam to eat of the tree, and so he turned to Eve as the weaker vessel, and she ate, seemingly to her disgrace.

How do we reconcile Eve's disobedience with our view that she acted as the first steward of the light in performing her foreordained role as the mother of all living? Does not her transgression in itself take away from the respect and honor we claim due her for her role in the Fall? We think not. Her reasons for eating the fruit and the very nature of her transgression reaffirms the view that she deserves our thanksgiving and praise for initiating the Fall.

Consider the reasons Satan gave Eve in order to convince her to eat the forbidden fruit and persuade Adam to partake also. Recall that when God commanded her and Adam not to eat of the tree of the knowledge of good and evil, he told them that "in the day thou eatest thereof thou shalt surely die," implying that as long as they remained obedient to Him they would enjoy their immortality. Satan assured Eve that she would "not surely die" if she partook of the fruit, promising her instead that she would be "as the gods" and her "eyes" would be "opened" so that she, like them, would come to "know good from evil" (Moses 4:10,11). Satan wanted to persuade her that gaining the ability to discern good from evil could not imperil her immortality, because it did not imperil the immortality of the gods. Eve found Satan's reasons very compelling, and we can understand why. The gods' knowledge of good and evil, which forms who and what they are, enables them to lay hold upon every good thing and as immortal beings enjoy fullness of life in the highest degree and have eternal increase (see, for example, Alma 32:28-42).

But how did Eve first learn of the gods' wisdom and the life it made possible? What experience instilled in her the desire to possess it for herself and to share it with Adam? Why did she believe that she and Adam could live as the gods do? Notice that Satan did not try to persuade Eve that the gods' wisdom was desirable and something she might possess. He did not find it necessary to give her reasons why she should get Adam to partake of the tree after she had done so, in order that he, too, would be wise like the gods. Satan assumed that Eve already desired the wisdom of the gods, not only for herself but for Adam as well, and he concentrated on convincing her that eating of the fruit was the only way she and Adam could acquire it.

There is only one other explanation of why Eve wanted to be as the gods. She and Adam were created in the image of God, and hence in the likeness of the gods, so she was predisposed to be like them with Adam. What must have awakened her desire was that she knew God in the Garden and He taught her and Adam that they should realize His likeness—that they should become as He is.[13] How else could she, in a state of innocence and alone with Adam, the veil having been drawn on their premortal life, learn about the wisdom of the gods and becoming like them?

We are persuaded that when God joined Eve and Adam together in celestial marriage He taught them somewhat concerning the conditions and promise of the marriage covenant, which are that if they remained faithful to Him they would become "gods" and, like Him, enjoy a "fullness" and "continuation of seeds forever and ever" (D&C 76:58-59; 84:38; 132:6, 19-20). Having learned of these things from her Father, Eve wanted the wisdom of the gods for herself and Adam, so they might become "wise and true" parents after His likeness.[14] Once God had planted that desire in Eve, her innocent heart was prepared for Satan to persuade her to eat of the fruit of the tree.

Satan spoke the truth when he told Eve that she and Adam must partake of the fruit of the tree of the knowledge of good and evil to become as gods. Given the plan of God and the situation in which He had placed them, there was no other way. Why there was no other way is a large subject, but suffice it to say here, in order for the spirit children of God to progress as immortal beings and by being faithful prepare to be gods, it was necessary that they enter mortality and as mortals come to know good from evil and choose that which is good. To do this, it was necessary that Eve and Adam begin their earthly existence in a state of innocence and pass from that state to one of temporal and spiritual death with its opportunity and promise of a greater life for themselves and their posterity. For this change to occur, it was necessary for them to transgress, for death can come about only as a consequence of transgression (2 Nephi 2:22, 25). So God devised the opportunity for them to transgress in the form of a tree whose desirable fruit he forbade them to eat and which He appropriately named the tree of the knowledge of good and evil.

Note that unless its fruit was forbidden, unless there was a divine command not to eat of it, the tree could not represent the opportunity to know good from evil. For if it were not a forbidden fruit, then eating it would not have constituted a transgression and consequently would not have resulted in temporal and spiritual death (Moses 6:55; D&C 29:39).

Eve was not willing to disobey her Father just because Satan told her that she and Adam must eat of the fruit to become like God, as impelling as his words to her may have been. Satan had to convince her further by saying, "*God doth know* that in the day ye eat thereof, then your eyes shall be opened and ye shall be as gods, knowing good from evil" (Moses 4:11; emphasis added). Satan's reasoning must have made sense to Eve, for she already believed her Father wanted her and Adam to become as the gods in wisdom and procreation. And it was Father who introduced her and Adam to the tree whose fruit He had made beautiful and good, indicating by the name He gave the tree that it represented the wisdom that He wanted her to have and that she now desired and telling her that she and Adam could choose for themselves whether to eat of it (Moses 3:17).

However, reason alone was not enough to persuade Eve to accept that God wanted her to eat of the tree, and thereby to convince her to partake of the fruit. In the end, Eve accepted Satan's words because she believed in him, and she believed in him because, as Jacob tells us, he "transformeth himself nigh unto an angel of light" (2 Nephi 9:9). In Latter-day Saint tradition, Eve did not realize who Satan was—he who rebelled against their Father—until after she had eaten of the fruit. Like true angels of light, false ones may come claiming to have a "message from God" (D&C 129:4-9), and though the messenger is false, the initial message may be true, as in the story of Eve.

To be precise, Satan did deceive Eve in part in his use of the words "ye shall not surely die," assuring her that she would be "as gods" who are immortal (Moses 4:10-11). But this was not the crux of his beguilement of her. The central feature was his pretending to be a messenger of righteousness with word from her Father (2 Corinthians 11:14-15). In this pretense, he convinced her that her Father wanted her to eat of the fruit, which was true. But Satan's desire was to turn her heart away from God to him, so that eventually she would "worship" and obey him instead of God (Moses 6:49).[15]

Indeed, in order for the Fall to occur as planned, it was necessary that Eve eat the forbidden fruit because Satan persuaded her to believe in him and not because she used her own reason to discover the truth about the tree of the knowledge of good and evil. To explain, we must begin by noting the peculiar nature of the commandment not to partake of the fruit: God commanded Eve and Adam not to eat of it with the intent and desire that they actually would partake in order to initiate His great plan of happiness. Whenever God commands someone to do or not to do something with the intent and desire that they disobey Him in order to bring about good, the success of His plan depends on those so commanded not knowing His purpose in giving it. If a subject of such a command learns of its purpose, then the will of God embodied in the purpose supersedes His will expressed in the command. If a person knowingly fails to keep the command in order to fulfill God's primary will in giving it, her act would be one of obedience rather than disobedience and would frustrate the purpose of giving the command in the first place. One underlying principle here is that if God wants a person to do or not to do something, all things considered, and that person knows or has good reason to believe this, then she is obliged to do or not to do that thing.

Suppose Abraham had realized that God, in order to test Abraham's faith and add to his righteousness, had commanded him to sacrifice his son Isaac with the intent that in the end he not do so. Abraham's prior knowledge of the plot would have spoiled the test situation, and even without further word from God, he would be obliged not to sacrifice Isaac. If the angel sent to stop Abraham had arrived late, and Abraham had succeeded in sacrificing Isaac as he had been commanded to do even though he knew God's real intent, he would have committed a great evil in God's eyes and would have been punishable for it.

Suppose Eve, after ample time had passed, figured out for herself from what the Father had taught her and Adam and from their by-now obvious stagnant situation in the Garden that her Father had commanded her and Adam not to eat the fruit with the intent that they partake of it in order to fulfill His purpose in their existence. Suppose further she shared her discovery with Adam. Their knowledge would have made it impossible for them to cause the Fall by eating the forbidden fruit. Both would know that if they did not eat the fruit, then they would fail to do what their Father wanted them to do. But if they partook of the fruit in order to fulfill His foremost will, their partaking would have been an act of obedience rather than a transgression. And if they "had not transgressed," they would have "remained in the Garden of Eden" forever and God's plan for his children's mortal existence would have been frustrated (2 Nephi 2:22).

Some might think that even if God wanted Eve and Adam to eat the fruit and Eve knew this, then her partaking of the fruit would still be a transgression unless God formally authorized it. So let us suppose Eve asked her Father about His foremost intent and what she and Adam should do. What could

He say to her? Being the God He is, He, in that situation, would be compelled to tell her the truth. Once He admitted to her and Adam that He did indeed intend that they eat the fruit, there would be no point in his iterating his command not to eat of it. But then they would realize they would not be disobeying him by partaking of it, and if they went ahead and ate the fruit anyway, their act would have been in obedience to His now-declared will. The upshot would have been that the Fall would not have occurred as planned.

It was Satan who made it possible for Eve and Adam to partake of the forbidden fruit as their Father wanted them to do and yet transgress at the same time. He did this by convincing Eve that he was an angel of light and by persuading her that she must partake of the still-forbidden fruit (and persuade Adam to eat also) in order to become wise like the gods (Moses 4:11). Submitting to Satan's will was was sufficient to constitute her transgression. Otherwise, what she did was a very good thing, as she later acknowledged (Moses 5:11), because it fulfilled the will of God and His plan of salvation. Though initiating the Fall involved a transgression, it was not a sin, for Eve's act was that of an innocent person who wanted to become like her Father, and not that of one who knows to do good and does it not (James 4:17).[16]

To better identify and evaluate Eve's transgression, we need to place it in its larger scriptural context. When God explained why He created the earth He said, in reference to His spirit daughters and sons, that He wanted "to prove them herewith, to see if they would do all things whatsoever the Lord their God shall command them" (Abraham 3:25). His foremost desire is that His children become "perfect" even as He is "perfect" (3 Nephi 12:48). Accordingly, the first commandment of the Father is that they "shall live by every word which proceedeth from [his] mouth" (see D&C 98:11; 84:44). As modern revelation tells us, when "God created man, male and female after his likeness," the very first "commandment" he "gave unto [Adam and Eve]" was "that they should love and serve him, the only living and true God, and he should be the only being they should worship" (D&C 20:18-20). Then He gave them particular commands, including the one that forbade them to eat of the tree of the knowledge of good and evil.

To obey God in all things, to love and serve Him and only Him (Exodus 20:3) meant that His daughters and sons should not obey Satan in anything. When Eve partook of the forbidden fruit because of Satan, she failed to obey God in all things. However, she was beguiled and her deed was otherwise good. What she did was the minimal transgression sufficient to initiate the Fall.

How then do we explain the fact that Eve failed to ask her Father about whether Satan's claims were true? She had not yet been temporally and spiritually cut off from her Father's presence and presumably, she could have discussed Satan's claim with Him before making any decision to eat of the fruit. And the fact remains that He had, in no uncertain terms, commanded her and Adam not to eat of the fruit of the tree of the knowledge of good and evil. What about the shame and guilt Eve felt when she became aware of her beguilement—feelings that caused her (and Adam) to hide themselves from the presence of the Lord for the very first time (Moses 4:13-14)? Perhaps there was more going on than we have yet recognized.

Scripture seems clear that Eve was indeed beguiled. In the book of Moses, the narrative of Eve's beguilement begins with a short account of Satan's fall and his *modus operandi*, which is "to deceive and to blind men" so he can "leave them captive at his will" (Moses 4:4). The narrative then continues with the account of Satan deceiving and blinding Eve so that she would eat of the tree (Moses 4:4-12). Still, it is possible that Eve was complicit in her own beguilement (see, for example, Alma 10:6; 30:53). She may have been guilty of self-deception motivated by a fear of what her Father might say or do if she did approach Him about eating the fruit of the tree she found desirable, of which he warned her not to partake (Moses 4:9-12). That would explain why she did not go to him to verify Satan's words to her, and why she felt the shame and guilt she did because of her disobedience.

We think this explanation of Eve's transgression is unlikely. As for her failure to consult with her Father, she had no reason to fear an audience with Him about eating the fruit to become as the gods. She knew He wanted her and Adam to fulfill His likeness by becoming as the gods. The Father may have spoken to them often about their eternal marriage and becoming like Him. Whether she believed that she and Adam must partake of the fruit of the tree comes down to whether she believed in Satan's presentation of himself as an angel of light. Either she was fully persuaded that he was what he appeared to be, or she harbored some doubts or simply did not believe him. Presumably, if she had not believed his pretense at all, she would not have been deceived in the first place and would not have eaten. If she was persuaded by Satan, then she had no reason to verify his words by going to the Father—he was what he appeared to be: an angel of light with a message from the Father (see 2 Nephi 9:9; 2 Corinthians 11:14-15; D&C 129:4-9). But if she had any doubts, there was no reason why she in her innocence should fear going straight away to her beloved Father concerning them. She had nothing to gain by not going to him, and if she ate of the tree, much to lose if she did not. She had no reason to deceive herself in order to avoid conferring with her Father.[17]

How then do we explain the shame and guilt she apparently experienced when her Father sought her and Adam out after they had partaken of the forbidden fruit (Moses 4:13-14)? The mere fact that she realized she had been taken in by Satan and disobeyed her Father would have provoked shame and guilt. But we also think what she felt was in part because she did not yet fully comprehend the significance of her and Adam's transgression in light of the gospel of Jesus Christ. Consider the reaction of those who disobey God and become aware of their sins in light of gospel truths in contrast to Eve's response to her and Adam's transgression. In the case of the former, the very thought of coming into God's presence afflicts their soul with "shame" so that they "dare [not] look up to him" and would "be glad" if they could "hide" from "his presence" (Alma 12:14-15).

When Eve first became aware that Satan had beguiled her, she felt shame and was afraid to face Him, so she and Adam "hid themselves from the Lord God amongst the trees of the garden" (Moses 3:25; 4:13-14; 3:25). But that was **before, not after**, God sent His angels to give them further light and knowledge concerning the plan of salvation. Once Eve grasped the larger picture, and understood the true significance of their disobedience, her response was dramatically different from her original reaction. Once they heard the angels' gospel message, both Eve and Adam "blessed the name of God" and were "glad" for their "transgression" (Moses 5:6-12)! And Eve herself tells us why in a short summary of the plan of salvation unsurpassed in all scripture: "Were it not for our transgression we never would have had seed, and never should have known good from evil, and the joy of our redemption, and the eternal life which God giveth unto all the obedient" (Moses 5:11).

As we ourselves reflect on the nature and import of Eve's transgression in light of the gospel, we should not cast blame or shame on Eve. Rather, we should be glad and bless the name of God for the transgression of our noble foremother. Indeed, we may have already done so. It does not strain the imagination to picture our presence in the heavenly host looking on as this drama unfolded on earth. When Eve partook, there was not weeping in Heaven and God was not wrathful because of what she had done, but all Heaven must have burst into rejoicing. And then all Heaven stood on tiptoes to see if Adam would hearken unto Eve's persuasion and partake as well. When he did, no doubt another shout of joy went up, with equal praise for Father's Adam.

The Cursing of Eve and Adam's "Rule Over" Her

When God summoned Eve and Adam to stand before Him after they ate of the tree of the knowledge of good and evil, He told Eve, "I will greatly multiply thy sorrow and thy conception. In sorrow thou shalt bring forth children, and thy desire shall be to thy husband, and he shall rule over thee" (Moses 4:19,

22). Though the record does not say so explicitly, it appears that God might have cursed Eve because she believed Satan and sampled the fruit. After all, he "cursed" the "serpent" because he "beguiled" Eve and he "cursed" the "ground" for Adam's "sake," so that "in sorrow" he would "eat of it" all "the day of his life," because he "hearkened unto the voice" of Eve (Moses 4:20, 23-25). So if our interpretation of the part Eve took in setting in motion the Fall is acceptable, then how do we explain this curse?

The answer is that God really did not curse Eve herself as he cursed the serpent himself (Moses 4:20).[18] Rather, He cursed her situation as a mortal and did so for her sake, just as He "cursed" Adam's situation (the "ground") for his "sake" (Moses 4:23-25), which indicates that He actually pronounced a blessing upon her. The fulfillment of God's words brought great blessings into Eve's life, and she knew as much when she later blessed His name (Moses 5:11). We see that this is so when we consider the several parts of the cursing of her situation.

Eve rightly regarded the fact that God would "multiply" her "conception" a great blessing. She wanted so much to be a mother and become an eternal parent like the gods. That, in part, is why she partook of the forbidden fruit. Accordingly, in the act of praising God for the Fall, Eve declared that "were it not for our transgression we never should have had seed" and "eternal life" with God (Moses 5:11).

Eve also understood and accepted that her Father would "multiply" her "sorrow" and that she would bear her children in pain, a blessing from Him. It is **true** that to become as the gods she had to acquire their wisdom, and to do so she had to experience the sorrows inherent in mortal existence. Referring to humankind in general and Eve and Adam specifically, the Lord tells us that "if they [Adam and Eve and their posterity] never should have the bitter, they could not know the sweet— Wherefore, it came to pass that the devil tempted [Eve and Adam]" and they "partook of the forbidden fruit and transgressed the commandment" (D&C 29:39-40). Furthermore, Eve evidently **believed** that undergoing earthly sorrow was necessary to become as the gods when she explained that if she and Adam had not "transgressed," they "never should have known good from evil" (Moses 5:11). Certainly, she believed it when God instructed her and Adam what to teach their "children" about preparing for "eternal life," saying that as their children began to "grow," they would "taste the bitter that they may know to prize the good" as part of mortal existence (Moses 6:55-59).[19]

We turn now to the most renowned part of God's blessing of Eve. He said, seemingly because of her leading role in the Fall, "Thy desire shall be to thy husband, and he shall rule over thee" (Moses 4:22). Many men, and many women as well, believe that in thus addressing Eve, God declared that men should have governing power over women, and husbands in particular over their wives, and that the wife, in submitting to her husband, should center her desires on him and serve his wants and needs. As some suppose, God would not have placed women under male rule unless women needed to be under the dominion of men for their own good, the good of their husbands and children, and hence the good of society. And presumably, some general weakness of character must be present in women requiring that men be given dominion over them, for why else would God deny women the same right to rule and conduct their lives as agents unto themselves as He gave men (Moses 6:56)? Did not Eve, who represents female nature, demonstrate that women should be governed by men when she allowed Satan to beguile her and persuade her to disobey a clear commandment of God?

Interpretations much like this one have been well received in the fallen world. They seem to explain and justify the existence of nearly universal male domination, which, even when benevolent in intent, has often proved to be a curse in the lives of women. But as reason proves and LDS scripture reveals, these ways of thinking are sadly mistaken.

How then do we interpret God's words to Eve, saying "thy desire shall be to thy husband, and he shall rule over thee"? What "desire" is referred to here? What does "rule over" involve? And what is the import of the "shalls" in the Father's instructions to Eve? The only desire of Eve that stands out in the story of her in scripture is her desire to be as the gods with Adam in the fulfillment of the divine likeness. We should expect this desire to figure prominently in scriptural narration since its object represents the foremost purpose of earthly existence and the primary purpose of the gospel. It is the desire that the Father Himself awoke in Eve in the Garden and that helped motivate her to eat the forbidden fruit. We see no reason to attribute any other desire to her. Certainly not a sexual desire for some man other than Adam which God needed to circumscribe![20]

What was God doing when he told Eve that her desire to be as the gods "shall be" to Adam her "husband"? It is instructive to note first what he was *not* doing. Obviously, the Father was not commanding Eve to pursue her desire to become as the gods with her husband Adam, for His desire that she do that was clear to her before she partook of the fruit and it motivated her to eat of it. Nor was He giving her permission to prepare for godhood with Adam, her husband, as she desired, for He did that when He married them for time and eternity. Nor was He commanding her to join with Adam in parenthood as husband and wife, for He had already commanded them to do that in the Garden (Moses 3:24). And of course, there was no point in predicting that her husband would be the one with whom she would strive to realize her desire to become as the gods. To explain what the Father *was* doing, we need to examine further the nature of Eve's desire and the conditions under which she would have to fulfill it now that she and Adam had partaken of the forbidden fruit.

Recall that Eve's desire to be as the gods and to realize the Father's likeness included becoming a wise and true parent like the Father. The Father indicated that Adam's and Eve's increase would be "many" (Moses 1:34; 4:26), and when He married them as a step in forming them in His own likeness, He commanded and "blessed" them to be "fruitful and multiply" (Moses 2:28; 3:24). As we know, Eve would bless

God for their transgression because it made it possible for them to have their own "seed" (Moses 5:11).

Then came the Fall, which transformed Eve's whole world. She found herself a mortal being and about to enter into what must have seemed like a very hostile environment compared to the Garden. Among other things, she realized this would be an environment in which she was to bring forth children, and that doing so would require her to shoulder enormous challenges and burdens. Her Father told her as much when he said that her sorrows would be greatly multiplied as she took on motherhood as a mortal in a fallen world (Moses 4:22). What is more, when Eve ate the fruit of the tree her "eyes" were "opened" and she became, as her Father said, "as one of us to know good from evil" (Moses 4:13, 28). Her new knowledge of good and evil no doubt awakened her to the tremendous moral responsibility that attends having and caring for children. The text indicates that she and Adam realized the enormity of her calling, not only as the mother of the first children in the mortal world, but as the mother of all human life to come.[21]

So it was that Eve found herself emerging from a state of innocence and leaving a life without cares to enter a harsh environment with a newly acquired sense of her moral responsibility as the first mother. Having just begun to know good from evil, and having not been taught much about the gospel (see Moses 5:5-6; 6:55-68), she did not yet have the bearings she needed to live in the strange new world. How were she and Adam, as wife and husband, supposed to go about raising children together and preparing themselves for godhood in that world? She needed further instructions from her Father.

So the Father gave Eve moral instructions in which He laid down the basic pattern of family and social life that she and Adam and their posterity must follow. He told her she should turn to Adam so that they might form a union like unto the unions found in the highest heaven and He indicated what the nature of that union should be, saying, "and he [Adam] shall rule over thee."

We are convinced that "rule over" is an unfortunate translation here, and for two related reasons. First, the Hebrew term rendered here as "rule over" can also mean "rule with." In fact, we understand that when the Hebrew word "*msh'l*" (usually translated as 'rule') is used in conjunction with "*bet*" (in most cases translated as 'with,' 'in,' 'by,' or 'at'), the better translation is "rule with" rather than "rule over."[22] The "rule" referred to here is that authorized by the Holy Priesthood (see D&C 84:17; 107:5, 40-44). Secondly, "rule" by means of the priesthood is rule according to the celestial order, the order of the gods, and that order is one of equal power (D&C 76:54-58, 94-95). In particular, it is an order in which couples who are married for eternity by the Holy Priesthood rule with one another as help-meets and equal partners on earth as well as in heaven.

We need not repeat here what has already been explained in previous chapters concerning the celestial order of equal power, except to say that women and men of God must learn to live together on earth having all things common and being equal in power. We know that Eve and Adam wanted to be as the gods and were eventually given the fullness of the gospel so that they could progress to that end. So reason alone leads us to conclude that they must have become the first people of Zion and lived together being equal in power, thereby setting the example for their posterity to follow.

We need not rely on reason to reach this conclusion; from the book of Moses we learn that Adam and Eve did indeed become the first people of Zion. Recall what Zion means: a people pure in heart who live according to the order of the highest heaven (D&C 97:21; 105:4-5). Moses indicates that Eve and Adam were "born of the Spirit," which is to say they were purified, or "sanctified from all sin," and were "born again into the kingdom of God," which on earth is the "kingdom of Zion" (Moses 6:59, 65; D&C 105:4-5, 32). They became "one" with God and were "after the order of him who is without beginning of days or end of years, from all eternity to all eternity" (Moses 6:67-68).

When God told Eve that Adam should rule with her, He introduced the idea of the order of the priesthood within which Eve and Adam would carry out their callings as the first parents and as the head of the human family. He was giving them a glimpse of how the gods truly live and rule. So it seems certain that Adam's rule was to rule *with* Eve and not *over* her as many in the carnal world continue to believe.[23] Theirs was an equal partnership that provides the prototype their posterity must follow in order to prepare themselves to be as the gods in eternity.

So God's word to Eve concerning her desire to Adam and that they rule together as first wife and husband actually constituted a great blessing. In fact, a dominant theme throughout the audience God conducted with her and Adam is that of a loving Father's concern for his daughter and her calling as the first mother. The interview begins when Adam admits that he had eaten of the fruit of the tree, saying he did so because Eve ate first and he ate in order to remain with her as God had commanded (Moses 4:15-17). Once the focus turns to Eve, it remains there until the end of the interview. Eve confesses she partook of the fruit because Satan beguiled her, so God curses the serpent for his deception of Eve by placing enmity between him and her and between his seed and her seed—which itself constituted a blessing (Moses 4:18-21). Then Father speaks to Eve again, telling her that she can now fulfill her desire to be a mother and learn to be as the gods. So it was when God addressed Eve, not Adam, that he first introduced the celestial order of family and social life within which a people can prepare for godhood.

Finally, with His concern for Eve in mind, God instructed Adam about his specific responsibility to provide for Eve and their family in their new environment by the sweat of his brow (Moses 4:23-25). That God had Eve's welfare and calling in mind when He spoke to Adam is borne out by how Adam responded, for his immediate and only reaction to God's instructions to him was to acknowledge Eve's high calling as the mother of all living. He solemnly repeated her name with a new awareness of its significance, the name given her as a sign of her momentous calling as the first woman, a name whose meaning God explained to Adam personally. In God's words dictated to Moses: "And Adam called his wife's name Eve, because she was the mother of all living; for thus have I, the Lord God, called the first of all women, which are many" (Moses 4:26).

Imagine! Eve as the Mother of All Living in the Almighty's great plan of progression and happiness for all humanity on earth! Surely Adam must have marvelled as the meaning and significance of her place in the grand scheme of things became apparent. We, too, marvel as we contemplate the calling of our noble foremother.

So the Father's recounting of Adam's recognition of Eve, which echoed the Father's own acknowledgement of her, felicitously concludes the narrative of the entire interview with the two of them, wherein the Father's loving concern for Eve stands out from beginning to end. One can hardly fail to notice two conspicuous omissions in how God concluded this account dictated to Moses (Moses 1:1; 2:1; 4:1; 32).. He makes no mention of what Eve must surely have felt about Adam's equally important calling as the first man and father of all living, nor does He mention specifically Adam's thoughts about the calling he had just received. The upshot is that the narration begins and concludes by recognizing Eve's calling rather than underscoring the view of many that the man Adam's needs and wants should be foremost and that Eve should submit to him and his rule. Do we have in this contrast a bit of divine irony?

Continuing the Work of Eve

Eve initiated her work as the first steward of the light and the mother of all living, but she did not complete it. Its completion has depended from the beginning on her daughters in every time and place. This earthly work will continue until the last child is born into mortality, raised in the ways of the light, and fulfills the divine image. In every gospel dispensation, the women of God, because of their greater light and knowledge, have been under special obligation to uphold and carry forth the labors begun by Mother Eve. This is particularly true of the latter-day women of God, who live in the last gospel dispensation, the dispensation of the fullness of times, when the knowledge of God has never been greater and when that old Serpent, the enemy of Eve and her seed from the beginning, has mustered all his forces to hinder and destroy her work. In their own families, in the communities of the Saints, and in the larger world of humanity, there exists opportunities aplenty for the women of God, whether or not they have children of their own in this world, to further the work Eve began. Whatever secures or promotes the ways of light, whatever preserves or enlarges the things that give life, whatever fulfills the image of God, can help fulfill the calling inherited from Eve.

Notes

1. The Hebrew word for God in the singular is *El* or *Elowahh*. The plural or honorific form takes the ending "*im*" as in *Elohim*, a term commonly used in the Hebrew bible which means "divine ones" or "gods" (male and female inclusive) in the plural form, or "god," "goddess," and "the true god" in the honorific form. See Francis Brown, S. R. Driver, and Charles A. Briggs, eds. *A Hebrew and English Lexicon of the Old Testament With an Appendix Containing the Biblical Aramaic, Based on the Lexicon of William Gesenius* as Translated by Edward Robinson (Oxford: Clarendon Press, 1977), 43.

2. The Proclamation on the Family states, "Gender is an essential characteristic of individual premortal, mortal, and eternal identity and purpose." "The Family: A Proclamation to the World," written by the First Presidency and Council of the Twelve Apostles of the Church of Jesus Christ of Latter-day Saints, was read by President Gordon B. Hinckley as part of his message at the General Relief Society Meeting held 23 September 1995 in Salt Lake City, Utah. Also found in *Ensign* 25 (November 1995): 102. See also a short work by Elder James E. Talmage, entitled, "The Eternity of Sex," in *The Young Woman's Journal,* October 1914. As Elder Talmage puts it, "The distinction between male and female is no condition peculiar to the relatively brief period of mortal life; it was an essential characteristic of our pre-existent state, even as it shall continue after death, in both the disembodied and resurrected states."

3. President Joseph F. Smith taught that "God instituted marriage in the beginning. He made man in his own image, male and female, and in their creation it was designed that they should be united together in sacred bonds of marriage, and one not perfect without the other." (*Gospel Doctrine*, fifth edition, 1939, p. 272).

4. Though the Only Begotten did not yet have an eternal partner, nevertheless His image as Lord and Savior includes female as well as male, particularly in their eternal relationship as wife and husband. This seems to be in harmony with Paul's teaching that "neither is the man without the woman, neither the woman without the man, in the Lord. For as the woman is of the man, even so is the man also of the woman; but all things of God" (1 Corinthians 11:11-12).

5. Prophets have taught that Adam and Eve were married by God and that that marriage was for all eternity. President Joseph Fielding Smith stated: "Here is a clear statement that the marriage covenant, when properly performed, is eternal. It is not to be annulled and come to an end at death. The first marriage performed on earth was the marriage of Eve to Adam, and this was before there was any death, therefore it was intended to be forever" (*Answers to Gospel Questions*, vol. 3 [Salt Lake City: Deseret Book, 1957-1963], 23). President Spencer W. Kimball also taught: "Adam and Eve were married for eternity by the Lord" (*The Teachings of Spencer W. Kimball*, comp. Edward L. Kimball [Salt Lake City: Bookcraft, 1982], 292).

6. In *The Gospel Kingdom*, President John Taylor identified the key roles that Adam and Eve played as the parents of all those who would come to this earth, as well as their eternal role as parents in the life to come. Of Adam he said, "He and his partner became the father and mother of lives—lives temporal, lives spiritual, and lives eternal, and were placed in the position to become Gods, yea, the sons and daughters of God, and to the increase and extent of their dominion there was to be no limit; worlds without end" (G. Homer Durham, ed., 3rd ed. [Salt Lake City: Bookcraft, 1944], 278-279).

7. President Gordon B. Hinckley taught that men and women will stand as equals in the celestial kingdom: "There are a few men in this Church—I'm glad there are not very many, but there are a few—who think they are superior to their wives. They had better realize that they will not be able to achieve the highest degree of glory in the celestial kingdom without their wives standing at their side equally beside them" ("Excerpts from Recent Addresses of President Gordon B. Hinckley," *Ensign* 26 [October 1996]: 73).

8. "Eve, Adam, Abraham, and others were among the noble and great ones involved with the creation of the earth. God foreordained her and named her Eve, 'the mother of all living'" (Daniel H. Ludlow, ed.

The Encyclopedia of Mormonism [New York: Macmillan Publishing, 1992] s.v. "Eve," by Beverly Campbell). Elder Orson F. Whitney also taught the principle that Adam and Eve were foreordained to their roles by God (*Collected Discourses*, ed. Brian H. Stuy, vol. 4 [Burbank, California, and Woodland Hills, Utah: B.H.S. Publishing, 1987-1992]).

9. President Wilford Woodruff believed that "Adam and Eve came to this world to perform exactly the part that they acted in the Garden of Eden; and I will say that they were ordained of God to do what they did, and it was therefore expected that they would eat of the forbidden fruit in order that man might know good from evil by passing through this school of experience which this life affords us." (Wilford Woodruff, *Journal of Discourses,* 26 volumes, London: Latter-Day Saints Book Depot, 1955-86, 23;125.)

10. The theme of Adam's awakening to the light through Eve is also found in Gnostic and Apocryphal accounts of Genesis. As Beverly Campbell notes, "The Genesis account begins by telling us that 'the Lord caused a deep sleep to fall upon Adam.' After the creation of Eve, Adam then is awakened. In the Gnostic gospels, Eve, or the feminine spiritual power she represented, is depicted as the source of this awakening, which is a spiritual awakening for mankind.

    "Recognizing that the gnostic gospels reflect only bits and pieces of selective truth, it is nonetheless informative to see the theme, prevalent in much of the Apocrypha, of Eve bringing light and awakening mind and spirit.

    "The Secret Book of John suggests that Adam 'suddenly awakens to the presence of the spirit hidden deep within,' which is embodied in the newly physical presence of Eve. This book concludes as Eve, 'the perfect primal intelligence, calls out to Adam [and in effect to you and me, the readers] to wake up, recognize her, and so receive spiritual illumination" ("Mother Eve: Mentor for Today's Woman: A Heritage of Honor," *The Journal of Collegium Aesculapium* [Spring 1994], 43). Of course, in our interpretation Adam comes to his own as a being of light only after Eve persuades him to eat of the fruit, which results in his coming to a knowledge of good and evil with the power to do good.

11. The English word "Eve" comes from a Hebrew root that signifies "to live, living, preservation of life, sustenance, to bring to life," among others. However, Eve's role as the "first of all women" and the mother of all humankind is best captured by those meanings that refer to one who "brings forth" and "sustains life," indicating that she is to be "the mother of all living" (Moses 4:26). See Ludwig Koehler and Walter Baumgartner, eds., *Lexicon in Veteris Testamenti Libros* (Leiden: E. J. Brill, 1958), 292-293.

12. Eve accomplished much in her role as the first woman which we have not mentioned. For instance, when Eve introduced into the mortal world the light as the power to know and realize good, she also made possible human freedom, not only for herself and Adam but for all their posterity. A free person is one who knows good from evil, can realize good, and are "agents unto themselves." As God explained to Adam and Eve, persons are "agents unto themselves" inasmuch as "they know good from evil" (Moses 6:55-56). So we may say of Eve that she was the mother of human freedom in the mortal world. What is more, the moral law became an operating part of that world when Eve introduced the light into it. The "light" is "the law by which all things are governed" (D&C 88:13), and so it contains the law designed to govern human existence. The light, which enables persons to discern good from evil, directs them away from evil and towards good (Moroni 7:16-23). This directionality is the moral law inherent in the light, and hence when the light is given to all who come into the world (Moroni 7:16; D&C 84:46), so is the moral law. Lehi apparently had this in mind when he taught that "men are instructed sufficiently that they know good from evil"— they have the light of Christ—and "the law is given unto men" (2 Nephi 2:5). So Eve is also the mother of the moral law. We cannot possibly describe fully, particularly in the few pages we have here, the contribution Eve made to humanity as the first steward of the light and the mother of all living.

13. The Prophet Joseph Smith taught that in the Garden "God conversed with him [Adam] face to face. In his presence he was permitted to stand, and from his mouth he was permitted to receive instruction." (Smith, Joseph, *Lectures on Faith*, Salt Lake City, Utah:Deseret Book Company, 1985, 13). We assume that Eve, too, enjoyed God's presence and received instruction from him along with Adam. After all, the Father's desire is that she and Adam together learn to be as the gods (D&C 132:19-20). To become as the gods, Eve and Adam would need the ability to "know good from evil" and then execute that ability to come to "a knowledge of good and evil" while in their mortal state (see, for example, Moroni 7:15-17; Alma 32:28-42; Moses 4:28, 6:55-56).

14. The Prophet Joseph Smith said, "Here, then, is eternal life—to know the only wise and true God; and you have got to learn to be Gods yourselves, and to be kings and priests to God, the same as all gods have done before you" (*Teachings of the Prophet Joseph Smith*, ed. Joseph Fielding Smith, Section Six 1843-44 [Salt Lake City: Deseret Book Press, 1938], 346).

15. One might suppose that Eve should have immediately seen through Satan's deception, since in beguiling her he spoke through the mouth of the serpent (Moses 4:5-8, 19), which should have tipped her off right away that here was a sly, deceitful, treacherous, and

unclean thing that cannot be trusted. But Eve obviously did not associate these traits with the serpent, since Satan succeeded in convincing her that he was a messenger of righteousness. One reason may be that she was an innocent, and she was in the Garden of Eden, where everything was good. She did not yet know slyness, deceit, treachery, and uncleanness, and certainly wouldn't have expected it in her state as an innocent in Eden. That aside, let us not overlook the fact that the serpent is a good symbol, as well as an evil one. In scripture, it represents the Savior—the one to whom all must turn for salvation (John 3:14-15; 2 Nephi 25:20; Helaman 8:14-15)—as well as Satan as an enemy of God (Revelations 12:9, Mosiah 16:3, D&C 76:28). Perhaps the devil picked the serpent as mouthpiece as a way of representing himself as the "Only Begotten" whom people should "worship" (see Moses 1:19, 4:1). The opposite meanings associated with serpent in conjunction with its reputation as being "more subtile than any beast of the field" (Moses 4:5), fittingly depicts the cunning by which Satan "deceiveth the whole world" (Revelations 12:9).

16. That Eve's disobedience to God was not a sin is a teaching of latter-day authorities. As Elder Dallin H. Oaks stated in a conference address, "[Eve's] act, whatever its nature, was formally a transgression, but eternally a glorious necessity to open the doorway toward eternal life." He further revealed that "the Prophet Joseph Smith taught that Eve did not 'sin' because God decreed it" ("The Great Plan of Happiness," *Ensign* 23 [November 1993]: 73). Elder Bruce R. McConkie said, for instance, "Adam and Eve could not commit sin while in the Garden of Eden, although laws of conduct had already been established, because the knowledge of good and evil had not yet been given them" (*Mormon Doctrine*, 2d ed., rev. [Salt Lake City: Bookcraft, 1966], 735).

17. According to Latter-day Saint scriptural tradition, in the story of Eve where Satan tempts her to eat the forbidden fruit, she asks him why he, her brother, was trying to persuade her to disobey their Father. Satan replies that he had said nothing about Father, which helped convince her to partake of the tree. Considered by itself, it might appear from this scriptural text that Satan was laying aside the issue of obedience to the Father when he attempted to persuade Eve to partake. But how, then, do we explain the fact that the innocent Eve, anxious as she apparently was to please her Father, nevertheless was readily satisfied with Satan's answer? We think the best explanation is to interpret his answer and Eve's response within the larger scriptural context we have been developing. Accordingly, when Satan told Eve that he had said nothing about Father, he spoke to her as one pretending to be an angel of light (2 Nephi 9:9) with the intention of blinding and deceiving her (Moses 4:4-12) by telling her (among other things) that the Father knew that by partaking of the fruit she and Adam would not die but

become as the gods in wisdom (Moses 4:12), as she already believed her Father wanted them to do. We believe Eve concluded that Satan's remark that he had said nothing about the Father meant to her that he had said nothing about disobeying the Father, but quite the opposite. Apparently with that remark, Satan finally satisfied Eve's concern that she obey her Father in all things, as the Father commanded her and Adam to do (D&C 20:18-19), and we infer that she was satisfied to the extent that she felt no need to inquire further of Satan nor to verify his words with the Father before partaking of the tree of the knowledge of good and evil.

18. Latter-day Saints reject the notion that Eve or her daughters were cursed for her transgression in the garden. Elder Dallin H. Oaks once explained: "Some Christians condemn Eve for her act, concluding that she and her daughters are somehow flawed by it. Not the Latter-day Saints! Informed by revelation, we celebrate Eve's act and honor her wisdom and courage in the great episode called the Fall" ("The Great Plan of Happiness," *Ensign* 23 [November 1993]: 73).

19. President Brigham Young taught that as Latter-day Saints we understand "why God permitted Mother Eve to partake of the forbidden fruit. We should not have been here today if she had not; we could never have possessed wisdom and intelligence if she had not done it. It was all in all the economy of heaven, and we need not talk about it; it is all right. We should never blame Mother Eve, not the least. I am thankful to God that I know good from evil, the bitter from the sweet, the things of God from the things not of God." (Brigham Young, *Journal of Discourses,* 26 volumes, London: Latter-day Saints' Book Depot, 1855-86, 13:145.)

20. A common interpretation of Genesis 3:16 is that Eve was cursed by God, and is required to submit to her husband as a result of the Fall. The verse states that "thy desire [shall be] to thy husband, and he shall rule over thee." Eve's, and woman's, "desire" toward her husband has been interpreted to mean sexual desire, a desire that makes her willing to be man's slave and to desire only that which her husband desires (see, for example, Mary J. Evans, *Woman in the Bible: An Overview of all the Crucial Passages on Women's Roles* [Downers Grove, Ill.: InterVarsity Press, 1983], 19).

21. Certainly after eating the fruit and as a result of his interview with God, Adam realized the greatness of Eve's calling as the mother of all living, for he was inspired to proclaim it (Moses 4:26). We must suppose from all we know about Eve that she was even more perceptive than Adam concerning her very own calling as the first woman, so we conclude that she, too, must have realized the magnitude of it.

22. We are indebted to Professor Donald Parry of Brigham Young University for pointing out this translation to us. (See Brown, Driver, and Briggs, *Hebrew and English Lexicon* (Hendrickson Publishing, Inc., Peabody MS: 1999), pp. 89-90).

23. In the previous chapter, we noted that the Melchizedek Priesthood is after the order of Enoch (the order of Zion), which is after the order of the Only Begotten Son (the order of the highest heaven) (D&C 76:55-56). We can now see that, as far as mortal life is concerned, the order of Melchizedek and the order of Enoch are in the first place after the order of Eve and Adam, who were the first people of Zion (see Moses 6:43-68).

CHAPTER 5

Women in the World

by
Valerie Hudson Cassler, with Alma Don Sorensen

The gospel of Jesus Christ, which gospel we teach and the ordinances of which we perform, is a global faith with an all-embracing message. It is neither confined nor partial nor subject to history or fashion. Its essence is universally and eternally true. Its message is for all the world, restored in these latter days to meet the fundamental needs of every nation, kindred, tongue, and people on the earth. It has been estab - lished again as it was in the beginning—to build brotherhood, to preserve truth, and to save souls.
—Howard W. Hunter

God's purpose is to bring to pass the immortality and eternal life of man (Moses 1:39; D&C 132:19-24). No matter the time period and regardless of the culture into which a spirit is born, every life is infinitely precious because God's purpose extends to every individual. God's orientation to human life is an expression of His love and is His way of being alive to human good. In the previous chapters, we have spoken of male-female relations in the perfect human society of Zion. I n this chapter, we wish to examine male-female relations in the imperfect societies across the world in which God's children live.

The Light, the Law, the Word
We begin with the situation humankind everywhere find themselves in, the universal human predicament introduced by the Fall, the grand possibilities of spiritual life and death in all their degrees in a world already infected by death (2 Nephi 2:27). Being in this situation constitutes the moral agency of

humanity (2 Nephi 2:16; 10:23; Alma 13:3; D&C 101:78) and it makes the aim of human existence clear: to pass from death into life in its highest degrees of fullness.

God has not left humankind alone and without guidance in their pursuit of life in its fullness. Because He loves human beings everywhere, He blessed them with the light of Christ. As scriptures say, "the spirit giveth light to every man who comes into the world" (D&C 84:46; 93:2). This light enables persons to "know good from evil" and to "lay hold upon every good thing" (Moroni 7:16-19). It is only by laying hold upon that which is good through the light within them that persons everywhere can move from death toward life and realize the universal aim of human existence.

The light contains a law inherent in it which gives life to all who abide the law. In D&C 88:13 we read that "the light which is in all things, which giveth life to all things" is "the law by which all things are governed." This law is moral law. Put in simple terms, the light of Christ directs persons away from evil toward good, and this directionality is the moral law inherent in the light. In Lehi's words: "Men are sufficiently instructed that they know good from evil"—God gives men everywhere the light of Christ—and "the law is given unto men" (2 Nephi 2:5). Only those who obey this law can begin to realize the purpose of human existence, the purpose of escaping death and realizing life in its fullness.

Though persons everywhere have the light with its law to guide them, there are a plurality of cultural manifestations of the human predicament and of the light and its law. The reason is that the light contains degrees of life and levels of law. This is true in eternity as well as mortality. In eternity there are "degrees" of "glory" and "fullness"—in the telestial worlds in particular the degrees are as numerous and different as the stars of heaven and each degree is governed by a level of law (D&C 76:98, 109; 88:22-24, 37-38). So there are many levels of law. We see the reflection of these heavenly worlds and levels of law here on earth where persons may live according to different degrees of light and law, and where the possibilities of their society are bound by the degree of light and law they live (D&C 93:2; 50:23-24; 82:3; 88:13).

What is more, good itself, in any degree which makes eternal life possible, has great variety and no one culture captures all that is good. Each great culture has a portion of the light and contains a unique manifestation of good in its art and architecture, literature and music, morals and law, and its styles and manners of living. All societies also contain elements of darkness and death. Indeed, we may say that in every earthly society there is a war between two loves: the love of light and the love of darkness. To every person is given the choice to cultivate a love of light or a love of darkness and society will reflect the choices of its citizens in this regard (D&C 29:45).

Though the light contains many levels of law and makes possible many degrees of fullness, it nevertheless directs all persons toward eternal life, which is the highest level of law (D&C 50:24; 84:46-37). This greatest of all human possibilities can grow up in every major society and culture by virtue of the light given to humankind everywhere. But persons can realize the highest possibility through their own culture only by having faith in Jesus Christ and by embracing the Word found in him. The Word in Christ is the divine exhortation to man to follow the light's moral law inherent in the plan of salvation and exaltation made possible by the Savior. The Word in Christ enables us to "lay hold upon every good thing" (Moroni 7:16-19). That is the testimony and central teaching of all scripture (3 Nephi 27:14-16). Faith in Christ and in his Word enables persons everywhere to realize fully that which is good and lovely in their own culture, and to enlarge upon that good until they do lay hold upon every good thing.

The light is present in all cultures, even carnal cultures and even though the Word of God may not be available to the members of a particular culture. This point is emphasized by scripture, "The Spirit giveth light to every man that cometh into the world" (D&C 84:46). No matter the era nor the culture, "men are instructed sufficiently that they know good from evil [and] the law is given unto men" (2 Ne 2:5). This light is the ability to distinguish good from evil.

The light contains a law inherent in this knowledge of good and evil—to cleave unto good and to shun evil. The scriptures teach us that the law is built into the light. In D&C 88:13 we read, "The light which is in all things, which giveth life to all things" is "the law by which all things are governed." Thus the light illuminates the difference between good and evil while simultaneously possessing inherent directionality toward the law. In a sense, then, we may speak of "the light and its law," because the purpose of the law—to define and organize human life so its highest possibility is realized and perpetuated in the divine image—is favored by the light.

The degree of fullness to which the law is abided by individuals may vary, but the law itself is ubiquitous. In his epistle to the Romans, Paul asserts that even the Gentiles, who do not worship the true God, show "the work of the law written in their hearts, their conscience also bearing witness" (Romans 2:15). In Doctrine and Covenants 88 we read that "all kingdoms have a law given" (vs. 36) and the kingdoms are differentiated by the degree to which their inhabitants abide by "the law which I [God] have given unto you, even the law of Christ" (vs. 21). Those who do not abide by the law of Christ "must inherit another kingdom, even that of a terrestrial kingdom, or that of a telestial kingdom" (vs. 21). We see the reflection of these heavenly kingdoms here on earth, where peoples may live the law to a greater or a lesser extent, and where the possibilities of their society are bounded by the degree to which the law is lived.

The Universal Deep Structure of Human Life

If the light and its moral law are ubiquitous, even though the full Word may not be available to all cultures at all times, there is a common basis for all human societies. Since all human existence was patterned after "the image of God" (Moses 2:27), both the light and its moral law are patterned after the image of God. Thus the moral law favors a way of life in the image of God's own life.

This underlying basis upon which all moral law and all moral orders are based is the universality of what we term "the deep structure of human life." The purpose of moral law is to advance a particular conception of the realization and perpetuation of the valued life, a conception patterned after divine existence. Indeed, a society cannot be viable without moral law reflecting, to a greater or lesser extent, the universal deep structure of life organized by God to bring to pass the immortality and eternal life of all mankind.

An examination of human life in light of God's purpose reveals the elements of the universal deep structure of every viable way of life in human society. Though there is a plurality of earthly manifestations of this deep structure, each manifestation contains at least three common elements. *First*, a viable society values life and consequently has a concept of human beings and how their lives should be lived. Human life is profoundly precious in such societies, and its loss is, in general, mourned. *Second*, viable societies acknowledge that human life has a two fold nature. Life is to be realized in its value and is also to be perpetuated. *Third*, every viable human society recognizes that perpetuation of human life is an integral and inseparable part of realizing and enjoying life. In such a society is found the understanding that any attempt to separate the two undermines the viability of the society.

We see the parallel to God's pattern of existence. Life is precious to God; He wishes every life to enjoy the fullness of its value; God desires life not only to be realized but to be perpetuated forever; and God's life is a life where the fullness of life and the perpetuation of life are inseparably linked. This is the universal deep structure of human existence because this is the structure of divine existence. We are God's children and God knows our greatest potential is to live as He does.

Because of the universal presence of the light and its law and the universality of the deep structure of human existence, judgment of diverse ways of living is possible. The nature of law is to order life, which it does by closing off some possibilities such as death and darkness. To break the law is to pursue the forbidden possibilities of death and darkness. Thus in every culture, ways of living may incorporate to various degrees the way of life or the way of death by the nature of the choices made in regard to that law which is "written" in the "heart" of every person (Romans 2:15). No one culture captures all good, and every culture has a portion of the light. There is a great variety of good in the world, for there is a great variety of viable societies in the world (2 Nephi 29:7-12). Goodness has great variety, not just in plants and insects and mountains, but also in art and architecture and literature. Likewise, since no one culture captures all good, earthly societies typically contain both elements of light and life and elements of darkness and death. Since light and life are "good" (Alma 32:35) and darkness and death are "evil" (D&C 10:21; 93:37), we can restate this to say that all earthly societies contain both good and evil.

What is the relationship between these earthly societies, containing as they do both good and evil, and the moral law, whose fullness is the Word? Since the moral law is given unto "all the nations of the earth" (2 Nephi 29:7, 11, 12), even though the fullness thereof may not be, each society has the means to distinguish between choices reflecting the way of life and choices reflecting the way of death as they occur within the society. This background of ethical opposition given by the moral law declares what is light and what is darkness. Satan and his followers are entirely without the law and thus entirely in the darkness because that is what they have loved (D&C 88:35; 10:21; 29:45; John 3:19). God, on the other hand, is full of light and loves light (D&C 67:9). Since every person is given the choice to cultivate a love of light or love of darkness, society will reflect the choices of its citizens in this regard.

If a society follows the moral law to any degree, realization and perpetuation of life can occur—i.e., the society will continue through time and perhaps even flourish. This is so because the law serves the purpose of the light and the content of the light is life. The light's measure of good is life—full, flourishing, and abundant life (John 1:4). In Alma's parable, we know the seed we have planted is good, light and real because it swells within us; the seed lives and grows and increases in fulness (Alma 32:32-35).

Because the moral law is universal and applicable to every earthly culture, it gives us a mode of reasoning whereby we can show that one way of living is better than another. Just as differentiations can be made between celestial life, terrestrial life, telestial life, and outer darkness based upon the amount of light manifest in each and the degree to which the law has been abided, so may we differentiate between earthly cultures on the very same basis. The very existence of the light and its law creates a boundary between light and dark and between life and death. Thus, a way of death is pointed out by every way of life as its opposite. The universal deep structure of human life cannot be rejected by a culture without a simultaneous embrace of death, both temporal and spiritual (Alma 5:40-42). We do not value and perpetuate life because we are mortal; we value and perpetuate life because we are descendants of God, and the light and its law are His way of living. The light, through its moral law, operates everywhere to define and order how people live, albeit in a plurality of ways, that civilizations might move towards the way of life of Him in whose image humankind was created.

The Perpetuation of Life

The perpetuation of life is integral to the universal deep structure of human life and to celestial life. Indeed, the highest level of existence, the celestial life, is set apart from all lesser ways of life, especially in reference to the perpetuation of life. Only in the celestial kingdom do they directly perpetuate life (D&C 132:16-17). Yet the work of those in the lesser kingdoms indirectly revolves around the perpetuation of life also, for their inhabitants act as ministering servants to those who do perpetuate life and whose purpose is to "bring to pass the immortality and eternal life of man" (D&C 132:17; Moses 1:39). So in all kingdoms of glory, perpetuation of life helps define labor therein.

The perpetuation of life in a human society is a complex thing. It involves the perpetuation of language, customs, literature, religion, skills, and other concepts of culture.

Perpetuation is thus more than giving birth to new members of the society. And yet the core of perpetuating life is bringing forth new life and nurturing it toward full personhood. All other sorts of perpetuation are but secondary to the perpetuation of new life.

Thus we may also say that the core part of all viable ways of living is the relationship and the division of labor between men and women, for it is through that relationship that life is perpetuated. In a very strong way the relationship and the division of labor between men and women in earthly societies determines not only the viability of the society, but also its standing before the Lord. These judgments can be made because the moral law is given to all.

Man and woman are both agents of the light and its law. It is as agents of the light and its law that man and woman perpetuate life. One without the other cannot perpetuate life; one without the other cannot become a god (D&C 132:19). Unlike other religious or secular beliefs positing the impermanence or malleability of gender, Latter-day Saint beliefs hold that our highest possibility is eternal life, a life characterized by eternal increase, which can only take place in the context of eternal gender. The proclamation on the family states, "Gender is an essential characteristic of individual premortal, mortal, and eternal identity and purpose."[1] If maleness and femaleness are permanent characteristics of our souls, and if maleness and femaleness are necessary to the perpetuation of life, what can we say about gender relations and the universal deep structure of human life?

The Relevance of Adam and Eve

We take again as our point of departure the story of Adam and Eve. The model applies to all men and women and thus does not represent the imposition of the traditions of any one particular culture upon the men and women of the world. Indeed, the story is given to us by the Lord as corrective to the traditions of earthly cultures. A standard critique of Western secular feminism is that it applies desiderata and cultural assumptions rooted in Western culture to the women of the world. Given the very high divorce rates in the West, and the fact that women and children make up the bulk of the West's poor, to claim that the women of the world would be better off if they lived, thought, and acted like Western women is suspect at best. Rather, we turn to the story of Adam and Eve as a means to find true role models that may lead us to the fullness of human flourishing.

One of the first lessons we learn from the story of Adam and Eve is that *gender relations are at the heart of life*. God created only two beings at the dawn of human history—one man and one woman. No male-male or female-female relationship can substitute for the critical importance of male-female relations. Hence, in examining any particular culture, we must train our powers of observation on the male-female relations in that society. We must not be distracted by histories or journalistic accounts that typically focus on male-male relations. The real "action" taking place within a culture is taking place between men and women.

Second, we learn that the appropriate relationship between men and women is called marriage. God married Adam and Eve in the Garden of Eden.[2] Their marriage symbolized that God intended that men and women be joined as one, that they love and commit to one another (D&C 42:22), and that their commitment to each other should exceed their commitment to any others, including parents (Moses 1:23-25). Just as male-female relationships are the centerpiece of any culture, so is marriage integral to the universal deep structure of human life. Loving, cooperative, committed relationships between men and women, approved by God through the marriage ordinance, are a hallmark of every viable way of living. As President Spencer W. Kimball wrote, "The Church will always hold aloft the banner of happy family life, for we can do no other. Family life is the best method for achieving happiness in this world, and it is a clear pattern given to us from the Lord about what is to be in the next world."[3]

Indeed, all those who inherit celestial life do so as married persons. And those who inherit lesser kingdoms inherit them as unmarried persons. There is no God without marriage. Heavenly Father could not be a god without being married to Heavenly Mother, who is also a god. Therefore, marriage is ordained of God for all His children, no matter where or when they are born into human life (D&C 49:15-16). As Brigham Young taught, "[Eternal marriage] is without beginning of days or end of years . . . We can tell some things with regard to it; it lays the foundation for worlds, for angels, and for the Gods; for intelligent beings to be crowned with glory, immortality, and eternal lives. In fact, it is the thread which runs from the beginning to the end of the holy Gospel of Salvation—of the Gospel of the Son of God; it is from eternity to eternity."[4]

Third, we understand from the story of Adam and Eve that *there is a division of labor in regard to the perpetuation of life.*

Motherhood

Though the exact division of labor between men and women varies greatly across cultures, in every culture women give birth to new life and, in an overwhelming proportion of cases, these mothers love and bond with their babies. Women nurture the light with its moral law as well as the life in their babies by loving them. In loving their babies, mothers point them towards the moral law. Women are alive to good—the good of their babies and their welfare. Thus, in the very first human relationship experienced on earth, new souls are prepared to see, recognize, and move towards the light and its moral law. Mothers prepare their babies in such a way that these new souls will have "the work of the law written in their hearts" (Romans 2:15). New souls will recognize and move towards the light and its moral law because these acts are familiar. They are based upon countless acts in early childhood of recognizing and moving towards the woman who provided life, love and nurture of the light within.

The spiritual significance of this work is profound, according to modern prophets. The caretakers of the light—the women—teach their children that there is love in the world and to seek that love. They teach them how to keep their second estate and give them the motivation to do so.[5] Indeed, President Gordon B. Hinckley has said, "There is no work closer to divinity than the work of nurturing God's sons and daughters." And President Joseph F. Smith said, "The love of a true mother comes nearer being like the love of God than any other kind of love."[6] In President David O. McKay's words, "Motherhood is just another name for sacrifice . . . No language can express the power and beauty and heroism of a mother's love."[7] The earthly kinship with the mother and the promise of eternal kinship with her are powerful motivators for a soul to yield to the moral law. Joseph F. Smith expressed this:

> *Only a little boy, . . . whenever temptations became most alluring and most tempting to me, the first thought that arose in my soul was this: Remember the love of your mother. . . This feeling toward my mother became a defense, a barrier between me and tempta-tion, so that I could turn aside from temptation and sin by the help of the Lord and the love begotten in my soul, toward her whom I knew loved me more than anybody else in all the world, more than any other living being could love me.[8]*

As President Thomas S. Monson has so eloquently put it, "Men turn from evil and yield to their better natures when mother is remembered . . . May each of us treasure this truth: One cannot forget mother and remember God. One cannot remember mother and forget God. Why? Because these two sacred persons, God and mother, partners in creation, in love, in sacrifice, in service, are as one."[9]

A mother is not a perfect vehicle of the light. Because she is a product of her culture, each mother imparts some darkness to her child as well. Women are often a conservative element in their society and may teach their children to love traditions of their fathers which are out of harmony with the ways of life. Certain women may be evil and may also love darkness and seek to awaken in their children a love of darkness. But in general, a mother wants good for her child, and there is a variety of good among mothers because they live in a variety of cultures. Each mother in every culture introduces new souls to agency and to the moral law. In general, women have not lost sight of the original woman, Eve, and what she stood for.

Getting Adam to Partake

There is an additional role played by Eve that is often overlooked when we speak of the division of labor regarding the perpetuation of life: getting Adam to partake. In this act, Eve persuades Adam that the realization of the fullness of life for himself is inseparable from the perpetuation of the fullness of life through future generations. To his credit, Adam hearkens to his wife, and by partaking, commits to life, to love, and to the perpetuation of life and love. The woman's love for her partner and the man's love for his partner unite them in a sacred cause, the perpetuation of love and life in their posterity. Eve's love for Adam, his love for her, and the fruit of that love represents movement towards the light and its law. It is the catalyst from which recognition of and desire for the light and its law is built in every civilization. And Eve is the root of this movement: she turns towards the light and persuades Adam to turn towards the light.

Interestingly, there is empirical support for this description, at least in our own religious community. A study of the religiosity of church-going Latter-day Saint persons across the life cycle, shows that the religiosity of the males in the study was typically low throughout youth but then took a sharp upward turn upon marriage.[10] Commitment to Eve created a turning towards the Word for these generally religious men that male experiences by themselves did not produce. This phenomenon did not occur in corresponding fashion for females in the study.

One of the dominant themes of a woman's life, besides the themes produced by maternal love, are those concerning "getting Adam to partake." Capturing Adam's attention, softening his heart, stimulating his commitment, and enlisting him in the cause of love and family preoccupy most women during their young adulthood. Our culture frivolizes this endeavor, claiming that women are selfishly and narrowly absorbed in "landing a man." Doubtless sometimes the enterprise does seem frivolous, and at times it is conducted unrighteously, but at its heart this female preoccupation with relationship to a male is not frivolous at all. It is profound and important and, if conducted for righteous intent through righteous means, it is sacred. Eve must get Adam to partake, must turn him towards the light, or the plan of salvation and exaltation will be frustrated. It is as much part of the divine stewardship of women as motherhood.

Roles of Husband and Father

And what of the role of man? The story of Adam and Eve provides a healthy role model for men as well. Just as Eve righteously persuaded Adam to partake, an important component of manhood is to hearken unto Eve and "partake." By so doing, a man commits to the cause of eternal life and becomes an agent of the light himself. Indeed, God is more approving of cultures in which men have "partaken" than of cultures where, despite the presence of the word of God, Adam's sons have not lived up to his good example (Jacob 3:5-7).

Since both men and women are creators of new life, both have an obligation to nurture that life. Adam helps in the nurturing and loving of new life, just as Eve does. Both share the responsibility of socializing their children in the degree of light present in their culture. Both Adam and Eve are agents of the light. But Adam has certain responsibilities in addition to these just mentioned. President Gordon B. Hinckley has spoken of the responsibility of fathers and husbands to provide for, protect, strengthen, and shield their families.[11] Thus in most cultures, men have the responsibility for the temporal security of the family. As noted in the Book of Mormon, the physical defense of one's wife and children is considered a "sacred duty" (Alma 44:5). And in the Doctrine and Covenants, we learn that economic support of one's wife and children is also considered a sacred duty, abrogation of which renders one "less than an infidel." (D&C 83:2).

When the word is had among a people, men not only hold responsibility for the temporal security of the family, they also hold responsibility for the spiritual security of the family. We shall turn to this topic in the next chapter.

We reiterate that the work of the man and the work of the woman are inseparable, because each is an agent of the light. Thus men nurture, while women are also vitally important in providing for the temporal and spiritual security of their families. Indeed, men and women would be remiss if they did not help each other in this way. Nevertheless, God has ordained that the primary responsibility of the woman is the nurturing of the children, and the primary responsibility of the man is the security of the family in all its facets.

Thus, even though we do not know how Heavenly Father and Heavenly Mother divide their responsibilities in the celestial kingdom, they have given us Adam and Eve as exemplars of how it is to be done in mortality.

Cultural Manifestations of Darkness

We have noted that there is a war taking place within every human culture, a war between the light and the darkness. At stake are the hearts of all God's children (D&C 88:40; 2 Nephi 26:10). The Lord laments the hold darkness has on the minds and hearts of His children: "For all flesh is corrupted before me; and the powers of darkness reign upon the earth, among the children of men, in the presence of all the hosts of heaven— which causeth silence to reign and all eternity is pained" (D&C 38:11-12).

There are ways of dying to the good in all cultures. Just as we recognize the work of the light in all cultures, so we may recognize the work of darkness. Just as the core of all ways of living is life and perpetuation of life, so the core of all ways of darkness is death (Alma 5:41-42). Lehi explains that "men are free according to the flesh; and all things given them which are expedient to man. And they are free to choose liberty and eternal life, through the great Mediator of all men, or to choose captivity and death, according to the captivity and power of the devil; for he seeketh that all men might be miserable unto himself" (2 Nephi 2:27). The choice for life or death is for every society to make.

As we have already noted, at the heart of life is the relationship between man and woman. Thus Satan and his followers must place at the top of their agenda the undoing of the God-ordained committed and loving relationship between men and women (2 Nephi 2:18, 27). If this can be accomplished, then it does not matter whether the culture is one in which the Word is had or not—in either case, the society will be destroyed because it is wicked (1 Nephi 14:7; 16; 17:37-38; 22:14; Genesis 6:7; Deuteronomy 7:2; 12:29-31; 2 Kings 16:3; Helaman 7:24; 13:14, 38; chapter 15).

Each way of life in the moral law points to a way of death as its opposite. The moral law closes off possibilities that would lead to death. When the moral law closes off a possible way of human existence, it is pointing out that way of existence as being a way of death and darkness. Given the universality of the moral law, then all social systems have closed possibilities —in other words, there are ways of living that are forbidden to societies that aspire to fullness of life. An analysis of these forbidden possibilities allows us to classify them by type according to which part of the moral law would be broken by their adoption within a human society. Types of societal deviations from the moral law would be historical signs that a human society is descending into darkness and ultimately death. A theory of the degeneration of human cultures can be built upon this basis.

It may take a long or a short time for a society to change from one that pursues life to one that pursues death. Remembering that we must focus in male-female relations to see the real spiritual action taking place in a society, several types of societal deviation from the moral law can be identified.

Type I Violations: Societal deviations from the moral law of marriage given to all cultures.

Every society has a concept of human life, how it is precious, and how it should be lived. This is the concept of the "realization of life" in a society. We have noted that the story of Adam and Eve makes plain that God intended the realization of life in every human society to involve marriage between a man and a woman. The marriage is a symbol of the type of relationship that should exist between the two essential creators of life. The relationship is to embody love and commitment and is to be understood as a relationship between two equals. Though there are many ways of loving and marriage in the world, encompassing differences in courtship, marriage ceremonies, and so forth, the centrality of marriage to the realization of life in society cannot be downplayed. It is central to the universal moral law given to all. Even in the context of such diversity, love between a man and a woman brings forth obligations from the light's law, an obligation to forsake all others and commit to the marriage partner, and an obligation to treat each other as equal beings of light. These particular aspects of marriage are also part of the moral law given to all.

Thus we may identify the first type of societal deviation from the moral law as a delinking of that society's conceptualization of the realization of fullness in life from marriage. Two subtypes of deviation can be identified in this regard.

Subtype I: The creation of a hierarchy in male-female relations.

The first step is to to create a hierarchy in male-female relations and thus pervert the concept of marriage as a loving, committed relationship between a man and a woman who stand before each other as equals. In this stage, a society begins to conceive a woman as fundamentally different from a man. Because she is not like them, men can begin to treat a woman differently from how they would treat another man.[12] Without exception, women in carnal and fallen societies are treated as inferior to men, not only as physically inferior, but as intellectually and spiritually inferior as well. As Elder James E. Talmage put it, "[Woman] has suffered the greatest humiliation during periods of spiritual darkness, when the Gospel of Christ was forgotten."[13]

Because women have been conceptualized as different, they become the means to men's ends rather than ends in themselves. Men begin to see women as instruments whereby their own wants, needs, desires, and lusts can be satisfied.[14] Women no longer hold full human value in such societies and male empathy for women becomes very difficult. Women in such cultures may be denied certain fundamental human rights, their agency may be constrained, and they may be the subjects of behavior that would never be applied to men (e.g., sex-selective infanticide, wife beating, polygamy).[15] Their labor and their contribution to society will almost always be rendered invisible and thus comparatively valueless.[16]

Economic dependence of the woman on the man in such cultures thus becomes a way to ensure the subservience of women to men. Marriage between men and women is still the societal goal, but it would be impossible to envision marriage in such cultures as a partnership between equals. Indeed, it eventually becomes impossible to envision love as the core of marriage. The sons of Adam do not follow the righteous example of their noble forefather, and, in a sense, they refuse to partake of that which Eve offers. Typically, commitment and fidelity in marriage for the woman is obligatory and deviation therefrom is met with the sternest punishment, whereas commitment and fidelity in marriage for the man becomes optional and deviation therefrom may not only not be punished but may actually be celebrated in male society.[17]

Obvious gender inequality and a double standard of fidelity, then, are the two primary hallmarks of this first subclass of societal deviation from the moral law concerning marriage (see Appendix A for additional annotated descriptions).

Subtype II: The elimination of marriage as the societal goal.

The second subtype of societal deviation from the moral law concerning marriage is to reconceptualize what is meant by the realization of life so that it excludes fundamental characteristics of what God meant by "marriage." In addition to stripping male-female relations of loving commitment and equality, as in the first subtype of violation of the moral law, the second subtype of violation goes further and may involve claims that marriage is unnecessary or harmful,[18] that fidelity in marriage and chastity outside of marriage is unrealistic,[19] and that same-sex sexual relations can be an appropriate part of the society's concept of realization of life.[20]

Partly in a natural reaction to the first subtype of societal violation of the moral law of marriage, women may begin to see marriage as an oppressive institution, because they have never experienced it as otherwise.[21] Indeed, cultures engaging in this second subtype of violation typically have less obvious gender inequality than those engaging in the first subtype of violation. Nevertheless, the devaluation of marriage signals a more subtle and insidious form of gender inequality. It signals that society has begun to believe men and women cannot be equal in the context of a relationship together and they can only realize equality separately. Oppressive marriage of the first subtype of violation and cultural descent is replaced by abandonment of marriage in a quest for equality. When women are freed in significant measure from the oppression of the first subtype of violation, and become able to support themselves as economic actors in their own right, they will eschew what they understand to be marriage—carnalized marriage between unequals as conceptualized in cultures engaged in the first subtype of deviation. This is perfectly understandable and natural. However rather than reconceptualizing marriage according to the divine model, what results is a relinquishing of marriage as a societal goal. In second-stage cultures, departure from marriage, whether in the form of cohabitation without marriage or divorce from marriage, becomes societally normal.[22] Promiscuity becomes celebrated for both men and women and is viewed as normal and even healthy human behavior.[23] The meaning and significance of marriage is almost completely lost in cultures engaged in the second subtype of deviation from the moral law of marriage, and marriage may even be viewed as an anachronism. The home in which there was never a marriage to begin with may be the symbol for second subtype descent.[24]

Type II Violations: Societal deviations from the moral law concerning children given to all cultures.

The loss of marriage as the central element of societal existence is a tremendous blow to any society. A loving and equal partnership between men and women can hardly be conceived of in such cultures. Yet the true profundity of this loss has yet to be realized. In the next type of societal descent, the loss of marriage brings further devastating loss—the loss of societal capacity for the perpetuation of life. As integral to the universal deep structure of human life as the moral law of marriage is the moral law concerning the bringing forth of posterity (or the perpetuation of life). Indeed, these two elements of the moral law are so intertwined that the violation of one inevitably leads to the violation of the other. This second type of societal violation of the moral law will lead in an even more direct fashion to the society's descent into darkness and death. As we shall see, the value of the perpetuation of life begins to wane. Next, the value of what life is still perpetuated—that is, the value of the children of the society themselves—is diminished. Finally, the bonds of love that tie parent to child are undone. When that occurs, an ultimate devaluation of all life within the society is possible. As with the first type of violations discussed above, the initial delinking of the realization of life from the perpetuation of life typically begins with men.

Subtype I: The separation of sex from the perpetuation of life for men.

In this subtype of violation of the moral law, men within the society are no longer actively engaged in the perpetuation of life. Children are still born into the society, but for many men, those children are the unintended consequences of their sexual relations with women. The siring of a child may no longer produce any obligation to commit to or temporally support the child's mother so she can adequately care for the child. Likewise, unless compelled to do so, the fathering of a child may not produce in the man any feeling of obligation for the nurture or temporal support of the child created.[25] Indeed, many men may be enraged when they discover their sexual partner has become pregnant and the woman may be abandoned upon such a discovery. They may reason that the woman should provide recreational sex with no commitments attached.[26] If commitment-producing situations develop, they perceive that the woman has failed them. Thus, sex becomes a commodity wholly detached from the perpetuation of life. This commodity may be increasingly obtained by force in such societies, since forceful acquisition minimizes the possibility of commitment.[27] In addition, when women are viewed as commodity-providers for men and children are viewed as burdens, this lamentable objectification may lead to an increase in domestic violence.[28] Consequently, family units composed of women and children to whom no man has made a commitment become numerous.

Since men usually hold power over women and children in the fallen world, when the perpetuation of life holds little value for men, resource allocation to women and children in society is low.[29] Children and their mothers will be economically vulnerable and may be the poorest members of society.[30] Services such as teaching and caretaking will be undervalued in these societies.[31] The work of motherhood will not be considered work at all, and abandoned mothers will not be given the temporal security to attend to their mothering work first.[32] These attitudes culminate in a "crisis of caretaking," for it becomes economically irrational and harmful to elect to become a caretaker.[33] As a result, the society is hard pressed to meet its caretaking needs at all.[34] More valued in this type of society is productive economic activity that produces wealth.[35]

Children, mothers, and other caretakers do not fare very well according to this benchmark of value.[36]

Men, on the other hand, have a great advantage in the production of wealth in fallen societies.[37] Though this confers great temporal benefits to men, it also constrains men who still desire to commit to a woman and the children of their marriage. The need to create wealth often impairs a man's ability to nurture and bond with his wife and children.[38] His conception of what family life means may become impoverished and his capacity to nurture his family will follow suit. Thus the father-child bond, even among men who desire commitment and children, may become attenuated. Elder Jeffrey R. Holland put it this way,

> *It seems to me that if more fathers would focus on their marriage, home, and family with anywhere near the intensity they focus on their careers, we would not have so many women trying so frantically to get away from that marriage, home, and family . . . God will hold us accountable for our performance as fathers, sons, and brothers, and not for how we did as doctors, lawyers, and corporate chiefs. The community, the nation, the world are crying out for leadership in the home, stability in the family, safety for our children. And what do some men do? Stay a little longer at the office! That's a little unkind of me, and unfair to many good men, but I am trying to make a point. Society has some problems, and too often men have been part of that problem. A significant portion of the challenges women and children face in the world today will not be healed or helped or resolved until men are more of what God expects them to be—good and gentle and compassionate and reliable. In short, more as He is. [F]or some, the vicious cycle continues, with too many men trying to be superior at everything but what matters most—being a husband and father . . . I desperately want my children to see at least something*

in their earthly father that would encourage their belief in a dependable, compassionate, and loving God.[39]

The home in which there never was a father present at all may be the symbol of this subtype of societal violation of the moral law concerning children given to all cultures.[40]

Subtype II: The separation of sex from the perpetuation of life for women.

The final subtype of societal descent comes about when women's attitudes towards the perpetuation of life begin to mimic the attitudes of men. Given the context of societal violations of the moral law concerning marriage and children, it is probably inevitable that women come to regard children as unnecessary burdens as well. If the first three subtypes of descent have come about, then it may be possible to move to the *coup de grâce*—the undoing of the human bond upon which all human bonds are based, the love of a mother for her children, born and unborn.[41] When the sons of Adam refuse to partake, the context in which a woman conceives and brings forth new life is polluted. Instead of rendering her and their child committed and loving support and protection, he may leave them to fend for themselves. Worse, he may demand that the woman must spurn the child as the price for maintaining the male-female relationship. What woe and sorrow is visited upon society through such selfish fatherlessness! When showing Enoch the saga of human history, the Lord breaks down and weeps because men "hate their own blood" (Moses 7:33). Generally, this has been interpreted as male-male hostility. But given Adam's declaration that Eve is "bone of my bone and flesh of my flesh" (Genesis 2:23), is not a more poignant understanding of the Lord's lament that men hate their own lovers and children? And that in such a context, women may begin to hate themselves, their womanhood, their motherhood, and their children?

Consider the situation of the woman in a time when Adam has been persuaded not to partake—more correctly, when Adam's sons do not live up to the righteous example of their forefather. The men in this woman's society may expect sexual relations from her, but without any corresponding commitment. To fulfill her natural tendencies as part of the work of womanhood to form a bond with a man, she may agree to such a Faustian bargain, which may lead her to the psychological state where she may desire to prevent conception. Means symbolic of her desire to avoid bringing forth a new life are devised.[42] She may then realize as a result the pale counterfeit of the desirable life that her civilization permits; she has one or more relationships with men and can cope with their lack of commitment by providing for herself.

Now consider her situation if the devices of avoiding pregnancy fail and she becomes pregnant. Rather than an occasion for rejoicing, fear enters her heart. If the man is not committed to her, he will probably not commit to the child. Furthermore, he may consider her pregnancy as grounds for him to leave the relationship. She may be faced with a terrible choice: she must either return the relationship to the status quo or be prepared to commit to the child alone. An examination of the latter alternative reveals the pitfalls of that path. If she chooses to commit to the child, she will forfeit her civilization's pale version of the desirable life. She will lose the male-female relationship and she may have to provide for and protect both herself and her child without any help from the father. What a horrible context in which to be a woman!

The only security in such a civilization may be sterility, appropriately enough. She lives in a culture of death where she may be forced to choose between a relationship with "Adam" or a relationship with her baby, but she may not be able to have both.

When a civilization creates such a vicious dilemma for women, it creates a context for choice in which one rational response by a woman to the dilemma is to spurn commitment to her child. Abortion and infanticide have been all too frequent phenomena in the civilizations of human history.[43] When children become inconvenient or unwanted, no matter how primitive or advanced the society is, there will always be means for such children to be washed away. Robert Butterworth, a professional psychologist in Los Angeles, commenting on the rash of sensational infanticides in the United States in recent years, stated, "[T]he fetus becomes separated from [the mother] emotionally and physically—a foreign object to oust as quickly as possible. The baby murders [are] proof of a hedonistic culture where getting rid of things that stand in the way of pleasure is paramount."[44] When the scale upon which "Adam" spurns "Eve" is vast enough, such methods will gain the explicit approval and sanction of society and no longer be practiced in secret and with shame.[45] Indeed, in our own civilization we find society lauding men who accompany their lovers to the abortion clinic to "support" them as these women tangibly spurn commitment to the offspring of their "love." Is it any wonder God weeps?

In the end, children become inconvenient and unwanted only when we view the realization of the desirable life for ourselves as imperilled by the perpetuation of the desirable life through our posterity. As we have seen, when realization overshadows perpetuation, the result is civilizational suicide. The light of the civilization has been snuffed out, and it will die.

Interestingly, such a society will usually die by the hands of its children, for who will take revenge for what has been done to the mothers, who are the stewards of God's light? The children of those mothers will wreak revenge on the society that attacked the wellspring of their life and love. This will not be a conscious revenge and it will not be motivated by righteousness. This revenge is the revenge of those who suffered because their mothers were persuaded or prohibited from giving them the nurture, love, and guidance towards the moral law they deserved because, in turn, their mothers were not protected and provided for and supported and respected as they deserved. These children generally have no respect for life or love, as a result of their upbringing.[46] A culture of death is always unkind to motherhood, but ironically it is the children who ultimately "bite back."

Children past feeling, who bring death and destruction to themselves as well as their society, are the emblem of this final subtype of societal violation of the moral law which brings descent into darkness.

Women and the Possibility of Zion

Zion presents a stark contrast to the societies engaged in the various types of societal deviation and decline that we have reviewed above. When realization and perpetuation of the desirable life are integrally connected in a society, as in Zion, the moral laws concerning marriage and the bringing forth of posterity are honored, not violated. As a result, marriage is at the heart of social relations and there are no inconvenient or unwanted children. There is no extramarital promiscuity and all children are born through marriage. All children are welcomed and loved and supported by both their father and their mother, who in turn love and support and are faithful to each other. Women and children are not in a position of vulnerability—physical, economic, or legal—in such societies. All family relationships are committed, caring, and covenant. "Adam" has committed to "Eve," "Eve" to "Adam," and both "Adam" and "Eve" to the child who is the fruit of their love.

We should pause to consider how women help create the possibility of Zion in every society and in every time. (In the next chapter, we consider how men help create the possibility of Zion.) Even in societies without the fullness of the law, which fullness is the Word, it is possible to *turn towards the light* and embrace commitment to life and love. God sends the light to every civilization and every person, for the light is kindled within each breast by its caretakers—the women. Women create the possibility of Zion in every society by their work as mothers and by their work as the lovers of men. Just as the light is sent to all, the caretakers of the light are sent to all.

Let us examine how the work of women creates the possibility for Zion in every society. First, let us examine the work that women do as the mothers of all living. Motherhood can be a powerful subversive force to all the "words" which are not the Word and which are at odds with the Word of the Everlasting Light. When a mother embraces her baby, she passionately desires happiness and safety for that child. Sara Ruddick describes the desire of each mother for her children:

> *At [maternity's] center is the promise of birth. To threaten bodies—to starve, terrorize, mutilate, or deliberately injure them—is to violate that promise. Every body counts, every body is a testament to hope. The hope of the world—of birthing women, mothers, friends, and kin—rests in the newborn infant. The infant's hope resides in the world's welcome. As they take up the life that birthing labor has given, infants express what Simone Weil described as "this profound and childlike and unchanging expectation of good in the heart"—an expectation that she called sacred: "At the bottom of the heart of every human being, from earliest infancy until the tomb, there is something that goes on indomitably expecting, in the teeth of all expe - rience of crimes committed, suffered, and witnessed, that good and not evil will be done to him. It is this above all that is sacred in every human being." To respond to the promise of birth is to respect a birthing woman's hope in her infant and her infant's hope in the world.*[47]

A mother realizes the infinite preciousness of her baby's life and commits to protect and nurture that life and point it towards the moral law. This commitment to her child may extend to a growing commitment to all children and may lead her to the understanding that all persons, young or not, are children of some mother who felt the same as she does about her child. This deep and passionate commitment may lead her to subvert or rebel against "words" that harm or threaten her own or any other child's happiness or safety. As only the Word, being the fullness of the moral law, guarantees her child's ultimate happiness and safety, whether the individual mother knows the Word or not, her love for her child prepares her to find the Word, or at least to reject that which is inconsistent with the Word. Thus women in their work as mothers can become powerful cultural subversives, a touchstone for the Word when it is restored.

Second, women's work as lovers of men also helps create the possibility of Zion. As a woman loves a man he may hearken to her and "partake," thereby entering into the loving, committed relationship with her that we call marriage. This marriage is the foundation for the creation of children, whom the man will love and nurture. Men begin to step into their own role as agents of the light, and become committed to the physical and economic security of women and children. Men who love and value women and children are in a position to receive the Word when they hear it. And once they receive it, they are then entrusted by God with the leadership role in the sacred task of building a Zion society.

All of this is to say that righteous womanhood and motherhood are subversive to the "words," whose author is ultimately revealed to be the god of this world, or Satan. Satan hates women especially, because in doing that which comes naturally—seeking a love relationship with a man and having children with him—she naturally spreads and preserves and enlarges the light, which is the foundation for laying hold upon the Word. Remember that in the Garden of Eden, God proclaimed that He would place enmity between Satan and woman, in addition to enmity between Satan and her seed (Genesis 3:15). Thus it was recognized, even at the first, that women in their roles as wives and mothers would work in natural opposition to the plans of Satan.[48] As long as these natural tendencies are acted upon and women's roles are fulfilled, the threat of Satan's "words" will be subverted.

Throughout history, the most important battle Satan has waged is not to suppress the Word, but to suppress the light. The Word may be restored again and again in a civilization, but the light, once extinguished, can never be rekindled within the context of that particular civilization. The battle against the light, the spurning of the light, and the increasing power of those who hate the light, ultimately doom civilizations. When the great civilizations have fallen, they have fallen because they actively condoned the extinguishing of their own light.[49] And what is this extinguishing? It is the societal violation of the moral law given to all civilizations concerning marriage and the bringing forth of posterity.

Note that the root of the difference between a culture of death and a culture of flourishing life, such as Zion, is the difference in Adam's reaction to Eve. When men move away from the light and the Word, women and children become vulnerable. The degree of their vulnerability becomes a barometer of how extreme the societal departure has been.[50] When Adam spurns Eve, Eve may find it rational to spurn their children and the society dies.[51] And in turn, the root of Adam's spurning of Eve is inequality. To reject commitment to one who loves you means that somehow you have rationalized that they are not worthy of equal love and commitment, or that it is not incumbent upon you to return in equal measure their loving commitment. As noted in Chapter One and in Appendix A, sexual or gender difference is a common basis for treating another as unequal. And so we find in the cultures of death, including our own, many and longstanding traditions and philosophies of men—often mingled with scripture—that women are different and lower creatures than men. These traditions serve as rationalizations for those men to spurn "Eve" and refuse to partake. And this act of spurning eventually and inexorably creates a culture of death, where cold, hard hearts are capable of treating life cheaply, instead of as the infinitely precious thing it is. For if a man is capable of treating his lover as an inferior, who can not be treated as an inferior? Thus all types of hostility and violence become permissible within the society, for one feels justified in treating even the "bone of my bone and flesh of my flesh" with inequality and violence. We are even moved so far as to say that the roots of all inequality and all violence are to be found in inequality in the male-female relationship. The forces that seek to sever the link between women and their children—the final stage in the battle against the light—could never have acquired the power they now have without men having treated women as inferiors and not as equals for so long.

This is why the issue of gender equality is the final and ultimate question of any society. If it is a lesser thing to be a woman, then the light dims and darkness will begin to cover the land. The debate over the equality of women is no fringe issue, but rather *the* issue at the very heart of our future possibilities. It is a debate over the very meaning of life—both mortal life and eternal life. Whatever his sins, if a man agrees to partake of that which Eve offers, he will turn toward the light in the process and gain the wherewithal to forsake his sins and accept the Word when he hears it. On the other hand, even if a man is born in the Church, even if he has held positions of authority in the Church, if he spurns Eve or treats her as an inferior, the light cannot abound in him, and exaltation is beyond his grasp. The analogous choice faces every woman as well, but as we have seen, the catalyzing societal violations leading to descent in the fallen world center around deviation of the sons of Adam. To live gender equality is to live as a man and a woman who are worthy to be exalted to godhood. If godhood is our highest possibility, then those who cannot treat the other sex as equals deny themselves the fullness of life.

There may be elements of any culture that represent barriers to happiness regarding male-female relations. We are counselled to let our benchmark be the gospel of Jesus Christ. President Howard W. Hunter commented, "Measure whatever anyone else asks you to do, whether it be from your family, loved ones, your cultural heritage, or traditions you have inherited—measure everything against the teachings of the Savior. Where you find a variance from those teachings, set that matter aside and do not pursue it. It will not bring you happiness."[52]

Elder Richard G. Scott elaborated, "[Y]our lineage can provide a rich heritage and great reasons to rejoice. Yet you have the responsibility to determine if there is any part of that heritage that must be discarded because it works against the Lord's plan of happiness. . . Is yours a culture where the husband exerts a domineering, authoritarian role, making all of the important decisions for the family? That pattern needs to be tempered so that both husband and wife act as equal partners, making decisions in unity for themselves and their family."[53] Elder Alexander B. Morrison summed up the situation in one sentence, "The Church cannot bow down before any traditions that demean or devalue the daughters of God."[54]

In essence, the "woman question" is the most revolutionary of all questions. Who is Eve? Who is she to Adam, and how should Adam respond to her? To answer those questions correctly is not only of great importance to women, it is of great importance to men. Achieving gender equality is only possible if we truly understand what life is and why it is infinitely precious. Such an understanding can only be had through the Spirit of truth and the grace of God. Gender equality is not a maraschino cherry, placed last atop a Zion sundae. It is, rather, integral to Zion's existence because male-female relations are the very heart of Zion. Gender relations are a central part of the divine plan of happiness and eternal life, so central that the building of Zion cannot be culminated where gender relations are out of sync with the gospel of Christ. The "woman question," properly answered, transforms a culture of death into a culture of abounding life. It transforms mortality into eternity, and earth into heaven. The "woman question," in the end, is the question of who Heavenly Father and Heavenly Mother are and of what their work is. It is the question of who we are to them and how they feel about us. It is the question of eternal life itself.

Notes

1   "The Family: A Proclamation to the World," written by the First Presidency and Council of the Twelve Apostles of the Church of Jesus Christ of Latter-day Saints, was read by President Gordon B. Hinckley as part of his message at the General Relief Society Meeting held 23 September 1995 in Salt Lake City, Utah. Also found in *Ensign* 25 (November 1995): 102. See also a short work by Elder James E. Talmage, entitled, "The Eternity of Sex," in *The Young Woman's Journal*, October 1914. As Elder Talmage puts it, "The distinction between male and female is no condition peculiar to the relatively brief period of mortal life; it was an essential characteristic of our pre-existent state, even as it shall continue after death, in both the disembodied and resurrected states."

2   See footnote 5, Chapter Four.

3   Spencer W. Kimball, *My Beloved Sisters* (Salt Lake City: Deseret Book Company, 1979), 13.

4   Brigham Young, *Discourses of Brigham Young*, comp. John A. Widtsoe (Salt Lake City: Deseret Book, 1978), 195.

5   Spencer W. Kimball, *Woman* (Salt Lake City: Deseret Book, 1979), 84.

6   Joseph F. Smith, *Gospel Doctrine* (Salt Lake City: Deseret Book, 1975), 315.

7   David O. McKay, "Gospel Ideals," *The Improvement Era* (Salt Lake City: Deseret Book, 1967), 456.

8   Joseph F. Smith, *Gospel Doctrine* (Salt Lake City: Deseret Book, 1975), 315.

9   Thomas F. Monson, "Behold Thy Mother," *Ensign* (April 1998): 4, 6.

10   James T. Duke and Barry L. Johnson, "Changes in the Religious Devotion of Latter-day Saints throughout the Life Cycle," *BYU Studies* 36, no. 1, (1996-97): 139-158.

11   Gordon B. Hinckley, "Daughters of God," *Ensign* 21 (November 1991): 99.

12   An interesting treatment of the theme of the "alien nature" of women throughout the history of philosophy is presented in Diana H. Coole's *Women in Political Theory* (Boulder, CO.: Lynne Rienner Publishers, 1988).

13   James E. Talmage, "The Eternity of Sex," *The Young Woman's Journal* (October 1914): 602.

14 An excellent theoretical essay on the possible origins of this phenomenon is Maria Mies' "Social Origins of the Sexual Divisions of Labor," in *Women: The Last Colony*, ed. Maria Mies, Veronika Bennholdt-Thomsen, and Claudia von Werlhof (London: Zed Books, 1988), 67-95.

15 Such practices are manifold and are outlined more fully in Appendix A.

16 See Appendix A for more detail and bibliographic citations.

17 See Appendix A.

18 See, for example, Stephanie Coontz and Donna Franklin, "When the Marriage Penalty is Marriage," *New York Times*, 28 October 1997.

19 In what can only be described as a watershed, Ann Landers, an important voice of "cultural common sense" in the United States, declared in December 1997 that since teens could not realistically be expected to abstain from sex, but that sex in an age of AIDS and other serious sexually transmitted diseases is simply not safe, her advice to teenagers is to engage in mutual masturbation!

20 Gay and Lesbian Studies have become one of the fastest growing fields of academia in the United States. An overview might be Didi Herman's *Rights of Passage: Struggles for Lesbian and Gay Legal Equality* (Toronto: University of Toronto Press, 1994).

21 The work of Andrea Dworkin is a case in point. See Cindy Jenefsky with Ann Russo, *Without Apology: Andrea Dworkin's Art and Politics* (Boulder, CO.: Westview, 1997).

22 The proportion among men and women in the United States who will never marry "has risen to about 10 percent among whites and 25 to 30 percent among African-Americans. In addition, many more women are having children outside of marriage—32 percent of all births in 1995." (Andrew J. Cherlin, "By the Numbers," *The New York Times Magazine*, 5 April 1998, 39). In 2003, the figure was 33 percent of all births. (The United States Census Bureau, October 2003, http://www.census.gov/procl/2003pubs/p20-548.pdf.)

23 Lamentably, this attitude leads to tragic social consequences. "In a random telephone survey of 503 teenagers in grades 9 through 12, . . . 36 percent said they had had sexual intercourse, and an additional 5 percent reported having engaged in sex other than vaginal intercourse . . . . Among the sexually active teenagers, the average age they reported their first intercourse was just under 15 years" (*New York Times*, 18 May 1994).

24 About half of all U.S. marriages end in divorce. U.S. Census Bureau data show that of 69.6 million family households in America, about 12.5 million are headed by females with no husband. Of those 12.5 million families, 8.8 million include dependent children. About "24

percent of all children [in the United States] were being reared by unmarried mothers in 1996." (Andrew J. Cherlin, "By the Numbers," *The New York Times Magazine,* 5 April 1998, 40).

25 As mentioned in note 24, about one quarter of all children in the United States are being raised by single mothers. The percentages in various ethnic communities may be much higher. For example, the majority of African-American children in the United States are being reared by their mothers or other female relatives.

26 In a Harris Poll conducted in 1994, seventy percent of the men surveyed stated that men "were not responsible enough" to choose a birth control method because they "don't care" and because they considered birth control "the female's responsibility" (*New York Times,* 23 May 1995).

27 Assuming half the nation's population is women, 75.4 out of every 100,000 U.S. women (totalling over 100,000 victims) were reported raped in 1999. Utah's rate was the 13th highest in the nation (*World Almanac and Book of Facts,* 2001 [Mahwah, NJ: World Almanac Books, 2001]; most observers believe that only 1 in 10 rapes are ever reported to the authorities). Though Utah's crime rate in the categories of murder, robbery, aggravated assault, and burglary are all below national averages, Utah is higher than the national average in the category of rape. One-third of all rapes involve girls between 11 and 18. More than 80 percent of reported rapes are committed by someone the victim knows. (N. Hobbs, "Date Rape," *Salt Lake Tribune,* 21 November 1997). The attitudinal base for these figures was illuminated by Ann Landers (28 February 1997): In a survey of high school students, 56 percent of the girls and 76 percent of the boys believed forced sex was acceptable under some circumstances. A survey of 11-to 14-year-olds found this: 51 percent of the boys and 41 percent of the girls said forced sex was acceptable if the boy "spent a lot of money" on the girl. Thirty-one percent of the boys and 32 percent of the girls said it was acceptable for a man to rape a woman if she had past sexual experience. Eighty-seven percent of the boys and 79 percent of the girls said sexual assault was acceptable if the man and the woman were married. Sixty-five percent of the boys and 47 percent of the girls said it was acceptable for a boy to rape a girl if they had been dating for more than six months. In a survey of male college students, 35 percent anonymously admitted that under certain circumstances they would commit rape if they believed they could get away with it. In another survey of college males, 43 percent admitted to using coercive behavior to have sex, including ignoring a woman's protest and using physical aggression to force intercourse.

28 Domestic violence seems an anomaly in a society where women are guaranteed equal rights. But by the third stage of descent, a society's attitudes about male-female and parent-child relationships have

deteriorated to the point where domestic violence is not unexpected. Some statistics:

A study issued by the U.S. Department of Health and Human Services in September 1996 states the estimated number of children abused and neglected rose 98 percent from 1986 to 1993 (up to almost 3 million children).

A study presented by Hindus Against the Abuse of Women concluded that the number of murders of women committed by "intimate relations" in the U.S. is almost double those in India—15 per year per million population for the U.S., compared with 6.25 in India (*Salt Lake Tribune*, 30 August 1997).

In the state of Utah, a recent poll shows that 21 percent of the women surveyed state their children witness verbal abuse, and 7 percent stated their children witness physical abuse (*Salt Lake Tribune*, 11 November 1997).

For especially vulnerable women, women in poverty, the situation is even more bleak. Studies show that 83 percent of poor women have been physically abused in the home (*Salt Lake Tribune*, 30 April 1997).

29 Speaking here specifically of wives, "[T]he person who makes more income has more decision-making power, and the more distance there is between incomes, the greater the control the high earner has . . .[T]he low- or non-earning spouse has few rights concerning even what might be considered essential and elementary family resources. For example the author of a study of working-class families found that working class women systematically had less access to family cash and in fact lived less well than their husband. Women were less likely to have a car, less likely to eat the same amount as or as well as their husband, and less likely to have similar discretionary spending money or decision-making capacity." (Pepper Schwarz, *Peer Marriage* [New York: Free Press, 1993], 112, citing three empirical studies.)

30 According to the U.S. Census Bureau, the three poorest categories of households in America are 1) females living alone ($14,331 per year), 2) females without husbands living with dependent children ($16,235), and 3) females without husbands living with or without dependent children ($21,348). The lowest income for a male-headed household was "male living alone," with average annual income of $22,586. (Data presented in *Salt Lake Tribune*, 2 February 1997). One in four American children are born into poverty (*World Almanac and Book of Facts*, 1998 [Mahwah, NJ: World Almanac Books, 1997]).

31 Day-care providers and caretakers for the elderly generally make minimum wage, and their turnover rate is about 35 percent a year.

One study of child care in the United States evaluates it as "woefully inadequate" along four dimensions of commitment, quality, safety, and availability (*Salt Lake Tribune*, 15 August 1997). In one study, day care workers made less money than animal caretakers or parking lot attendants. Moving on to teachers, the average school-teacher in the United States makes about $21,000 per year.

32   A horrific example of this is in Michigan, where women on welfare have to go to work within six weeks of having a child or they lose their benefits (P. Kilborn, "Steps Taken on Welfare in Michigan," *New York Times*, 1 November 1995). In one expose, welfare mothers in New York City being forcibly shifted into workfare faced an acute lack of child care, with child care lacking for upwards of 70 percent of the children. These mothers were coerced by social workers to place their children in substandard, even dangerous child care, or else face a cut-off of benefits. (Rachel L. Swams, "Mothers Poised for Workfare Face Acute Lack of Day Care," *The New York Times*, 14 April, 1998.)

33   An excellent analysis of this situation is provided by Shirley Burggraf in her book *The Feminine Economy and Economic Man* (Reading: Addison-Wesley, 1997). Here's one quote: "The concept of economic man provides no clues as to how the human race survives the dependency phases of the human life cycle when the individual is unable to compete; and yet those phases have always claimed a substantial share of the economy's resources, the major resource being the efforts and labor of women. . . .Our culture is [now] profoundly threatened by the loss of what we have taken for granted for so long—the assumption that the necessary caretakers would always be there" (p. 20).

34   See Ted Conover's "The Last Best Friends Money Can Buy," *The New York Times Magazine*, 30 November 1997.

35   The inequitable treatment of wives in Social Security payments is a classic example. Women who interrupt their careers to become homemakers and care for dependents are penalized in the Social Security system. As a result, the poverty rate among women over 65 is twice that of men over 65. (Kathleen Feldstein, "Social Security's Gender Gap," *The New York Times,* 13 April, 1998).

36   Indeed, at least one group believes that caretaking will never be truly valued until men pay wages to their wives for housework. The Wages for Housework campaign, though not likely to be successful, exposes the caretaking conundrum faced by homemakers (Meki Cox, "Another Women's Movement: Wages for Housework," *The Salt Lake Tribune*, 19 April, 1998).

37   Women make about 76 cents to a man's dollar in the United States, and male-headed households are the wealthiest in the nation (U.S. Census Bureau). "White men, while constituting about 43% of the work force, hold about 95 of every 100 senior management posi-

tions," according to a report by the federal government (*New York Times*, 16 March 1995).

38 See, for example, "Obstacles for Men Who Want Family Time," by Susan Chira, *New York Times*, 21 October 1993. One expert quoted in the articles states the message to men is this: "Be more involved, but not to the point where it interferes with your job."

39 Jeffrey R. Holland and Patricia T. Holland, "Considering Covenants: Women, Men, Perspective, Promises," In S.F. Green and D.H. Anderson, *To Rejoice as Women: Talks from the 1994 Women's Conference* (Salt Lake City: Deseret Book Company, 1995), 113-114.

40 About one-third of all births in the United States are to unmarried mothers, according to the U.S. Census Bureau.

41 Though in this section, we will comment on the growing hardness of women's hearts towards children, we must recognize that there is an even more horrible version of the severing of the bond between mother and child. Some look forward to the day when men may reproduce without women. "Franklin E. Kameny, a retired government physicist and gay rights activist, has proposed developing a 'completely artificial' womb. 'You take the cell, put it in there, take care of it for nine months, open it, and voila, a clone,' Kameny says. 'No need for a uterus or a woman!'" (As quoted in "Better Make Mine a Double," *The New York Times Magazine*, 19 April, 1998, 19.)

42 We recognize there may be righteous reasons to avoid conception or otherwise use such devices for the sake of the health and strength of the woman involved.

43 See Valerie M. Hudson and Andrea den Boer's, "Bare Branches: Causes and Consequences of the Masculinization of Asia's Sex Ratios," a paper presented at the International Studies Association convention, Minneapolis, Minnesota, 16-21 March 1998.

44 As quoted in "Recent Cases of Abandoned Babies Highlight Issue of Teen Pregnancy," by Steve Stuebner, *The Salt Lake Tribune*, 4 March, 1998.

45 In the U.S. in 1995, there were 311 abortions for every thousand live births, for a total of approximately 1.2 million abortions that year.

46 The literature on this subject is just beginning to reach a critical mass. How a child is treated during its first few years can determine to a great degree whether the child will ever develop empathy and self-restraint. Without those two characteristics, the child is much more likely to be violent and anti-social. For example, an abused child is 1500 times more likely to abuse as an adult. Suicide rates for children from troubled homes are also much higher. Interesting studies about this phenomenon are reviewed in D. Goleman, "Early

Violence Leaves Its Mark on the Brain," New York Times, 3 October 1995; R. Hotz, "Study Shows Growing Up Without Love Harms Kids," *Salt Lake Tribune,* 28 October 1997; J. Mohlman, "Mothers and Infants," *Insight 12,* no. 2 (Winter 1997): 25-32.

47 Sara Ruddick, *Maternal Thinking: Toward a Politics of Peace* (Boston: Beacon Press, 1995), 217-218.

48 We recognize that not all women will have the opportunity to be wives and mothers in this world; however, the prophets have repeatedly taught that no blessing shall be denied them if they remain faithful (see, for example, President Gordon B. Hinckley, "What God Hath Joined Together," *Ensign* 21 [May 1991]: 71). It is also important to note that the work of the caretakers of the light is not limited to their roles as wives and mothers. All women can look to Eve as their role model by partaking of the light, perpetuating it, and nurturing it in others. Elder Jeffrey R. Holland reaffirmed this in a recent general conference address: "'No blessing shall be withheld' from the faithful, even if those blessings do not come immediately. In the meantime we rejoice that the call to nurture is not limited to our own flesh and blood" ("Because She is a Mother," *Ensign* 27 [May, 1997]: 35).

49 An example of the destruction of a civilization due to the extinguishing of the light is found in the Book of Mormon. The Nephites, having the Word but having lost the light, were destroyed by the Lamanites, who, having lost the Word, retained the light and, therefore, life. In chapter 3 of Jacob, Jacob writes that because the Nephites practiced whoredoms and spurned their wives and children, they were less righteous than the Lamanites, who did not commit whoredoms and showed love to their wives and children. Indeed, Jacob implies that because of Nephite whoredoms, God will destroy the Nephites by the hands of the Lamanites while preserving the Lamanites (Jacob 3:3).

50 In an analysis of the Book of Mormon, Donna Lee Bowen and Camille Williams come to the conclusion that "[in the Book of Mormon], the behavior and treatment of women were seen as an index of social and spiritual health" (Daniel H. Ludlow, ed. *The Encyclopedia of Mormonism* [New York: Macmillan Publishing, 1992], s.v. "Women in the Book of Mormon," by Donna Lee Bowen and Camille Williams).

51 The rate of divorce is often used to measure the degree of the demise of the family, or Adam's spurning of Eve, within society. However, divorce rates are not indicative of the whole story; societies in which divorce is uncommon (or difficult to obtain, particularly for women) are not exempt from civilizational suicide. The question we must ask is whether or not the marriage relationship is one built upon love, commitment, and equality.

52 President Howard W. Hunter, "Counsel to Students and Faculty," Church College of New Zealand, 12 November, 1990.

53 Richard G. Scott, "Removing Barriers to Happiness," general conference address, April 1998.

54 Comment made at the annual meeting of the International Society, Provo, Utah, August 1994 (question and answer session).

CHAPTER 6
True Patriarchy and False Patriarchy

by
Valerie Hudson Cassler

*You see that boy of mine? Though but five, he governs
the universe. Yes, for he rules his mother, his mother
rules me, I rule Athens, and Athens rules the world.*
                                                    —Themistocles

The Importance of Getting It Right

The principles expressed in the last several chapters lead us
to believe that men and women are both agents of the light.
They both serve the same Master and are equal before him.
Furthermore, they participate in a system of equal power and
understand that the spiritual work of one is meaningless
without the spiritual work of the other. While having different
primary spiritual responsibilities in mortality, they are to
regard each other as equal partners in doing the work of God.
Conditions other than these preclude communities or individuals from living a Zion existence.

We see then, how fundamental gender relations are to the
plan of salvation and exaltation and how important it is to
understand how these relations should be conducted in a
manner pleasing to God. If the purpose of the kingdom of God
on earth is to prepare us for eternal life, then a vital part of that
preparation is to bring about a community wherein gender
relations become righteous in the eyes of the Lord.

With that perspective in mind, let us expand upon the principles spoken of in the preceding chapters so we may see their
application to more concrete interactions between men and
women living the law of Zion. Let us explore these ideas by

elaborating in more detail the work of the women and men—how the work is alike, how the work differs, and how the principle of gender equality persists nevertheless.

Ariel's Next Question

In the spring of 1996, I was driving my then nine-year-old daughter, Ariel, to judo class. She was unusually quiet and I knew why. For years, when anyone had asked her what she wanted to be when she grew up, she would answer, "President of the United States, prophet of the Church, a mother, a botanist, a teacher, and a ballet dancer." This had been the topic of conversation just before we got in the car and her older brother had cavalierly informed her that there was no way she could be prophet of the Church—that only men could be the prophet. We drove along in silence for several blocks and then she turned to me, her chin quivering, and asked, "Mom, is it true? Is it true women can't be the prophet?" I told her it was true. She began to cry in earnest. I realized this was a major turning point in my daughter's life. For the very first time, she saw that her gender constrained who she could be. My heart broke for her, broke for the loss of something she might never regain—the feeling that who Ariel was was more important than the fact that she was a girl. Through my own pain I determined that I could not leave her with this bald, isolated, soul-withering fact when the context in which it was embedded gave her so much richer possibilities. I pulled the car over to the side of the road and turned off the engine.

I asked her if she felt God loved her. She nodded. I asked her if she felt God loved her brother, Ben, more than He loved her. She shook her head. I asked her if she thought God felt Ben was smarter or braver or wiser or more trustworthy or more spiritual than she was. That got a smile and an "Of course not!" I asked if she thought the prophet, Gordon B. Hinckley, was brave, wise, and spiritual. She said yes. I asked her if she thought he was braver, wiser, and more spiritual than his wife, Marjorie Hinckley. She took a few moments to mull this over and then said, "I don't know, but I don't think so." I asked, "So how come he's the prophet and she will never be?"

Having discarded the possibility that women were somehow flawed or inferior to men in virtue or in the love of God, Ariel was now puzzled instead of pained. She wiped away her tears. "I don't know, Mom. How come?"

I pulled out a piece of paper and a chewed-up pencil and began to sketch a diagram. What follows is a recreation of how I sketched the diagram and what I said to Ariel as each part of the diagram was drawn.[1]

This is the celestial kingdom, where Heavenly Father and Heavenly Mother live. They love each other very much and they treat each other as equals. He is not above her and she is not above him. He is the King of Heaven and she is the Queen of Heaven. All beings who live in the highest level of the celestial kingdom are equal and full of love for each other. This is where we are all striving to go.

The work of Heavenly Father and Heavenly Mother is to increase the number of spirits who are able to receive a fullness of joy and inherit eternal life by bringing forth children and guiding them in the path whereby they, too, might become gods and live in happiness and equality and have their own children. Bringing forth children and creating families is the very heart of the work of God, and thus these works continue in mortality even when and where there is no priesthood and no conception of the gospel of Christ, as we have seen in Chapter Five. Knowing that "gender is an essential characteristic of individual premortal, mortal, and eternal identity and purpose" (a statement that cannot be applied to any other difference between humans), scripture makes plain that male-female relations are the central element that make the work of God happen (D&C 132: 19-20).

Why might this be the case? Why is bringing forth children and creating families the essential defining work of gods and gods-in-training? Since God is a being with a fullness of life, what is left to be desired? What could be the treasure of such a being? The only possible answer is more fullness of life. But since God has a fullness of life already, how could there be more? There could only be more if there were more beings having a fullness of life. So the work of God is to bring to pass the existence of more beings having a fullness of life. It is the work of God's love, for He desires that all who are worthy share in the fullness of joy He experiences. Since even God cannot create intelligence, God must organize and nurture and guide intelligence through the various stages necessary to reach the point where such intelligence can obtain the fullness God has.

The work of God is to bring other intelligences to a level equal with God's own. Once again, we see the integral connection between equality and the work of God. God's greatest treasure is not gold and jewels and castles, but rather God's immense circle of treasured intimate equals—God's friends. Indeed, the phrase "peculiar people" in the scriptures really has a meaning more akin to "mobile treasure"—those who love God are God's mobile treasure.[2] God's work is a work of love, and God's love is a love which works to bring an inferior into a position of equality with the superior, which equality is the prerequisite of full intimacy.

Though God guides our intelligences along the path to a fullness of life, in the end, God does not intend to keep us as servants or even as His little children. Our God intends to have us as friends and equals! That is God's work and God's glory, that we might be brought into a fully intimate friendship and equality with Him (D&C 84:77; 88:107).

Thus we see that "the continuation of the seeds" is a defining characteristic of godhood. It is the work of God (D&C 132:19). Those who do not obtain a fullness of life will not have "continuation of the seeds." The "continuation of the seeds" may also be understood as "bringing to pass the immortality and eternal life of man" (Moses 1:39). In this work of God we can also expect a system of equal power between the two indispensable elements that make the work possible—an exalted man (a god) and an exalted woman (a goddess). The work of God is equally the work of God the Father and God the Mother.

There was a place or a time we now call the premortal existence. In the premortal existence our intelligences were organized into spirits and we became the children of our Heavenly Father and Heavenly Mother. In the premortal existence, we were nurtured, and we grew and developed. We wished to progress to the next stage of development where we would test our ability to discern good from evil while apart from our Heavenly Parents. Two-thirds of us accepted this plan and the offering of Jesus Christ to be our Savior.

Those of us who accepted the plan were permitted to pass through the veil that shrouds mortal life. We know women play an important role in the passage through the veil; they escort every soul through the veil, even the soul of the Savior of mankind. In a sense, they serve as the gatekeepers to our mortal world. Perhaps this service is a sign of their apprenticeship to their Mother in Heaven. Presiding over those who passed through the first veil, they clothed each traveller with a physical body and introduced them into mortality and agency through personal suffering and sacrifice.

In this mortal world the women, in their work as mothers, nurture our young souls and keep alive the desire to be reunited with the light. In a sense, *our mothers become **care-takers of the light** within us, and more broadly, caretakers of the light within a society.* They teach those to whom they give birth that there is light and love in this world, and to seek it. In this way, young souls are prepared to recognize and be receptive to the moral law and its fullness, the Word. Furthermore, in their work as lovers of men, women persuade men to partake and thereby commit to the cause of life and its perpetuation.

When the young soul has grown into accountability, the soul's main task is to choose good over evil. The young soul possesses both physical life and agency, and in order to intro-duce accountability, the moral law, whose fullness is the Word, is given. The moral law, as we have seen in Chapter Five, is the dividing line between good and evil and light and darkness and is given to all men regardless of era or culture. It provides for life that abides the law, the only life permitting eternal flourishing. Following the moral law means drawing nearer to the light. Loving the light means receptivity to the Word when it is heard. Christ, the apprentice of his Father, was the Word. He imparted stewardship over the Word to His own apprentices in all ages and gave them authority to preach and to judge according to its precepts. These apprentices are male officers of the priesthood who have hearkened unto "Eve" and committed to life and its perpetuation, and it will be their privilege and duty to preside over the second veil, through which those of God's children who are righteous will regain the presence of their Heavenly Parents. Again, in a sense, *our fathers are* **caretakers of the Word** *in our service, and more broadly, caretakers of the Word within a society.*

Stewardship over the Word involves personal sacrifice so that mortal agents may be cleansed from sin and become sanctified, justified agents and thus have eternal life. Furthermore, those agents—mortal or otherwise—who are not cleansed from sin must be placed within the bounded spheres of their respective competences by the stewards of the Word. These stewards, or caretakers of the Word, are the gateway from mortality to eternal life. Through righteous judgment by those whose stewardship it is to provide such, a person may be admitted into godhood. The caretakers of the Word will have the opportunity to teach and minister it unto those who have accepted the lessons and sacrifice of the caretakers of the light. The caretakers of the Word make plain the opposition that is the foundation of our agency: blessings and cursings, abundance and chastenings, dunging and pruning, vengeance and mercy, protection from the wicked and leaving us to our own strength (DC 97:7, 9). Through the great personal sacrifice of the caretakers of the Word, they may claim kinship with those they serve (Hebrews 2:10-13; Mosiah 15:12). It was not until Christ had made such a sacrifice that He was entitled to call us His children (Mosiah 5:7, 8).

Without divine power, the sacrifices of both sets of care-takers would be without effect. The sacrifices of the caretakers of the light would not result in life, and the sacrifices of the caretakers of the Word would not result in sanctification. The Word without the light is sterile; the light without the Word is doomed to darken and die. Jesus Christ fulfilled the promise of the sacrifices made by both types of caretakers. Two things were conquered in the Atonement: Christ conquered death[3], the archenemy of the caretakers of the light, and He conquered sin, the archenemy of the caretakers of the Word. Without Christ, those who give birth do so in vain; all their works (their children) will die. With Christ, virtually all who have be given life by the caretakers of the light will retain it forever; they will obtain immortality regardless of the extent to which they abided the moral law. It is significant that the resurrected Christ appeared first to the woman Mary, one of the caretakers of the light, to announce that death had been overcome. Because of Christ, the work of the caretakers of the light, as mothers and as lovers of men, is not in vain.

Without Christ, the caretakers of the Word work in vain for the sanctification of souls; all their efforts are fruitless. With Christ, virtually all will receive a measure of sanctification, and some will receive a full measure of sanctification and become gods. Without Christ, there are no kinship ties of lasting import created by the caretakers. But with Christ, the kinship sealing promise offered by the caretakers of the light and the care-takers of the Word becomes real and eternal. By the power of the Atonement, Christ claims kinship with us all (Hebrews 2:10-13; Mosiah 15:12).

Looking at the complete diagram, we see things not seen before and we begin to suspect how equality persists between the work of the caretakers of the light and the caretakers of the Word. The two gateways, the two sacrifices, the two steward-ships—is one higher than the other? No. There is a perfect equilibrium of the power of the gateways, the power of the sacrifices, the power of the stewardships. The caretakers of the light and the caretakers of the Word are both ultimately agents of the light, and their works are both the works of light.

Because of the unity of their works as agents of the light, the tasks of the two sets of caretakers bear some important similarities. Each stewardship involves, a) sacrifice on the part of the caretaker, b) the possibility that those on whose behalf the sacrifice is offered may decline the offer, c) glory and thanksgiving for caretakers who willingly undergo the suffering and sacrifice, d) the opportunity to teach and minister to those on whose behalf the sacrifice is made, e) the promise through Christ of kinship with those on whose behalf the sacrifice is made (if they accept the sacrifice) and, f) equal potential for progression towards Godhood for the faithful caretakers and for those who faithfully accept the offering of the caretakers. In a sense, the caretakers and their sacrifices become recognizable landmarks on the way to eternal life. The caretakers are our guides and our gateways to God and godhood.

Yet there is a sequence to the stewardships which leads to misperception of the absolute equality of the stewardships. The caretakers of the light, in their work as mothers, must perform their work for an individual before the caretakers of the Word perform their work for an individual, else, as we have seen, there is no agency, and no potential for eternal life or godhood. Because of this fact, the full drama of the work of the caretakers of the light is muted. We do not see how some accepted the offering made by the caretakers of the light in their work as mothers and how some did not. Thus every individual on earth has accepted the offering of the caretakers of the light, and thus the sacrifice of the caretakers of the light seems common. Their very sacrifice in their work as mothers is concealed because of its perceived commonness. Pregnancy, labor, delivery, and breast-feeding are concealed as far as their full drama and their full glory are concerned. The sacrifice of blood and water— sometimes even the very sacrifice of life itself by a caretaker of the light[4]—is usually not seen by the family or the community, but rather by a birth professional—a doctor or midwife. The ministry of the caretakers of the light in their work as mothers, which includes nurturing bodies and spirits subsequent to birth, is likewise hidden by its very commonness. The keeping of the first estate and the entrance into the world of mortality through the caretakers of the light are past for every adult. We no longer see the drama and we value less the gateway and the sacrifice that brought us here. Even the caretakers of the light themselves begin (as a result of the descent into cultural darkness as explicated in Chapter Five) to view their work as mothers as ordinary, menial, and dirty instead of as the glorious stewardship it really is. Only young children seem to recognize the importance of the work of the caretakers of the light and reward it with complete devotion.

Two dramas appear to be highlighted from our vantage point past past the first veil and en route to the second. The first is the drama of the caretakers of the light in their work as lovers of men. The drama of "getting Adam to partake," as we have seen in Chapter Five, is no frivolous endeavor. R a t h e r , when it is undertaken with righteous intent through righteous means, it is a key element of the plan of salvation and exaltation.

Not all women will have the opportunity to have children in this life,[5] but all women will have the opportunity to love men, even if that love does not culminate in marriage. The theme of movement toward a loving union between man and woman occupies much attention in all cultures. Art, literature, music, myth, film, and advice columns center around several major themes in all cultures, but certainly one of those themes is love between men and women. It is a core preoccupation in all civilizations because it is a core element of the moral law given to every society and thus the universal deep structure of all human existence.

The drama of the caretakers of the Word is the second drama adults see and with which they are preoccupied. Will an individual accept the moral law, be receptive to the Word when it is heard, come into the fold, and become a sanctified person? Will an individual give up his or her sins, offer appropriate repentance, and turn his or her life around? Will an individual accept the sacrifice of the caretakers of the Word and enter into eternal life, or will eternal life be denied to that individual by righteous judgment? The focus is placed on knowing the moral law, what one must do to receive and accept the Word, how one is to act as a caretaker of the Word, and so forth. The guidance we seek is guidance to the second gateway, not the first, and so we seek wisdom from the presiding caretakers of the Word. The caretakers of the light do not preside over the second gateway, and we perhaps overlook them and do not remember the sacrifice and the ministry in their work as our mothers and as the lovers of men. Yet if we ponder our motivation to make it through the second gateway, is not an important part of that motivation to remain true to the love and the promise of eternal relationship with the caretakers of the light, whether as mothers or as lovers—those who, in the words of Joseph F. Smith, have "loved me more than anybody else in all the world, and more than any other living being could love me?"[6]

The centrality of Christ to the work of both types of caretakers is worth pondering more deeply. The Atonement of Christ visibly shows both types of sacrifice. In the Garden of

Gethsemane, Christ took upon himself the sins and sufferings of the world. He groaned in agony and sweated water and blood. Hebrews 5:1-10 helps us understand that a high priest is one who offers sacrifice for sin and that Christ was the great High Priest. If a high priest is similar to those whom have been called "caretaker of the Word," then Christ shows the type of sacrifice the caretakers of the Word make for those they wish to bring through the second gateway. It will not be a sacrifice of pigeons or lambs, but a sacrifice infinitely more personal, a sacrifice that is like the one made by the caretakers of the light (Hebrews 10:11-12). After the Garden of Gethsemane, Christ was crucified on the cross and gave forth blood and water unto death. Very much like the ordeal the caretakers of the light in their work as mothers, Christ's death was birth for others—very much like the situation of more than one half million women around the world each year who die in childbirth amid water and blood. Christ died so the deaths and the offering of death on the part of the caretakers of the light is glorified with its fulfillment—immortality for virtually all whom the caretakers of the light have brought forth.

But Christ's sacrifice not only typifies the sacrifices made in relation to children, it also typifies the sacrifices made by women who love men and men who love women. Christ is also a groom and husband to the Church, which is his bride and wife (D&C 65:3; Revelations 21:9). Christ "partakes" of that which His bride offers and commits to the life of his bride and of their resulting children. This is symbolized by the allegorical marriage of God's Son. We see that Christ sets the example for all men in His work as the lover of His bride as well as the father of His children. Christ gives His life for that which nurtures His children: the Church. For that sacrifice, the Church promises to hearken unto Christ and to subject her children to the judgments of Christ. The Church is the home of the children of Christ and is protected and loved by Christ. And thus in all marriages in the new and everlasting covenant, the husband hearkens unto his wife and partakes and thereby commits to life and its perpetuation. He offers to lay down his life to protect and save his wife and children, both physically and spiritually. These elements represent the work of the caretakers of the Word as lovers of women and as fathers of children and are a type of Christ's actions.

Likewise, the wife, in similitude of the Church as bride, brings forth children to lead them to the husband and the Word, with its resulting judgment. Her work as a lover of men and her work as a mother to her children are as integrally connected as the work of the husband as a lover of women and as a father to his children. Eve's promise to hearken unto Adam was more than all we have previously said, it was also the offer to subject the life it was in her power to give to the righteous judgment consequential to the exercise of agency. What a profound offering to be made by the caretakers of the light! Here we see the beauty and power of the marriage bond between a woman and a man. The woman who loves the man gives all she has to bring forth new life and ushers that life into agency. The man who has hearkened unto the woman and committed to life gives all he has to save that life from the ill effects agency can bring and will usher that life into eternal life if possible, which is also the dearest desire of the caretakers of the light for their children. In seeking for the immortality and eternal life of man, the woman and the man are indispensable partners and their purpose becomes one. The love between the woman and the man and the love between them and their children ensures both mercy and justice will be satisfied. That love ensures eternal kinship and eternal increase.

The relationship between the man and the woman is to be one of equality, where the man labors so the labors of the woman will not be in vain and the woman labors so the labors of the man will not be in vain. They serve each other equally, they serve their children equally, they serve God equally. They are both agents of the light. The woman, as a lover of man, serves him by persuading him to partake, by participating in a system where the Father and his sons on earth are to guard the bounds between right and wrong, and by subjecting the life she brings forth in her work as a mother to that system of judgment.

The woman serves the man who serves God the Father. On the other hand, the man as a lover of woman serves her by partaking and committing to life and its perpetuation and by creating and administering a system where life can be had forever, and whereby life can be had abundantly and with eternal increase. The man serves the woman who serves God the Mother. The righteous woman and the righteous man are perfect equals and indispensable partners or in other words, essentially they are lovers.

Indeed, *eternal marriage and exalted motherhood are the full measure of priestesshood, just as the full measure of priesthood is eternal marriage and exalted fatherhood.* Thus it is incorrect to see priesthood as some special "extra" given to men, or to insist that women lack priesthood.[7] To reach this erroneous conclusion is to fail to understand the purpose of priesthood, which is to make of a man a heavenly father. Because of the equitable division of labor we have described in this volume, it is not necessary that a woman be given a stewardship in the work of the Word (i.e., to be a priest) for her to become a heavenly mother. The work she does in mortality as a steward of the light, whether one wishes to call it wifehood or motherhood or priestesshood or womanhood, is fully sufficient to render her worthy of exaltation and eternal increase, to make of a woman a heavenly mother.

It is worth quoting extensively from the fine conference address (General Relief Society meeting) of Sheri L. Dew, entitled, "Are We Not All Mothers?" reprinted in the November 2001 *Ensign* magazine. Her remarks clarify these points:

> *While we tend to equate motherhood solely with maternity, in the Lord's language, the word mother has layers of meaning. Of all the words they could have chosen to define her role and her essence, both God the Father and Adam called Eve "the mother of all living" —and they did so before she ever bore a child. Like Eve, our motherhood began before we were born. Just as worthy men were foreordained to hold the*

*priesthood in mortality, righteous women were
endowed premortally with the privilege of mother -
hood. Motherhood is more than bearing children,
though it is certainly that. It is the essence of who we
are as women. It defines our very identity, our divine
stature and nature, and the unique traits our Father
gave us. . . . Elder Matthew Cowley taught that, "men
have to have something given to them [in mortality] to
make them saviors of men, but not mothers, not
women. [They] are born with an inherent right, an
inherent authority, to be the saviors of human souls
. . . and the regenerating force in the lives of God's chil -
dren. Motherhood is not what was left over after our
Father blessed His sons with priesthood ordination. It
was the most ennobling endowment He could give His
daughters, a sacred trust that gave woman an unpar -
alleled role in helping His children keep their second
estate. As President J. Reuben Clark Jr. declared,
motherhood is "as divinely called, as eternally impor -
tant in its place as the priesthood itself." . . . Elder John
A. Widtsoe [said}: "Women who through no fault of
their own cannot exercise the gift of motherhood
directly, may do so vicariously." . . . Like the Savior,
"who for the joy that was set before him endured the
cross," Eve, for the joy of helping initiate the human
family, endured the Fall. She loved us enough to help
lead us. As daughters of our Heavenly Father, and as
daughters of Eve, we are all mothers and we have
always been mothers . . . . We are all mothers in Israel,
and our calling is to love and help lead the rising
generation through the dangerous streets of mortality
. . . No woman who understands the gospel would ever
think that any other work is more important or would
ever say, "I am just a mother," for mothers heal the
souls of men.*[8]

Some may argue that this vision of woman reduces her to her biological sexual and procreative functions. We do not agree. Divine love enlarges and humanizes the body by limiting its lawful exercise. Thus, expressing a woman's highest potential in terms of eternal marriage and exalted motherhood does not reduce her to her bodily functions, but rather enlarges and enhances our understanding of what those functions really mean. Those who hate or devalue or dismiss the body and its functions always find themselves in enmity with women, for women give us our bodies through the physical effort and suffering of their own bodies. A remarkably reliable generalization concerning religions is that the greater the expressed longing to shed the body and the greater the identification of a heavenly state with "bodylessness," the lower the status of women and the greater the contempt for women.[9]

Seeing Women

Although exalted mother and father stand as equals, our situation—being past the first gateway and en route to the second—skews our perspective. God the Mother seems absent. Man's service to God the Mother through serving woman is not seen clearly. What the woman does may seem of little importance.

One important area where this relative invisibility may cause women to conclude that God is less interested in them than in their brethren is in the holy scriptures.[10] Indeed, some even go so far as to say that women's relative invisibility in the scriptures casts doubt on the truth claims of the gospel, since if the gospel is sexist, then it cannot be true. But we assert there is a faith-supporting reason for this relative invisibility, while simultaneously forwarding the notion that there is room for a more complete discarding of certain distorting practices that do not come from God but from the wickedness of the world.

The question is, given all we know about the fundamental nature of gender equality in the plan of salvation and exaltation, why aren't women as visible as men in the scriptures as we now have them? If the division of labor we have outlined is not far off the mark, then at least part of the answer is that this division will impose patterns of visibility and invisibility on men and women. Because of his stewardship concerning the Word, Adam (representing all men) is to hearken unto God and is to impart God's Word to Eve (representing all women) and their children. Adam gained this stewardship and this right by first hearkening unto Eve and demonstrating his commitment to the light and those who are its stewards. Indeed, Adam's hearkening unto Eve is a natural precursor of his calling in connection with the Word. Nevertheless, because of his stewardship over the Word, the Word Adam imparts seems to have a maleness about it because the conduit is man. Indeed, we would expect the holy scriptures to comprise a record of the joint stewardship of men here on earth with men beyond the veil. We would expect the written text to be mostly men on the "other side" talking to men in mortality about this joint stewardship. That is indeed what we find, but it does not imply that God is any less interested in His daughters than His sons.[11]

Many women fall prey to this faulty conclusion not only from the relative invisibility of women in the scriptures but even from the language of certain holy ordinances. Without a fuller understanding it is easy to see how this may happen. For example, the endowment for our adult mortal life is the endowment to prepare us for the second gateway. It emphasizes the role of the Father and the service of women to men who serve the Father. It emphasizes the steps to the second gateway, which steps are presided over by men, the apprentices of their Father in the work of the Word. It emphasizes the second gateway itself, which is man. What we seem to see is men, men, men and their power and priesthood and presiding. This is completely natural and appropriate, given our situation of being past the first gateway and en route to the second, but it is wholly incomplete with respect to the totality of our life, past, present, and future.

When the veil was drawn over our minds, the impact on the relative visibility of men and women in the plan of salvation and exaltation might have been very great. Suppose, for example, women played a large role in premortal life. Drawing the veil at birth would then result in a distinctive and predictable pattern of relative invisibility of women in the work of God. Perhaps this skewedness is simply balanced out when we remember all in the hereafter. Nevertheless, if this skewedness so depresses and discourages the caretakers of the light in this life that the first gateway is imperilled and contaminated, we will see the disintegration of the family and the imperilling of the second gateway as well. It benefits no one, especially not the caretakers of the Word, for the caretakers of the light to suffer under such a gross misperception. It may be time for the stewardship of the caretakers of the light to be brought into illumination somewhat more than it has been to date. All men and all women will find joy in this greater light and knowledge and hearts will be knit together in love and equality. We will set the stage for Zion to be built in our midst, for surely in Zion there is an accurate perception of the role of the caretakers of the light—the servants and daughters of God and apprentices of Heavenly Mother.

A significant amount of the relative invisibility of women in holy scripture and in holy ordinances is explainable by the division of labor we have elaborated; nevertheless, the remainder of that invisibility may be a distortion. For example, new analyses of the Dead Sea Scrolls indicate that scriptural verses concerning women or mentioning women in pro-active or positive roles have been deleted or distorted in the relatively modern compilation we know as the Old Testament.[12] Furthermore, several Hebrew and Aramaic words indicating reference to groups comprising both men and women have been rendered in the King James version of the Bible as English words that refer only to men. For example, "b'nai" often translated as "sons" in verses referring, for example, to "the sons of God," in the original language can refer to persons of both sexes. These distortions are lamentable and any action we as a people can take to rectify error or misperception should be undertaken. Latter-day Saint General Authorities have led out in this regard by adding the phrase "and daughters" to scriptural verses making reference to the "sons of God" they cite in the semi-annual general conferences of the Church.[13] Joseph Smith once said, "When we say brethren, we mean those who have continued faithful in Christ, men, women, and children."[14] We should follow this example in personal and family scripture study. Doubtless there are other ways for handling more serious distortions created by the carnal and fallen state of certain male editors of the Bible.

Another area in which we should emulate our General Authorities is in developing a greater recognition and valuation of the work that women do as stewards of the Light. Recent conference addresses by President Gordon B. Hinckley, Elder Richard G. Scott, and Elder Jeffrey R. Holland are excellent examples of this movement.[15] Visibility does impact how we carry out our roles as helpmeets to one another. When women are invisible or devalued, the role of helpmeet that men play is impoverished. Likewise, when women are visible and valued, men's responsibilities as helpmeets in her work and men's responsibilities as the lovers of women become enlarged. Men will increasingly begin to understand they are to love and cherish women and assist them in nurturing children and caring for the home; and they learn that such help is a priesthood duty. Men will begin to re-envision and magnify their roles as husbands. They will also begin to re-envision their fatherhood role and see themselves as much responsible for the socialization of the children as the mother. The work and duty of being with the children may be primarily the mother's before the age of accountability, but it becomes equally the father's work and duty after the age of accountability has been reached. Last, treating women as the focus of decision and initiative in their individual stewardships, and understanding they have an equal and equally valued say in all common stewardships, are essential elements of right conduct in the community of the Saints. Just as husbands and wives stand before each other as eternal equals, so also brothers and sisters stand together as eternal equals.

Regaining a proper perspective concerning men and women is a sign that an individual or a community is moving closer to Zion. As one grows closer to Zion, the skewed perspective of seeing only men is replaced. The women are "seen" rather than overlooked or taken for granted; our Mother is no longer as invisible as she once was. We now see both men and women in equal relief. In addition to being a sign, replacement of the skewed perspective is also a cause of sifting. Those who cannot treat caretakers of the light with respect and equality and love cannot enter Zion and will not experience the "seeing" of women and our Mother. These things will be kept from them as a token that a sifting has taken place. As Christ exclaimed to others whose understanding was not what it should be, "Having eyes, see ye not?" (Mark 8:18). We believe this is the primary reason why so little about Mother in Heaven is spoken of by our prophets. Those who have Zion eyes will see and those who have not will not. The key to seeing Mother in Heaven is to see her apprentices here on earth, to really see and value and support the women in our own lives and the role they have played as caretakers of the light.

True Patriarchy

Perhaps no other word has caused such pain and confusion to the women of the Church as "patriarchy." As noted in Chapter One, one young woman summed up the problem very nicely by asking, "Doesn't patriarchy just mean 'men rule forever'?" Given all that we have expounded in this and other chapters, it is clear that patriarchy cannot mean an eternal hierarchy of men over women. The system of equal power between men and women that characterizes the eternal life of flourishing would be undone if patriarchy had such a meaning.

Let us begin our discussion of patriarchy with a statement by President James E. Faust: "Every father is to his family a patriarch and every mother a matriarch as coequals in their distinctive parental roles."[16] Let us add the observation that a man may not enter into the patriarchal order of the Melchizedek Priesthood without being sealed to a woman in

the new and everlasting covenant of marriage. Stated differently, the patriarchal order of the Melchizedek Priesthood
could not exist without women. As previously noted, the patriarchal order means the family order.

There is a tiny minority of men in the Church who would
agree with all that has been said in the last paragraph, but for
the wrong reasons. The attitude, which fortunately is very
uncommon, is that these statements are true because the patriarch needs a servant who will function as a womb for him. In
this viewpoint, the woman, as the servant of the man, will
undergo the pain and suffering to bring forth children into
mortality so that the patriarch need not concern himself with
that portion of his children's "begetting." As one Latter-day
Saint man put it, "[My wife] is but a biological vessel to
increase my priesthood kingdom." To this man, his wife is a
piece of equipment—a walking womb—that he must acquire
before requesting entrance into the celestial kingdom. This
loathsome interpretation is completely at odds with the spirit
of the plan of salvation and exaltation. As President Gordon B.
Hinckley has said,

> *Your wives are indispensable to your eternal progress.*
> *I hope you will never forget that. There are a few men*
> *in this Church—I'm glad there are not very many, but*
> *there are a few—who think they are superior to their*
> *wives. They better realize that they will not be able to*
> *achieve the highest degree of glory in the celestial*
> *kingdom without their wives standing at their side*
> *equally beside them. Brethren, they are daughters of*
> *God. Treat them as such.*[17]

Furthermore, the great atoning sacrifice of Christ in "begetting" us, or in bringing us forth as his sons and daughters, was
sealed by sacrifice of blood and water through suffering
(Mosiah 5:7). Christ was not above the type of sacrifice that
women make in their work as mothers in bringing forth their
children. Additionally, it is hard to conceive of a Christ who
would say, "Suffer the little children to come unto me," but yet

be "above" changing their diapers or other menial and dirty tasks related to childcare. Indeed, President Howard W. Hunter exhorted husbands to share with their wives the duties of childcare and housework.[18] If Christ is the role model for patriarchs, then the attitude that women exist so patriarchs need not make messy personal sacrifices for their children amounts to a rejection of true patriarchy.

If we discount interpretations of patriarchy that suggest women are not equal to men, or that women exist as menial-duty appendages to men, then patriarchy, whatever it means, must preserve a system of equal power and dignity between men and women. How can a system termed "patriarchy" do that? Since we acknowledge that men are patriarchs and women are matriarchs in the home, why are we to live a "patriarchal order" and not a "matriarchal order" when we talk about eternal life in a family order? How are we to understand that a man is the head of the family, though he and his wife are equal partners in the leadership of the home?

Remembering that women and men are united in their work as agents of the light, if we translate the term "patriarch" into "a caretaker of the Word" and "matriarch" into "a caretaker of the light" as these terms have been used in this chapter, we see not only how patriarchs and matriarchs are equal in power and in dignity in their distinctive parental roles, but we also see with new eyes what a "patriarchal order" might mean.

As discussed in an earlier chapter, God's exalted children form an eternal and governing family in heaven. The order of family government in eternity is sometimes referred to as the patriarchal order of heaven. We know that "the Church of the Firstborn is the divine patriarchal order in its eternal form."[19] President Ezra Taft Benson described the patriarchal order as the order of family government based on the new and everlasting covenant of marriage.[20] It may be somewhat misleading to call the governing order of heaven "patriarchal" because how the term is used in the fallen world may cause some to believe that among God's exalted daughters and sons some men rule over other men and men have dominion over women. But this is clearly not the case. All relations that form the order of the eternal family grow out of the relationship of equality that exalted beings have with one another through Christ (D&C 88:107; D&C 50:27-29; 84:37-38; 76:94-95). This is true not only of the relationship between brothers, but also between sisters, between brothers and sisters, and between husbands and wives. The patriarchal order arises out of and embodies these relations of equality. The patriarchal order is a way of ordering the work of gods, all of whom—male and female—are joint heirs and equals.

We suggest the family order of heaven is sometimes referred to as the "patriarchal order" because of the special role men play in creating and preserving that immense network of relationships of equality that characterizes the order. Let us see how this might be by extending our discussion of "patriarchy" and "patriarchal order" using the allegory given by Elder Boyd K. Packer in the October 1993 General Conference. The Lord gives a man one key and tells him he is to "protect at all cost" a vault wherein lies a priceless treasure. He gives him a second key and tells him it is the key to the treasure, and if he is a faithful guardian, he should feel free to use his second key and enjoy the treasure. The man enters the vault and attempts to open the door to the treasure, only to find he needs two keys. A woman holds the other key and they can open the treasure only together. Her job is to guard the treasure; his job is to guard the vault. There is not hierarchy between them, but heterarchy in a system of equal power.[21] The man and the woman each have an important responsibility and stewardship. He helps and serves her and she helps and serves him in this work. Furthermore, they are equal partners in the treasure.

This allegory speaks great truth and illuminates beautifully the system of equal power between men and women. The purpose of the priesthood is to bless the lives of the children of God and to invite and bring those who are worthy into "the vault"—the kingdom of God—through the saving ordinances of the gospel which constitute the door, or gate, to the vault. Male priesthood power and authority, as we have discussed, are based upon divine love and thus, are not about hierarchical power but about allowing the greatest number of God's children to move closer toward a godly way of existence. The guardian of the vault cannot force people to enter the vault. The guardian of the vault has no power over those who are worthy to enter the vault. The guardian enjoys no greater blessings than those who enter the vault. Yet male priesthood power and authority does include guardianship, with the power and authority to forbid unworthy individuals from entering the vault.

However, we must remember the purpose of this "power and authority to deny entrance"—this guardianship—or we will grossly misunderstand it. *The purpose of guardianship is to create a realm wherein guardianship need not be exercised.* The man's guardianship makes possible a place (the vault) where the treasure may be enjoyed in safety and equality with the woman, who is also worthy to enjoy the treasure. This guardianship is therefore a form of nurture toward those who live within the vault. Without guardianship to deny admittance, (the vault) would be contaminated and destroyed. That guardian "father power," creating as it does an order under the guardianship of the patriarchs, is the interface between Zion and not-Zion. Only it stands between the possibility of Zion and the impossibility of Zion.[22]

The order under the guardianship of the patriarchs, or "patriarchal order," works as a divine system of equal power. Any power and authority given to male priesthood holders is given for the purpose of bringing to pass the opportunity for all worthy individuals to live in equality as gods, including worthy women. Guardianship authority makes Zion possible, but in Zion, unlike the world, such authority does not seek to perpetuate its prerogatives at the expense of equality. When the guardian takes off his armor at the end of the day and enters the vault to be with the worthy people who live in the vault (Zion), he does not claim to be "above" them or to act as a "Gentile prince" to them (Matthew 2:25-28). Indeed, what he desires is to live in peace and equality with them as one of them. This is not only the basis of male-male relations in Zion, but it is the basis of male-female relations in Zion. This is how we are to understand how it is that a father "presides" in the home, yet his wife is his full and equal partner. There is no paradox or contradiction whatsoever.

If the caretakers of the Word (the patriarchs) establish order through exercising righteous guardianship, the patriarchal order established by them will not mean "male power over women," as the fallen world assumes. The patriarchal order means *the order established by men, by virtue of their male priesthood power as caretakers of the Word, to create a space where the full equality of men and women in the work of God may have its expression.* Indeed, we may go so far as to say that this priesthood power restores equality between men and women. Thus women should rejoice at the restoration of the priesthood because that restoration signifies not only the reestablishment of right relations between man and God, but also the reestablishment of right relations between man and woman. Only in the context created by the patriarchal order of the priesthood will the conditions necessary for a celestial life be achievable.

How is this so? The patriarchal order, in establishing the Word of God, divides the light from the darkness. Consider our universe. If there was no division between light and darkness, the universe would be a uniform mixture of light and dark. Given the expanse of dark comprises an estimated ninety percent of the known universe according to astronomers, it would be a very dark place indeed. But if one divides the light from the dark, then astounding creations such as suns appear, which illuminate the universe and its worlds. The division of light and dark creates places where light can abound. Similarly, the division between righteousness and unrighteousness created by the patriarchal order creates places where righteousness—and equality—can abound.

Women are not the passive recipients of the blessings of the patriarchal order. Women reciprocate through the exercise of their matriarchy (i.e., by serving as caretakers of the light). The blessings of their matriarchy are indispensable to the existence of patriarchy and to the work of God. Without matriarchal succor there will be none to inherit the kingdom of equals guarded by the patriarchs.

In viewing the whole system we are moved to cry out, "How exquisite and beautiful is the divine system of equal power that characterizes male-female relations! How wondrous that the work of males achieves the equality of females, and that the work of females achieves the equality of males!" Where the sensibilities of a fallen world see only hierarchy and a sham of equality, those with "eyes to see," see a perfectly balanced system in which each party works to the benefit of the other in equal power and dignity.

Counterfeits of Patriarchy in the Community of Saints

The fallen world and its god (Lucifer), are capable of twisting divine concepts to the end of rendering them useful to the "plan of misery." Satan has had much success twisting the concept of patriarchy so that it no longer resembles true patriarchy, or the patriarchal order, found in heaven. Indeed, what Satan substitutes is a patriarchy based on fallen values of power and control and pride. This is lamentable, for it alienates many from the heavenly principle, when what is in truth alienating is the fallen perversion of patriarchy. We have examined egregious perversions of patriarchy to be found in the fallen world in Chapter Five and also Appendix A. However, in this chapter we wish to hit a little closer to home. Are reverberations of fallen notions of patriarchy to be found in our own community, the community of Saints? Yes, despite the best and bluntest efforts on the part of our General Authorities, there are still a few who cling to worldly counterfeits of patriarchy. Let us examine several syndromes of perversion and false patriarchy occasionally found among members of the Church.

Syndrome #1. *Men are to rule over women because men are wiser, not as easily deceived, better than/more virtuous or*

more righteous, less emotional or less sentimental, and less
parochial than women. Men are the shepherds and women
are the sheep they guide to the celestial kingdom. That is why
God does not require men to hearken to their wives; he only
requires that wives hearken to their husbands. Paul said the
man was the head of the woman as Christ is the head of the
man; a hierarchical relationship should therefore exist
between man and woman.

These views are inconsistent with the gospel of Christ.
Women are capable of being as wise, as brave, as virtuous, as
full of reason, and as inclusive as men. As we have explained
earlier, men are not given the priesthood as a prize that women
were not worthy to obtain. In Chapter Four, we discussed how
Eve's partaking of the fruit was an important task foreordained
specifically to her. Though Satan deceived her regarding his
own identity and motives, Eve was not deceived in her judgment that partaking of the fruit was what she should do. We
have commented previously on the hierarchy that exists
between men and women in the divine scheme and contrasted
this with fallen notions of hierarchy. As President Gordon B.
Hinckley has put it, "God our Eternal Father ordained that
[men and women] should be companions. That implies
equality."[23]

Elder M. Russell Ballard elaborates:

Men and women joined together in marriage need to
work together as a full partnership. However, full and
equal partnership between men and women does not
imply the roles played by the two sexes are the same in
God's grand design for His children. As the
Proclamation to the World on the Family clearly
states, men and women, though spiritually equal, are
entrusted with different but equally significant roles.
These roles complement each other. Men are given
stewardship over the sacred ordinances of the priest -
hood. To women, God gives stewardship over
bestowing and nurturing mortal life, including

providing physical bodies for God's spirit children, and guiding those children towards a knowledge of gospel truths. These stewardships, equally sacred and important do not involve any false ideas about domi - nation or subordination.[24]

Regarding Paul and the covenant about "hearkening," we suggest this refers to men's role past the first gate, which is presided over by women. Past the first gate (symbolized by Eve's partaking of the fruit and Adam's hearkening unto Eve and partaking of the fruit), all should hearken unto the care-takers of the Word as they endeavor to lead us further down the path toward godhood. That the work of the caretakers of the Word appears the primary drama of this life does not mean that they or their work is superior to that of the caretakers of the light. It means that to them is given the responsibility to create a space where all may become gods. They are the "head" in the sense used by Mosiah to describe Christ. He is our head because He makes us free through His dividing of light and darkness, which dividing we call the Word (Mosiah 5:7-8).

As we have seen, the patriarchal order makes possible a type of life in which all, including women, are free and equal. Paul's comment should be interpreted as supporting the divine system of equal power between men and women, not as under-mining it (see also Appendix B). John A. Widtsoe sums up this point nicely, "It is but a small and puny-souled man who could wish to humiliate women as a class and keep them as an infe-rior sex; for men can never rise superior to the women who bear and nurture them."[25]

Syndrome #2. *A wife's God-ordained duty is to obey her husband. She sins if she does not obey him. A husband has the right to overrule his wife because he is the head of the house - hold and holds the priesthood. If God wishes to speak to a woman, he will speak to her through her husband. That is why women's faces are veiled—as a symbol that it is the man who has direct communication with God, and women should subordinate themselves to the men to hear God's will.*

A man who honors his priesthood does not require obedience from his fully equal partner and lover. He requires that she allow him to discharge his duty before God as someone who bears the responsibility for imparting the Word, for providing guardianship, and for judging between righteousness and unrighteousness within their household. If he is worthy in his role, she should "hearken" unto him; she should seriously listen to and thoughtfully consider what he says. As noted earlier, this is not a coercive power. To use a phrase of Elder Boyd K. Packer, a man should never attempt "to pull priesthood rank on his wife."[26] Why? Because what will follow is a heavenly "amen" to the priesthood of that man (D&C 121:37).

The head of the household does not have the right to overrule his equal partner. Household decisions should be made in unanimity, as all collective decisions are made in the units of Zion (D&C 107:27-29). As President Howard W. Hunter stated, "A righteous husband and father will accept his wife as a full partner in the leadership of the home, including full knowledge of and full participation in all decisions relating thereto. The Lord intended that [the wife] be a companion equal and necessary in full partnership. For a man to operate independent of or without regard to the feelings and of his wife in governing the family is to exercise unrighteous dominion."[27]

Furthermore, if the head of the household willfully disconnects himself from "the powers of heaven" through unrighteous dominion (D&C 121:36), a woman no longer has the responsibility to hearken unto him. Indeed, she has the responsibility *not* to hearken unto him.

The mutual obligation of men and women to counsel with each other is not limited to the family, but also extends to the Church. "[No] marriage of family, no ward or stake is likely to reach its full potential until husbands and wives, mothers and fathers, men and women work together in unity of purpose, respecting and relying upon each other's strengths."[28] Elder Marvin J. Ashton once said, "Our women are companion-leaders to help all our members receive the benefits of the

Church and the watch care, development, and refuge from the world that the Church provides."²⁹ Elder M. Russell Ballard suggests:

> *I would urge the priesthood brethren who preside over ward and stake councils to draw upon the great power, insight, and wisdom that women can bring with them to these council meetings. . . . It is a short-sighted priesthood leader who does not see the value of calling upon the sisters to share the understanding and inspiration they possess. . . . It is easy to under - stand why many sisters are frustrated when they sit in council with priesthood leaders and are not invited to make substantive contributions to the council. They have much to offer in finding real solutions to the problems facing priesthood leaders . . . Sisters, be prepared both mentally and spiritually to discuss the needs of those who fall within your stewardship. Be bold. Be assertive. Feel confident about raising weighty issues and concerns. You have as much right to input and inspiration as any other council member. The priesthood leader to whom you report will be strengthened more than you can imagine if he hears what you have to say. You will in many cases view the needs and concerns of women, youth, children, and families with greater empathy and insight than will your priesthood leaders. . . . [M]en and women express themselves differently and tend to have different skills, talents, and points of view. When either viewpoint is taken in isolation, the resulting image may be blurry, one-dimensional, or otherwise distorted. It is only when both perspectives come together that the picture is balanced and complete. Men and women are equally valuable in the ongoing work of the gospel kingdom . . . . [O]ne who lays claim to special privilege through the priesthood doesn't understand the nature of his authority. Priesthood is about service, not servitude;*

compassion, not compulsion; caring, not control.
Those who think otherwise are operating outside the
parameter of their authority and are gravely
mistaken.[30]

The insistence of some men in the Church on obedience can
at times take on a very coercive nature, reminding one of
Satan's repeated desires that men "worship" him and obey him.
Lest we be misunderstood, we believe that obedience to the
Word of God is vitally important. Obedience is a good thing if
it is not coerced but instead is done because one loves the
Word. Indeed, obedience is using one's agency to choose good.

However, when a person attempts to coerce another into
obedience, or when a person is more interested in having
others obey him than in guiding them toward godhood and
equality, or when a person demands obedience to his own will
instead of God's, then we are not talking about obedience but
unrighteous dominion over souls made free through Christ.
This type of dominion is a grave sin. As Elder Jeffrey R. and
Sister Patricia T. Holland stated, "Never let it be said of any
Latter-day Saint man that he has contributed to the 'injustice
that womanhood has endured in mortality,' to use Elder
Talmage's searing phrase."[31]

Probably the most eloquent statement on the subject was
made by the Prophet Joseph Smith, who stated:

It is the duty of a husband to love, cherish, and nourish
his wife, and cleave unto her and none else; he ought to
honor her as himself, and he ought to regard her feel-
ings with tenderness . . . [He is] not to rule over his
wife as a tyrant, neither as one who is fearful or
jealous that his wife will get out of her place, and
prevent him from exercising his authority. It is his
duty to be a man of God (for a man of God is a man of
wisdom) ready at all times to obtain from the scrip-
tures, the revelations, and from on high, such
instructions as are necessary for the deification and
salvation of his household.[32]

Syndrome #3. *Men and boys are more valuable and require more attention and concern than women and girls. A sign that God feels a family is righteous or should be blessed is that the family will have many sons.*

We were appalled to discover that this third syndrome still exists in our culture. Nevertheless it does, but hopefully to a limited extent. One woman, after having four daughters, gave birth to a son. Her father, a lifelong member of the Church commented, "Well, honey, you finally did something right!" Another woman, the mother of daughters, commented to someone who had just had her second son, "You are so blessed to have sons!" One strong Latter-day Saint father commented, "I have six sons and three daughters. Thank goodness it isn't the other way around!" The clear implication of such remarks is that somehow having sons is a "better" blessing than having daughters. This attitude can affect the self-esteem of young girls directly and may affect decisions later in the girls' lives as well. Some mothers of daughters have, in previous times, lamented the perceived lack of opportunities for development for their daughters in Church programs. One said: "My daughter would love to learn the skills the boys learn in the scouting program. My daughter gets the feeling she's not worth the type of investment the Church makes in the boys, simply because she is a girl." Thankfully, the Church has begun to address this perception brought on by the contaminating influence of false patriarchy in the world by providing "Achievement Days" for young girls and stronger programs for older girls.

This syndrome dies hard, though it is the syndrome most clearly at odds with Church teachings. God loves His daughters just as much as He loves His sons. If He sends His daughters to our families, do we think He is happy when they receive a less enthusiastic welcome than their brothers? For shame! Our daughters should feel as loved and as valued as they did when they lived with Heavenly Father. As President Gordon B. Hinckley put it, "Do you think the God our Eternal Father loves his daughters less than he loves his sons? No man can demean or belittle . . . a daughter of God without giving offense to her Father in Heaven."[34]

Syndrome #4. *Gender roles should be strict in definition. Women should not be missionaries and men should not change diapers. Women should not take up scarce slots in universities or paying jobs that should go to male breadwin - ners. Women should never be statesmen or leaders; it is a disgrace to the men. If a woman has something to say, she should talk to her husband in private about it and not intrude into affairs which should be decided by men.*

As we were writing the chapters for this book, we were afraid that someone would misinterpret our words as support for this syndrome. Any time one puts forth an argument that a man's primary responsibility is X and a woman's primary responsibility is Y, one finds conceptually simple persons who insist that only men should do X, and they had better not do any Y either; and only women should do Y, and they had better not do any X. To say such things denies the unity of the work of our Heavenly Parents. Furthermore, at its foundation, one finds a striking lack of charity in this position.

Sometimes arguments like these take on a ludicrous cast. One young Latter-day Saint man, very sincere, explained to me that men could not bear to change diapers because they were not "genetically wired" to be able to stand the smell. Of course, God made women capable of standing the smell, so they should be the ones changing the diapers! Another man stated proudly that even though he and his wife had had numerous children, he had never changed a diaper in his life.

Not surprisingly, arguments about who should be doing what typically center around male tasks viewed as granting privilege and status and female tasks viewed as distasteful and menial. We sense the message of hierarchy creeping in; males should be off deciding great matters and are "above" menial tasks of childcare and homemaking. The minute someone is "above" doing something, even if they attempt to justify it as being God's will, we are observing a disconnection from the powers of heaven (D&C 121:36). Recall Christ's comment as his disciples protested that the Son of God was "above" the dirty task of washing their feet: "Ye know that the princes of the Gentiles exercise dominion over them, and they that are great exercise authority upon them. But it shall not be so among you: but whosoever will be great among you, let him be your minister. And whosoever will be chief among you, let him be your servant: even as the Son of man came not to be ministered unto, but to minister, and to give his life a ransom for many" (Matthew 20:25-28).

Elder Boyd K. Packer hit the nail square on the head when he proclaimed: "There is no task, however menial, connected with the care of babies, the nurturing of children, or with the maintenance of the home that is not his [the husband's] equal obligation. The tasks which come with parenthood, which many consider to be below other tasks, are simply above them."[35] And Elder M. Russell Ballard has elaborated, "We know that a father's role does not end with presiding, providing, and protecting family members. On a day-to-day basis, fathers can and should help with the essential nurturing and bonding associated with feeding, playing, story-telling, loving, and all the rest of the activities that make up family life."[36]

I will never forget a conversation that brought this point home to me. I had a new baby and a toddler and my home looked like a tornado had hit it. I couldn't bear to look at my house, it was so messy. I lamented on the phone to a dear friend that I felt ashamed, for were we not to keep our homes in such a state that if the Savior walked in, we would feel no embarrassment? My wise friend said, "Valerie, if the Savior came to your home, He would help you clean your house and take care of your little ones." The Spirit bore witness to me at that moment that that was exactly what Christ—a man among men—would do, and tears filled my eyes.

This brings us to our first assertion that no one is "above" the distasteful and menial tasks that go with caring for God's children. Indeed, probably nothing brings one a greater measure of the power of heaven, as Christ intimated, than to perform these tasks for those who cannot help themselves. It is fine to be a guardian and judge in Zion as caretaker of the Word, but a guardian or judge who forgets that God's children must be nurtured and cared for as well as guarded and judged is missing the point of God's work. Indeed, such an attitude leads to perversions that those who are not guardians and judges are inferior to those who are.[37] How can one remain a righteous guardian and judge without assisting in the work of nurturing and caring for God's children? We feel it is for this reason that President Howard W. Hunter stated that a righteous husband and father "share[s], as a loving partner, the care of the children. Help [your wife] to manage and keep up your home. Help teach, train, and discipline your children. . . . [O]ne of the greatest things a father can do for his children is to love their mother."[38] Without providing such assistance, a husband and father may fall prey to some of the fallen perversions of patriarchy. He may lose the charity that Christ would express to women and to children.

Our second assertion is that the gospel of Christ calls all persons to labor diligently as God's stewards, according to their various talents, to accomplish the purposes of Zion. This requirement implies that all persons are to have the opportunity to enlarge and exercise the talents with which God has blessed him or her for the building up of the kingdom of God. Scripture tells us that God is "no respecter of persons" and He "denieth none that come unto him," neither "male nor female" (D&C 38:16; 2 Nephi 26:33; Galatians 3:28). In His Zion, God gives women and men equal opportunity for growth and development.[40] Both men and women, provided they will come unto the Lord, have equal chances to develop and use their talents as He needs and requires such of them in order to guide them in preparation for eternal life.[41]

Thus, women may have special talents to preach the gospel, and may be called by the Spirit to go on a mission, though they do not have the sacred responsibility that the young caretakers of the Word do. Women may have special talents as statesmen, as lawyers, and other seemingly "male" occupations. They should have the right to develop such talents. Men may have special talents as nurturers, teachers, and other seemingly "female" occupations, and they should be given the opportunity to express such talents. Currently, there are only a handful roles out of an infinity of roles that apparently are gender-exclusive: priesthood holder, father, husband, wife, and mother.[42]

Men and women have primary responsibilities for which they are held accountable before God. This is what God requires as a minimum for each man and woman, insofar as they have been taught correct principles and have been given opportunities to function in these roles.[43] However, those roles do not represent the maximum an individual man or woman can do as a righteous son or daughter of God. God gives a talent so it can be used, even if it does not directly pertain to one's primary responsibilities as caretaker of the Word or caretaker of the light. The work of our Heavenly Parents is not rigidly and artificially divided, but is unified and one in purpose. Men and women are both agents of the light. Thus, the righteous exercise of all talents supports the work of God, regardless of the gender of the person to whom the talent is given. Insofar as full exercise of a talent may impede one's role as a caretaker, the talent should be put on hold until one's primary responsibilities are fulfilled.[44] Nevertheless, one's talents and responsibilities should not be seen in zero-sum terms—that is, one either develops one or fulfills the other—but rather should both been seen as worthy endeavors, one of which has higher priority than the other.

President Gordon B. Hinckley put it this way:

There must be respect for the interests of one another. There must be opportunities and encouragement for the development and expression of individual talent. Any man who denies his wife the time and the encouragement to develop her talents, denies himself and his children a blessing which could grace their home and bless their posterity.[45]

In sum, those who suffer from this syndrome deny themselves charity and fail to understand the unity of the work done
by each of our Heavenly Parents. Fortunately, artificial and
rigid gender roles passed down by tradition are less persuasive
to the rising generation, who seem to be more responsive to
individual circumstances than previous generations.

Syndrome #5. *Patriarchal lines are all-important, both
here and in the hereafter. Matriarchal lines are not spiritually
or temporally significant. A woman becomes a member of her
husband's line and does not continue her own family's line.
After all, nobody names or counts their daughters in the Old
Testament; they only name and count their sons. Our patriar -
chal blessings tell us the tribe, defined in terms of Jacob's sons,
to which we belong. Matriarchal lines do not matter.*

Though this syndrome might seem fairly innocuous
compared to the syndromes previously discussed, the error it
contains becomes the seed for practices and traditions that
actively harm women. For example, by conceptualizing one's
daughter as not fully part of one's family line, one draws near
to traditions that claim that daughters are but "houseguests" in
the family, and that "raising a daughter is like watering a plant
in another man's garden." These attitudes lead to inferior care
and concern for the lives of daughters. Furthermore, by stating
that one's patriarchal lineage is all that matters, one implicitly
states that who one's mother and grandmother and foremothers were is of no consequence. In 1997 in Brigham Young
University's own Family History Library, our research assistant was chastised by a brother for working on her matriarchal
line first, since it was her patriarchal line that was "more
important!" The contribution of one's foremothers to a soul's
development is thus deemed as naught next to the contribution
of the fathers, grandfathers, and forefathers.

However, even in the Old Testament, a document not
known for expressing the full equality of women in a fashion
comprehensible to the twenty-first century mind, it does
appear to matter greatly who one's mother and foremothers
were. Abraham had several sons, but only Isaac, not even his

firstborn, was the child of promise, for he was the son of Sarah. David's lineage, through which the Savior entered mortality, was enhanced by the presence of Ruth and Tamar as his fore-mothers. It mattered that Joseph was the firstborn of Rachel, even though he was not Jacob's firstborn. Indeed, in most ancient cultures a man gained the right to the kingship based on the identity of the woman he married.[46]

Furthermore, in latter days, men of God have been inspired to recount the importance of the spiritual legacy left by their foremothers. To give but one example, Elder William Rolfe Kerr of the Seventy imparted the following in the October 1996 general conference:

> *The power and influence one person can have is enor - mous. It was one Sarah Anne Meeks who paid what seemed to be her ultimate sacrifice as she stood alone on the doorstep of her home in far-off England nearly a century and a half ago. Her father met her there with a small bundle containing a few of her belongings and with these words, "You join that church and you must never set foot in my home again." Unfortunately that was the last she saw of her family. Alone? Very much alone! She could have bowed to that impossible, heart-wrenching rejection. But no—she loved the Lord. She had been touched by the Spirit and knew that the gospel of Jesus Christ had been restored to the earth in its fullness. She knew that she must stand as a witness to the truthfulness of this message. She knew that she could make a difference.*
>
> *From that one stalwart woman has sprung a progeny of faithful Latter-day Saints difficult to number. Literally hundreds of her descendants have stood as witnesses all around the world testifying to the reality of the Restoration of the Gospel—the same message she embraced as she stood alone. One of those descendants now stands here as an especial witness of the Savior Jesus Christ.* [47]

Clearly, it mattered that Elder Kerr was in Sarah Ann Meek's matriarchal line.

Though perhaps the importance of patriarchal lineage appears in the forefront of our minds because of our position in the plan of salvation past the first gate and en route to the second gate, we suspect that as we move closer to Zion, the importance of our matriarchal lines will be more visible to us. A family does not "lose" a daughter to another line—two family lines are "rejoined" when a daughter (or a son) marries. After all, we are all brothers and sisters, both spiritually and temporally, through our common parentage in Adam and Eve and in our Heavenly Parents. The ties to the mothers are as important as the ties to the fathers in our eternal life, and we feel this will be made more plain as time passes. We can help in this process by preserving as much about the lives of our foremothers as we preserve about the lives of our forefathers, so our children will feel the righteous influence and example of both. There is no excuse for discounting or devaluing the contribution of fully one-half of one's heritage on the basis of gender.

"Patriarchy" and "patriarchal order" do not mean "men rule forever" over women. No hierarchy or coercive power should result from the true exercise of these heavenly principles. The purpose of the patriarchal order is to establish a space where the full equality of men and women can flourish and eternal life can be enjoyed. Likewise, the purpose of matriarchy is to lift both men and women closer to godhood's equality and the fullness of life. By seeing the divine system of equal power behind male-female relations, we become free to discard worldly perversions of true patriarchy that have plagued and haunted mankind through the centuries. We become free to experience a spiritual ascent in our Latter-day Saint culture. As we do so, we make it possible that when we meet the inhabitants of Enoch's Zion, we will fall upon each other's necks. They assuredly will not wish to fall upon our necks if we still labor under dark distortions concerning the position and value of half their citizens—the women of Zion.

The strongest and most progressive force for women in the world is the gospel of Jesus Christ. And the most profoundly feminist act that a person can commit is to spread the gospel of Christ and thereby help build the kingdom of God on this earth.

Notes

1   Plus material I have added in the course of writing this book.

2   We are indebted to Professor Stephen Ricks of Brigham Young University for this exegesis.

3   In connection with death, Christ also conquered suffering (Alma 7:12), which is also the enemy of the caretakers of the light.

4   At least 585,000 women die from childbirth every year, according to the World Health Organization (June, 1996).

5   Authorities of the Church repeatedly tell us that no blessing will be denied the faithful, whether it be marriage, children, or other blessings not attained in this life. President James E. Faust recently reaffirmed this: "Some faithful women have been denied that which is at the very center of their souls. In the eternal plan, no blessing will be kept from the faithful" ("Woman, Why Weepest Thou?" *Ensign* 26 [November 1996]: 54).

6   Joseph F. Smith, *Gospel Doctrine* (Salt Lake City: Deseret Book, 1975), 315.

7.   As President Harold B Lee put it, "Pure womanhood plus priesthood means exaltation. But womanhood without priesthood, or priesthood without without pure womanhood doesn't spell exaltation." *The Teachings of Harold B. Lee* (1996), p. 292. In a way, then "priesthood" means "pure manhood."

8.   Sheri L. Dew, "Are We Not All Mothers?" *Ensign*, November 2001, pp. 96-98.

9   Another interesting fact to ponder is that not only can Satan never have a body, he also cannot ever be married to a wife, or have children and be a father. This may help explain his antipathy towards all the roles that women occupy in the plan of salvation and exaltation. We are indebted to Cheri Loveless for this insight.

10   In a 1991 address to the women of the Church, President Gordon B. Hinckley read and responded to a letter from a fourteen-year-old girl. Unable to find any scriptures which stated that women could enter the celestial kingdom, the girl asked, "Are men more important than women?" President Hinckley assured her that women are as eligible as men to enter the celestial kingdom and added that the

when the Lord speaks of attaining the blessings of the gospel, he is referring to "His daughters as wells as His sons. Infinite shall be the reward of each, and everlasting shall be his or her glory." President Hinckley also affirmed the importance of women: "You occupy a high and sacred place in the eternal plan of God, our Father in Heaven. You are His daughters, precious to Him, loved by Him, and very important to Him. His grand design cannot succeed without you" (Gordon B. Hinckley, "Daughters of God," *Ensign* 21 [November 1991]: 97-100).

11   Another useful idea is to search for scriptures describing the role of the light and then to understand that women are an important "text analog" of these scriptures, given their stewardship concerning the light.

12   We are indebted to Donald Parry, professor of Hebrew Language and Literature at Brigham Young University, for this information.

13   President Gordon B. Hinckley asserted that we should "not be disturbed. . .by the fact that the word *man* and the word *men* are used in scripture without also mentioning the words *woman* and *women*. I emphasize that these terms are generic, including both sexes" (Gordon B. Hinckley, "Daughters of God," *Ensign* 21 [November 1991]: 98).

14   *Teachings of the Prophet Joseph Smith*, comp. Joseph Fielding Smith (Salt Lake City: Deseret Book, 1977), 128-9.

15   President Gordon B. Hinckley, "Women of the Church," *Ensign* 26 (November 1996): 67-69; Elder Richard G. Scott, "The Joy of Living: The Great Plan of Redemption," *Ensign* 26 (November 1996): 73-75; and Elder Jeffrey R. Holland, "Because She Is a Mother," *Ensign* 27 (May 1997): 35-37.

16   James E. Faust, "The Prophetic Voice," *Ensign* 26 (May 1996): 6.

17   Gordon B. Hinckley, "Excerpts from Recent Addresses of President Gordon B. Hinckley," *Ensign* 26 (October 1996): 73.

18   Howard W. Hunter, "Being a Righteous Husband and Father," *Ensign* 24 (November 1994): 49-51.

19   Daniel H. Ludlow, ed. *The Encyclopedia of Mormonism* (New York: Macmillan Publishing, 1992), s.v. "Church of the Firstborn," by Ivan J. Barrett.

20   Ezra Taft Benson, "What I Hope You Will Teach Your Children About the Temple," *Ensign* 15 (August 1985): 9.

21   The concept of "heterarchy" is the closest that our discipline of political science can come to understanding a system of equal power between individuals with differences. Heterarchies are "complex systems in which elements have 'the potential of being unranked . . . or ranked in a number of ways, depending on systemic

r e q u i r ements. . . . In contrast, hierarchies are those in which some elements, on the basis of certain factors, are subordinate to others" (Carole L. Crumley, "Historical Ecology: A Multidimensional Ecological Orientation," in *Historical Ecology: Cultural Knowledge and Changing Landscapes*, ed. Carole L. Crumley [Santa Fe: School of American Research Press, 1994], 12).

22   Indeed, this "father power" is necessary in the family because the family is a curious mix of Zion and not-yet-Zion. The relationship between the husband and wife is (should be) patterned after Zion, but the husband and wife are bringing into the family children who are not yet able or ready to live a Zion existence. The children are not yet equals, and with the help and training provided by the parents they must prove themselves worthy to be considered equals. In this probationary mortal life, the interface between Zion and not-Zion can be within the home, as well as between the home and the outside fallen world. For these reasons it is not a contradiction to say that the father is the head of the household and that the husband and wife are equal partners in the leadership of the family. "Father power" is necessary in relationship to the children's status, but "father power" has no place in the husband-wife relationship. For example, we know that Heavenly Father took one of his children, Lucifer, and "threw him out of the house," so to speak; but such an interaction is unthinkable between Heavenly Father and his beloved and equal partner, Heavenly Mother. Confusion over the place of "father power" in the home is a common wellspring of unrighteous dominion in marital relationships.

23   President Gordon B. Hinckley, "Cornerstones of a Happy Home," an address given at a satellite broadcast fireside for husbands and wives on 29 January 1984. In that same address, he also stated, "It is commonplace with us to say that we are sons and daughters of God. There is no basis in the gospel for inferiority or superiority as between the husband and wife. Do you think that God our Eternal Father loves his daughters less than he loves his sons? No man can demean or belittle his wife as a daughter of God without giving offense to her Father in Heaven."

24   M. Russell Ballard, "The Sacred Responsibilities of Parenthood," BYU Education Week Devotional address delivered 19 August 2003, accessed at http://www.desnews.com/cn/view/1,1721,380002177,00.html on 11 September 2003.

25   John A. Widtsoe, *Priesthood and Church Government* (Salt Lake City: Deseret Book, 1939), 89.

26   Boyd K. Packer, "The Father and the Family," *Ensign* 24 (May 1994): 20. Elder Packer stated: "When there is a decision to be made that affects everyone, you and your wife together will seek whatever you might need, and together you will prayerfully come to a unified

decision. If you ever pull priesthood rank on her you will have failed in your leadership." Quoted in Carlfred Broderick, *One Flesh One Heart: Putting Celestial Love Into Your Temple Marriage* (Salt Lake City: Deseret Book, 1986), 32. During the April 1998 session of general conference, Elder Packer stated, "In the home it is a partnership with husband and wife equally yoked together, sharing in decisions, always working together. While the husband, the father, has responsibility to provide worthy and inspired leadership, his wife is neither behind him nor ahead of him but at his side" ("The Relief Society,"*Ensign* 28 [May 1998]: 73).

27 Howard W. Hunter, "Being a Righteous Husband and Father," *Ensign* 24 (November 1994): 49-51. President Spencer W. Kimball stated the same thought in this manner, "When we speak of marriage as a partnership, let us speak of marriage as a full partnership. We do not want out Latter-day Saint women to be silent partners or limited partners in that eternal assignment! Please be a contributing and full partner!" (*My Beloved Sisters* [Salt Lake City: Deseret Book Company, 1979], 31; emphasis added).

28 Sheri L. Dew, "It is Not Good For Man or Woman to Be Alone," *Ensign*, November 2001, p. 13.

29 Elder Marvin J. Ashton, Address at Regional Representatives' seminar, 31 March 1989, p. 2.

30 M. Russell Ballard, *Counselling with Our Councils,* Salt Lake City: Deseret Book, 1997, pp. 53, 57, 94-95, 57.

31 Jeffrey R. Holland and Patricia T. Holland, "Considering Covenants: Women, Men, Perspective, Promises," in S.F. Green and D.H. Anderson, eds. *To Rejoice As women: Talks from the 1994 Women's Conference* (Salt Lake City: Deseret Book Company, 1995), 109.

32 Joseph Smith, "On the Duty of Husband and Wife," *Elder's Journal of the Church of Jesus Christ of Latter-day Saints* (August 1838): 61.

33 It is noteworthy that the veiling of women takes place during an endowment of power given during the mortal phase of life, where, as we have seen, the first gate presided over by the caretakers of the light is past, and the second gate, presided over by the caretakers of the Word, looms before us. Another key may be found in Exodus 34:28-35.

34 President Gordon B. Hinckley, "Cornerstones of a Happy Home," an address given at a satellite broadcast fireside for husbands and wives on 29 January 1984.

35 Elder Boyd K. Packer, "A Tribute to Women," *Ensign* 19 (July 1989): 72-75.

36 M. Russell Ballard, "The Sacred Responsibilities of Parenthood," BYU Education Week devotional address delivered 19 August 2003, accessed at http://www.desnews.com/cn/view/1,1721,380002177,00.html on 11 September 2003.

37 Here is one example from the U.S. Air Force: "Freedom—a feeling the protected will never know."

38 Howard W. Hunter, "Being a Righteous Husband and Father," *Ensign* 24 (November 1994): 49-51.

40 M. Russell Ballard, "Equality through Diversity," *Ensign* 23 (November 1993): 90; first delivered at the 1993 General Relief Society Meeting.

41 Ibid. 89.

42 Please remember that we regard the full measure of priesthood as being an exalted spouse and father and the full measure of priestess-hood as being an exalted spouse and mother. Thus these gender-specific roles are intertwined.

43 There will be some who do not receive opportunities to perform even this minimum in their mortal lifetimes. Divine justice demands that they receive such opportunities in their eternal lifetimes.

44 President Howard W. Hunter's relinquishing of his musical career is a good case in point. See Elder James E. Faust's biographical article on the prophet, "The Way of an Eagle," *Ensign* 24 (1994): 2-13.

45 President Gordon B. Hinckley, "Cornerstones of a Happy Home," an address given at a satellite broadcast fireside for husbands and wives on 29 January 1984.

46 We are indebted to Dan Belnap for this observation.

47 William Rolfe Kerr, "Behold Your Little Ones," *Ensign* 26 (November 1996): 81.

CHAPTER 7
Polygamy

by
Valerie Hudson Cassler

During the time when members of the restored Church were commanded by the Lord to practice polygamy, some practiced it without any discernible hardship, and others with great pain. Contemporary Church members may look back upon that period with acceptance, indifference, or discomfort.

We do not see the diversity of feelings itself as harmful. Rather, since the new and everlasting covenant of marriage is at the heart of the work of eternal life and of godhood, confusion about the nature and form of lawful marriage ordained by God is harmful. Women (and men) may think that gender equality is compromised by the doctrine of polygamy.[1] So we ask, what is the principle and purpose of marriage in God's work? What is the law (or rule or unrestricted form) of marriage? What is the lawful exception to the law of marriage? What is the nature and the status of the lawful exception?[2] The overarching question we pose is whether God has revealed His mind about these matters. We believe that He has, specifically in Jacob 2 and in Doctrine and Covenants 132.

These scriptures come to us without taint of translation and interpretation over millennia, in contrast to the Bible. Therefore, mistranslation cannot have occurred and we assume misinterpretation should be at a minimum.[3] In that case, we must either conclude that God revealed to Jacob something contradictory to that which He revealed to Joseph Smith, or we must assume that these two scriptures do not contradict one another. We choose to assume the latter. We believe these two scriptures are not only not in contradiction but in fact reinforce, affirm, and parallel one another.

Marriage as an Eternal Principle

God commands His children to marry (D&C 49:15-16) and He married Adam and Eve in the Garden of Eden before the Fall (Moses 3:25). Scripture asserts that persons must be married to inherit the fullness of the Father in the celestial kingdom and those who are not worthy of the celestial kingdom live as unmarried persons (D&C 132:4-6, 17-21). Furthermore, not only are persons to be married, but they are to be married in the new and everlasting covenant. The Lord states this type of marriage is "by my word, which is my law" (D&C 132:19). In Latter-day Saint culture we colloquially refer to marriage in the new and everlasting covenant as "temple marriage." From all of this we understand that marriage in the new and everlasting covenant, or temple marriage, is an eternal principle of the highest importance. This is so because of the purpose of such marriage.

The purpose of marriage in mortality is to raise up right-eous seed to God, which merits the marriage partners the right to a "continuation of the seeds forever and ever" as godly marriage partners in the hereafter (D&C 132:19). God's work consists of raising up His seed unto righteousness—of endeav-oring to produce a righteous eternal increase unto Himself (Jacob 2:30). We are His servants in this task. Even though we experience each other in this life as fathers and mothers and sons and daughters, we must recognize that we are all brothers and sisters as Heavenly Father's seed. We serve His purpose by being parents to His children and by striving to point them in the direction of righteousness. In doing so, we parents, who are also His children, are established in righteousness to God. Though in mortality we may bear children with our bodies, and tend their bodies and spirits, the reality is that they are not our eternal increase—they are the Lord's eternal increase. As President Gordon B. Hinckley has recently stated, "Never forget that these little ones are the sons and daughters of God and that yours is a custodial relationship to them, that he was a parent before you were parents and that he has not relin-quished his parental rights or interest in these little ones."[4]

Through the work of marriage in mortality, we are preparing for the time when we will have our own eternal increase and our own children—when we ourselves are gods. Marriage under the new and everlasting covenant was "instituted for the fullness of my [God's] glory" (D&C 132:6), to further in mortality God's work of raising up His seed unto righteousness, but it is also a preparation for our own existence in the future as gods with eternal increase of our own (D&C 132:19-20). In a sense, the marriages into which we enter here on earth, even within the temple of the Lord, are probationary marriages. As earthly parents, we are acting *in loco parentis* to our children, whose true parents are divine. Only if we acquit ourselves well in the roles of spouse and parent in this probationary state are we entitled to perpetuate those roles in an eternal marriage state in the hereafter. In mortality, then, the purpose of marriage is to raise up a righteous seed unto God, and in fulfilling this first purpose, the second purpose of marriage pertaining to the hereafter is also brought about. Thus the spiritual rationale which underpins the eternal principle of marriage in the new and everlasting covenant is God's overarching work of love for His children "to bring to pass the immortality and eternal life of man" (Moses 1:39) "that they might have life and that they might have it more abundantly" (John 10:10).

Given this eternal principle of marriage, what is the law (or rule or unrestricted form) of marriage? Is there a lawful exception? What is the nature and status of that lawful exception? Let us first turn to Jacob's sermon.

Jacob's Sermon on Marriage

What is the form of Jacob's discussion of marriage? First, Jacob notes a social problem of great severity. The men of the time are taking many wives and concubines and "seek to excuse themselves in committing (these) whoredoms, because of the things which were written concerning David, and Solomon his son" (Jacob 2:23). These great men of the scripture were doing one thing, but God is now saying that those who follow David and Solomon's example are committing iniquity (Jacob 2:23). How are we to understand this apparent contradiction?

In answer to that question, the Lord notes that these men "understand not the scriptures" and err when they "seek to excuse themselves" in emulating David and Solomon (Jacob 2:23). The Lord continues, "David and Solomon truly had many wives and concubines, which thing was abominable before me" (vs. 24). Immediately following this frank judgment, the Lord states, "*Wherefore* . . . I have led this people forth out of the land of Jerusalem, by the power of mine arm, that I might raise up unto me a righteous branch from the fruit of the loins of Joseph. *Wherefore*, I the Lord will not suffer that this people shall do like unto them of old" (Jacob 2:25-26). The use of the word "wherefore" in these two scriptures reveals that part of the purpose in separating the Nephites from the civilization of their origin and bringing them across the ocean to the promised land was to raise up a righteous people who would not succumb to the moral errors of David and Solomon.

And how would the children of Lehi act if this purpose had been fulfilled? In the very next verse we are given the answer to that question. In verse 27 Jacob expounds the law of marriage—the rule or unrestricted form of marriage: "*Wherefore, my brethren, hear me, and hearken to the word of the Lord: For there shall not any man among you have save it be one wife; and concubines he shall have none*" *(Jacob 2:27)*. The general law (or rule or unrestricted form) of the eternal principle of marriage is monogamy and is found in several places throughout the scriptures. To take but one example, the Lord says in Doctrine and Covenants 49:16 "Wherefore, it is *lawful* that he [man] should have one wife, and they twain shall be one flesh, and all this that the earth might answer the end of its creation." In the beginning, when the earth was empty and sorely needed replenishing, God gave Adam but one wife that the pattern of His law of marriage might be set from the dawn of time in the very first human marriage on earth (see also Moses 5:3).[5] Joseph Smith said, "I have constantly said no man shall have but one wife at a time, unless the Lord directs otherwise."[6] Bruce R. McConkie concurs: "According to the Lord's law of marriage, it is lawful that a man have only one wife at a time, unless by revelation the Lord commands plurality of wives in the new and ever-lasting covenant."[7] Of course, taking a plurality of wives outside of being commanded to do so by the Lord, is always a grievous sin.[8]

Jacob teaches us that monogamy is the general law of marriage and polygamy is an exception to the general law, which exception must be commanded by the Lord before it can be practiced. Furthermore, Jacob reveals the reason the Lord will command polygamy to be practiced: "For if I will, saith the Lord of Hosts, raise up seed unto me, I will command my people [to practice polygamy]; otherwise they shall hearken unto these things [to take but one wife and have no concu-bines]" (Jacob 2:30, 27). Recalling that the two-fold purpose of marriage is to raise up a righteous seed unto God here in mortality and to prepare the marriage partners for eternal increase in the hereafter, the Lord specifically links the lawful but exceptional commandment of polygamy to the first of these purposes. This explicit linkage to an underlying spiritual purpose of marriage is to be expected. If God proclaims both a law of marriage and a lawful exception in marriage, then the rationale for both the law and the law's exception must be a spiritual rationale, for as the Lord says, "Wherefore, verily I say unto you that all things unto me are spiritual, and not at any time have I given unto you a law which was temporal . . . . For my commandments are spiritual; they are not natural nor temporal, neither carnal nor sensual" (D&C 29:34-35).

With this understanding of the purpose of marriage and the law and the lawful exception of marriage in mind, Jacob's sermon is profound, despite its brevity. God commands men and women to marry (D&C 49:15). In general, He commands them to marry monogamously (Jacob 2:27; 3:5; D&C 49:16) but sometimes He will command them to marry polygamously (Jacob 2:30). Both the giving of the general law and the commandment to depart from the general law are motivated by

God's love for us. But one thing is also clear from Jacob's sermon: *God is not indifferent concerning how His children marry. He actively and severely restricts the practice of polygamy, while leaving monogamy unrestricted.* One can be destroyed for practicing polygamy without God's sanction, becoming "angels to the devil" and "bring[ing] your children unto destruction, and their sins heaped upon your heads at the last day," but no such punishment attends the practice of monogamy (Jacob 2:33; 3:5-6, 10-12).

Unfortunately, Jacob does not provide us sufficient information about the exception to discuss its nature and its status in the eyes of God. We are not given reasons for the remarkable difference in degree of restriction between monogamy and polygamy made by the Lord. Our next question, for whose answer we must turn to Doctrine and Covenants 132, is simple: Why is God not indifferent between the practices of monogamy and polygamy, severely restricting as he does the second while leaving the first virtually unrestricted?

Doctrine and Covenants 132

Doctrine and Covenants 132 is one of the deepest and most thought-provoking scriptures in our canon. It concerns the new and everlasting covenant of marriage and its place at the heart of the plan of salvation and exaltation. Without its restoration, the fullness of eternal life would be unobtainable. Thankfully, as noted in D & C 132:40, the Lord gave Joseph Smith an appointment to restore all things, and therefore, he restored the new and everlasting covenant of marriage. This much is indisputable. What is often in dispute in our culture is what exactly this means.

Given the over 150 years that have passed since the receipt of the revelation now known as Doctrine and Covenants 132, we are in a better position to settle that dispute. Joseph Smith restored marriage for "time and all eternity" (D&C 132:18), which we now colloquially call "temple marriage." In restoring the principle of temple marriage, Joseph Smith restored *both* the general law of marriage and the lawful exception as elucidated by Jacob centuries before. Put more precisely, Joseph Smith restored the general law of monogamous temple marriage but he also restored the lawful exception of polygamous temple marriage. At the time of the revelation (most scholars say prior to the date given for D & C 132), God commanded Joseph Smith to command the Church membership to practice polygamy. By so doing, God activated the lawful exception to the general law of marriage. Thus, polygamous marriages entered into in the temple after that commandment was given by the Lord were "without condemnation on earth and in heaven" (D&C 132:48). Putting Jacob's teachings together with Joseph's teachings, the commandment to practice polygamy was given by God at that time for the purpose of raising "up seed unto me [God]" (Jacob 2:30).

However, in 1890 God rescinded the commandment sanctioning the lawful exception to the general law of marriage. Polygamous marriages would no longer be recognized by the Lord, and indeed would be grounds for excommunication from the Church. This rescinding did not "unrestore" the new and everlasting covenant of marriage, or temple marriage. Temple marriage is a mainstay of our religion and will never cease to be our ideal. The new and everlasting covenant of marriage is still among us, but the commandment to live the lawful exception to the general law of marriage is no longer among us. Thus the "restoration of all things" does not demand that polygamy be actively practiced among the Saints. It merely demands that the possibility of God commanding polygamy (which possibility demands the restoration of temple marriage and sealing keys) exists. And so it does to this day. As long as there are temples and sealing keys among our people, God can command His people to practice polygamy. But the presence of temples and sealing keys does not conversely demand or necessitate that God actually issue the command to practice polygamy. Our contemporary situation is perfectly described in this manner and explains how Bruce R. McConkie could conclude that polygamy cannot be a requirement for exaltation.[9]

Thus we see that God's lack of indifference concerning the manner of marriage among His children which we noted in Jacob 2 persists in Doctrine and Covenants 132. Even with the restoration of temple marriage, God is still not indifferent between monogamy and polygamy. He persists in actively and severely restricting polygamy despite the presence of temples in our midst. Absent a commandment from the Lord to practice polygamy given through the prophet, a member of the Church would be excommunicated for attempting to practice it. The illegality of polygamy in the United States is not really the issue here, for such an excommunication would take place even if the Church member were living in a land where polygamy was a legal practice according to the law of the land. Even if polygamy were to be legalized in the United States itself, the Church would still excommunicate members who attempted to practice it, unless the Lord issued the required commandment through the prophet. *God persists in making a strong discrimination between monogamy and polygamy, even in the context of the restoration of all things.*

We come now to a very important question: Why is God not indifferent between monogamy and polygamy? Though Jacob 2 does not provide any insight on this matter, D & C 132 sheds great light on this topic, and we go so far as to say that in this scripture the Lord freely reveals His mind to his children.

Isaac and Hagar

One of the marvelous elements of D & C 132 is the insight this section provides into how the Lord reasons. The argument the Lord puts forward is meant to be understood by His people. It is reasonable to begin with the assumption that God meant what He said in this scripture and that God wants us to understand what He meant. In D & C 132, the Lord attempts to reason with Joseph Smith in order to help him understand the principles involved in marriage. In D & C 50:10-13, the Lord describes how he will reason:

> *And now come . . . by the Spirit, unto the elders of [my] church, and let us reason together, that ye may under -*

stand; Let us reason even as a man reasoneth one with another face to face. Now, when a man reasoneth he is understood of man, because he reasoneth as a man; even so will I, the Lord reason with you that you may understand. Wherefore, I the Lord, ask you this ques - tion.

The Lord will reason with us and present arguments that we may understand, and on the issue of polygamy, the Lord will begin His chain of reasoning with a question, which He will then proceed to answer. The Lord states at the beginning of the revelation:

You [Joseph Smith] have inquired of my hand to know and understand wherein I, the Lord, justified my servants Abraham, Isaac, and Jacob, as also Moses, David, and Solomon, my servants, as touching the principle and doctrine of their having many wives and concubines—Behold and lo, I am the Lord thy God, and will answer thee as touching this matter (D&C 132:1-2).

What is the form of the argument concerning the law of marriage in this scripture? The form is virtually identical to Jacob 2, which demonstrates the consistency and unchanging nature of the Lord's reasoning on this matter. D & C 132 parallels Jacob 2 and serves as a detailed exposition and affirmation. The same historical question serves as the catalyst for section 132 as it did for Jacob 2: What are we to make of the practice of David, Solomon, and other great patriarchs of old having many wives and concubines (D&C 132:1)? This time the inquirer is Joseph Smith—he who had previously translated the Book of Mormon, including Jacob 2.

This inquiry is again met by a setting forth of the general principles of marriage in the new and everlasting covenant, followed by a more specific explanation of the lawful exception of polygamy. Hyrum M. Smith's commentary on the Doctrine and Covenants states, "The Revelation is divided into two parts. The first, comprising vs. 3-33, deals mainly with the principle of celestial marriage, or marriage for time and all eternity; the second, comprising the remaining verses, deals with plural marriage."[10] As to the first part of the revelation, concerning the principle of marriage in the new and everlasting covenant, the Lord explains that all bonds and covenants "not by me or my word" (vs. 13) are of no effect after death, including the bond and covenant of marriage. He then goes on to explain that there is a marriage "by my word, which is my law, and by the new and everlasting covenant" (vs. 19) and that this marriage covenant remains in effect after death. Furthermore, parties to this special marriage covenant inherit the fullness of his glory (i.e., which glory shall be a fullness and a continuation of the seeds forever; (vs. 19)). That is to say, those who enter this covenant are able to have their own eternal increase in the hereafter. Having eternal increase renders them "gods, because they have no end" (vs. 20), and they shall have "all power" (vs. 20). Thus, only marriage within the new and everlasting covenant fulfills the two-fold spiritual purposes of marriage: to raise up a righteous seed unto Him in mortality and to prepare His children to be eternal godly marriage partners and have eternal increase. All who choose not to enter this special marriage covenant remain "separately and singly" (vs. 17) after death and cannot have eternal increase. Because they cannot have eternal increase, they cannot be gods but "are appointed angels in heaven, which angels are ministering servants" (vs. 16). Now that this revelation has been given, all those who choose to marry outside the new and everlasting covenant though they were able to marry within that covenant are "damned; for no one can reject this covenant and be permitted to enter into my glory" (D&C 132:3).

In the setting forth of this general principle of eternal marriage there is no mention of polygamy. Indeed, the whole issue of David and Solomon is not even raised in the verses where the Lord discusses in general what eternal marriage is, why He commands eternal marriage, and why those who reject it are damned. Additionally, this marriage covenant is described in the terms "if a man marry a wife" (vs. 19), using a singular article. Logically, of course, this phrasing does not preclude a man marrying more than one wife, but neither does it imply the same. We cannot say, then, on the basis of verses 3 through 33 where the general principles are expounded, how the Lord views the two possible forms of temple marriage—monogamy and polygamy. We can only say that He is stating a clear preference for marriage in the new and everlasting covenant as versus marriage outside of it.[11] However, what comes after verse 33 reinforces that monogamy is the general law and that polygamy is a departure from the rule. The Lord is definitely not indifferent between the two.

It is not until the second half of the revelation, starting with verse 34, as Smith and Sjodahl note, that polygamy is addressed. The Lord begins by explaining that because of Abraham's righteousness in receiving all things by revelation and commandment, Abraham "hath entered into his exaltation and sitteth upon his throne" (D&C 132:29). As a result, Abraham's seed will continue and will be "as innumerable as the stars" (D&C 132:30). A key element of Abraham's righteousness was to enter into the "law," which provides for "the continuation of the works of my Father, wherein he glorifieth himself" (D&C 132:31). The law referred to here is the new and everlasting covenant, or temple marriage. And again the Lord warns, as He did in verses 3, 17, and 21, "Enter ye into my law and ye shall be saved. But if ye enter not into my law ye cannot receive the promise of my Father, which he made unto Abraham" (D&C 132:32-33). Entering into the new and everlasting covenant of marriage (temple marriage) is a requisite of exaltation for all, including Abraham and Joseph Smith.

Finally, starting with verse 34, the Lord turns to the topic of polygamy. He begins the discussion with a statement of fact: "God commanded Abraham, and Sarah gave Hagar to Abraham to wife." In the verses that follow, the Lord will answer the question He then poses: "And why did she do it?" (D&C 132:34).

The Lord explains His reasoning on polygamy in terms of a specific analogy between two situations that occurred to Abraham. The Lord's subsequent explanation centers around an analogy the Lord himself posits between his commandment to Abraham to sacrifice Isaac and his commandment to Abraham to marry Hagar polygamously. In verse 36 the Lord explains: "Abraham was commanded to offer his son Isaac; nevertheless it was written: Thou shalt not kill. Abraham, however, did not refuse, and it was accounted unto him for righteousness" (D&C 132:36). Given the importance of His children having a correct understanding of their Father's mind on this topic, we cannot believe the analogy was chosen without great care. God wishes us to see how and why He views the two situations as analogous. By choosing the story of Isaac the Lord reveals His mind to us and constrains forever and irrevocably any discussion we, His children, might choose to have on the subject of polygamy. We must understand correctly why the Lord elects to use this particular analogy or we are likely to seriously err in our understanding of the role and place of polygamy in God's plan for His children.

The first and most telling point to note about the analogy is that the story of <u>Isaac is a story of sacrifice</u>. The Lord is telling us that the term "Abrahamic sacrifice" refers not only to the story of Isaac but applies to the story of Hagar, as well. Hyrum M. Smith and Janne M. Sjodahl, in their authoritative Doctrine and Covenants commentary, concur:

*"Section 132 contains (1) an introductory statement (1-2); (2) a reminder to the Prophet that knowledge demands obedience (3-6); (3) a definition of the celestial law (7-14); and (4) how the law applies to marriage covenants (15-20); (5) a demand for obedience (21-7); (6) the Law of the priesthood (28-33); (7) the doctrine of plural marriage (34-40); (8) a declaration that plurality of wives is not adultery (41-9); (9) **that it is a sacrifice** (50-7); (10) that it is a law of the priesthood (58-66)."*[12]

Before the Lord even delves into the analogy, His very positing of an analogy between the Isaac situation and the Hagar situation is revealing. Of all the possible analogies of sacrifice God has commanded in history, He chooses the most wrenching sacrifice He has ever commanded to serve as the analogy wherewith to instruct us concerning polygamy—the sacrifice of one's own innocent child by one's own hand. This choice of analogy by the Lord is meant to reveal to us that in the Lord's eyes the Hagar situation is no light matter but rather is like unto the heaviest and most heart-wrenching of all sacrifices He has ever required of man.

Four Types of Sacrifice

Though sacrifice is one of the first principles of the gospel, there are various forms of sacrifice of which the Abrahamic sacrifice is the highest and heaviest. Let us see why this is so.

A first type of sacrifice represents our choice to sacrifice to obtain a desired goal. For example, we might speak of "sacrificing" to send a child on a mission. The sacrifice is by our choice and the goal is one we desire to see realized.

A second type of sacrifice might better be understood as accepting persecution as a reaction of the unrighteous to our decision to follow God. We might be ostracized or even oppressed because of our beliefs and behavior by those who believe and behave otherwise. In some cases, the unrighteous might even seek to take our lives. Our choice to pursue a desired goal leads to choices by the unrighteous, which we cannot control, to inflict suffering upon us.

A third type of sacrifice appears from our mortal perspective not to involve our agency, though perhaps from an eternal perspective agency did indeed play a role at a prior point. These are sacrifices of adversity, for example, where an innocent child is born with an imperfect body or accidents or illness take the health or life of persons. These sacrifices come to us without conscious mortal choice on our part, and the element of a desired goal in such a context is often obscure, as it was obscure to Job.

But the heaviest sacrifice a person can ever be called upon to make—the Abrahamic sacrifice—is slightly different from these other three types. In the Abrahamic sacrifice, we are asked by God to make a conscious choice in a situation in which what He requires of us cannot be regarded as a desired goal from all that we know about God's laws. We can all understand how obedience to God's laws, for example to the Ten Commandments, brings a happier, richer, and more peaceful life. But what if God were to command us to break His law? Reason alone would tell us we would lose the happiness and peace that come from obedience to the law. But the test of the Abrahamic sacrifice is not a test of reason. It is a test of faith—indeed, it is the ultimate test of faith.

Remember for a moment what an Abrahamic sacrifice represents. An Abrahamic sacrifice involves at least three elements found in the story of Abraham being commanded to sacrifice Isaac: 1) God makes plain to Abraham a law ("thou shalt not kill" [D&C 132:36]); 2) God then requires Abraham, an innocent and righteous man, to depart from that law ("sacrifice Isaac"), and the choice to depart therefrom would seem to erase the joy that naturally follows from the law; and 3) God provides a means of escape from the departure from the law (the angel sent to stay his hand and the ram in the thicket; Genesis 22:11-13), which allows renewed joy from being able to live under the law once more.

The Abrahamic Sacrifice Concerning Hagar

With that understanding in mind, let us turn to where we left off in D & C 132. Remember that in verse 34 we begin a discussion of polygamy. We discover that God commanded Abraham to have children (in this case, one child) with Hagar, who was not his wife at the time of the commandment and who was handmaiden to his wife, Sarah. Abraham took Hagar to wife, thus entering into a God-commanded polygamous union. Fortunately, rather than leaving us with just this fact, the Lord helps us to greater understanding through the discussion that follows. The Lord asks "why" this was done (vs. 34), and then proceeds to answer: "Because this was the law; and from Hagar sprang many people. This, therefore, was fulfilling, among other things, the promises" (vs. 34). Does this mean that in God's eyes polygamy is the general law and that He is indifferent between monogamy and polygamy after all? We will see that this is not what the Lord is saying.

The Lord's exposition does not end with verse 34. To make sense of verse 34 we must view it in conjunction with the remainder of the section, especially the verses that specifically mention Abraham (verses 35-37, 50-51). Immediately after verse 34 the Lord asks, "Was Abraham, therefore, under condemnation?" (vs. 35). If we accept the position that the Lord is indifferent between monogamy and polygamy, this question is a non sequitur, and indeed, the very question itself makes no sense. How can someone practicing a form of marriage about which God is indifferent be perceived to be "under condemnation"? God cannot be referring to some type of cultural condemnation by Abraham's peers. Remember, we are not talking about Joseph Smith's time, when polygamy was culturally unacceptable. In Abraham's time, polygamy was commonplace and well accepted. No one in Abraham's cultural setting would be condemning him for practicing polygamy, so why does the Lord ask, rhetorically, if Abraham was under condemnation? The Lord's question raises a puzzle for us, and to understand it we must look to the scriptures that immediately follow.

Verse 36 is the key to the puzzle. In this verse the Lord posits the direct analogy between his commandment to Abraham to marry Hagar and his commandment to Abraham to sacrifice Isaac. Remember that in verse 36 the Lord explains: "Abraham was commanded to offer his son Isaac; nevertheless, it was written: Thou shalt not kill. Abraham, however, did not refuse, and it was accounted unto him for righteousness."

The general law God commands all to obey is: "Thou shalt not kill." Then, to one innocent and righteous man at one time, he gives a commandment to kill his own son (not a stranger, not a criminal, not an enemy soldier. There is no justification possible for killing one's innocent young son). God has commanded something exceptional of this man—something that goes against all he knows of God's law and for which he can find no possible justification. God is asking Abraham to depart from the law He Himself gave. In this sense, God asks Abraham to perform a Christlike sacrifice in similitude of the sacrifice of God and his own perfectly innocent Son in the Atonement.

We know from the account in Genesis that Abraham's choice was felt by him as a sacrifice of happiness; Abraham was not happy to hear the commandment to sacrifice Isaac. Indeed, we believe he felt great sorrow and perhaps even confusion.[13] Yet Abraham was determined to obey God, even if great sorrow and grief befell him as a result. Because Abraham obeyed an exceptional commandment of God and departed from the law, it was counted unto him for righteousness. But that obedience did not turn the departure from the law into the law. God has never since commanded any person to sacrifice their child. In fact, God provided Abraham an escape from killing his son, despite the original exceptional commandment to kill Isaac. In returning to the law ("thou shalt not kill") after having to depart from it ("sacrifice Isaac"), Abraham felt renewed joy and relief in regaining Isaac. Though he undoubtedly felt paradoxical joy in submitting to God's will in all things, Abraham's joy was not full until the test was over and the escape made.

Why is the Lord making the sacrifice of Isaac a direct analogy to his commanding Abraham to take Hagar to wife? We conclude that in this situation, as in the situation concerning Isaac, God commands a departure from the law—something that is, as a general rule, a thing to be *condemned* by the Lord. That is why the Lord asks, "Was Abraham, therefore, under condemnation?" According to the general law of monogamy in the new and everlasting covenant of marriage set forth by God himself (and not the cultural norms of the time; see Jacob 2:27), and given that God is not indifferent between the two forms of marriage, Abraham *is* under condemnation— otherwise the Lord's question makes no sense. But the Lord answers his own question in this fashion: "Nay [he was not under condemnation]; for I, the Lord, commanded it" (vs. 35), thus creating the supersessionary but still exceptional "law" of verse 34. There would be no puzzle and nothing to ask or answer if God was indifferent between monogamy and polygamy. But if God is *not* indifferent between monogamy and polygamy, then a puzzle does arise—a puzzle that is answered by the Lord with reference to an obvious case of a commandment by God to depart from the general law and follow a lawful exception. This is the strongest possible scriptural evidence that D & C 132 is in complete harmony with Jacob 2, and that the general law or rule of marriage is monogamy and the lawful exception is polygamy. Furthermore, God maintains as strong a discrimination between the two forms of marriage in this dispensation as he did in Jacob's time.

We can now say why it is that God is not indifferent between monogamy and polygamy. In the Lord's eyes, monogamy is not a sacrifice, whereas polygamy is.[14] And we are not talking about just any sacrifice. The Lord tells us that polygamy is an Abrahamic sacrifice, but monogamy is no sacrifice at all. No matter what the human inventory of emotions toward polygamy—joy, sorrow, or joy and sorrow mixed—the most mature and most knowledgeable viewpoint is that of the Lord, who appears to be stating that He views it as an Abrahamic sacrifice. The Lord reveals His mind on this matter through His analogy between Isaac and Hagar. All other things being equal, God is not indifferent towards the type of sacrifice Abraham was required to make because it involves Christlike suffering. However, as with Abraham's sacrifice, sometimes Christlike suffering is the greater good and the most loving course of action because it brings good to others who would not otherwise obtain it. Thus, in a sense, despite the suffering involved in a Christlike sacrifice, there is a joy which comes from knowing that sacrifice is, in God's eyes, the right and loving thing to command. Furthermore, there is a joy which comes from suffering in God's cause, because it immeasurably deepens our hope and trust and faith in His goodness and equity. But notice that the presence of joy in a sacrificial act does not remove that act from the category of "sacrifice" to the category of "non-sacrifice" in the Lord's perspective. We will explore this topic further in a moment.

The Abrahamic sacrifice would mean very little if we did not passionately discriminate between our desire for the happiness God's law gives us and our antipathy towards abandoning that happiness even if God commands it. If Abraham were indifferent to whether Isaac lived or died, God's commandment to sacrifice Isaac could not have constituted a test of Abraham's faith. Likewise, if God were indifferent as to whether Isaac lived or died, there would have been no angel and no ram in the thicket. But an Abrahamic sacrifice is no cold and passionless event. Quite the contrary, it is the greatest passion the human heart can feel. This is an innocent person consciously choosing to release what he knows to be true happiness under God's loving laws because he loves God more dearly than his own true happiness. This is a sacrifice not justified under the law of God because both Abraham and Isaac were innocent, and though this sacrifice brings a paradoxical joy that comes in choosing faith in God above all, *the joy is not complete until the escape is made.* Once His test was passed, Abraham's reward, among other things, was to not have to sacrifice Isaac. Indeed, in a sense Abraham's reward for offering to sacrifice Isaac was to regain Isaac forever. Though the test was probably given to Abraham because he was so very righteous (Abraham 3:23), his reward for passing the test could not have been perpetuation of the sacrifice. We belabor this point for a good reason, to be discussed shortly.

This combination of suffering and joy applies equally well to the Hagar situation. Abraham was not happy at the prospect of killing Isaac, and though sacrificing the joy that flowed naturally from obeying the law prohibiting murder, Abraham obeyed. It was counted unto him for righteousness and deepened the joy that he found in his loving relationship with the Lord. Since the Lord tells us the Hagar situation is analogous, then none of the parties—Abraham, Hagar, Sarah (or for that matter, Ishmael and Isaac)—should have been exempt from suffering in this situation, though the paradoxical joy that accompanies sacrifice would have been present as well. In the Lord's eyes, all five persons were sacrificing. And what were they sacrificing? The natural joy that comes from the law of marriage—monogamy in the new and everlasting covenant of marriage. Genesis makes plain that was the case; no one was happy, and Hagar and Ishmael were forced to leave (Genesis 16, 21). Indeed, God sanctioned their dismissal from the camp, while at the same time miraculously saving Hagar and Ishmael from death in the desert. God didn't seem to expect or require that they all be happy—He only expected that they trust and obey Him, in which obedience they would find the paradoxical joy mentioned above and further His works here on earth.

Furthermore, since Abraham offering to sacrifice Isaac was counted unto him for righteousness, the offering on the parts of Abraham, Sarah, and Hagar to depart from the law of marriage was also counted unto them for righteousness.[15] No doubt Abraham, Sarah, and Hagar eventually felt the peace and joy that comes from obeying God's commandments, all of which— even those commanding Christlike sacrifice—are rooted in God's perfect love for all His children. Nevertheless, being happy about such a commanded departure from the law does not seem to factor into the counting of one's obedience to the same commandment unto one for righteousness. After all, a sacrifice remains a sacrifice despite the paradoxical joy experienced.

We know this principle from many situations in the holy scriptures. "Murmuring" against the Lord or rebellion against His will is not acceptable (1 Nephi 2:12; 1 Nephi 7:6-8), but crying out to the Lord in innocent anguish—anguish felt as a result of obeying God's commands—is completely acceptable. In murmuring, one feels the pain of obedience in sacrifice and responds by resenting and even hating God for it. Such a reaction drives a wedge between oneself and God, and even the paradoxical joy that comes from obeying God is lost. Instead of paradoxical joy, the murmurers feel only bitterness of spirit. On the other hand, the righteous may cry out in innocent anguish when they feel pain in obedience and in sacrifice, but this pain causes them to throw themselves on the mercy and goodness of God. It brings them closer to God and allows them to feel the paradoxical joy of sacrifice, though they still also feel the sacrifice keenly.

We know Christ himself cried out in pain and anguish in the Garden of Gethsemane. He cried out in pain and anguish upon the cross at Calvary. He initially felt to shrink from drinking the bitter cup (Mark 14:36; D&C 19:18), and even asked Heavenly Father why He had forsaken Him (Matthew 27:46). Christ was making *a sacrifice not justified under the law,* because Christ consented to be killed even though He was completely innocent before God and man. His death was a departure from divine law and justice in His own case, but this departure allowed Him to fulfill the demands of justice that would otherwise fall on man. His departure from the law in His own case brought about great good for countless others, since all of God's sons and daughters would otherwise fall to sin by their agency. If Christ Himself was not thought less of by God for expressing suffering caused by a departure from divine law, then why would God require mere mortals to be stoic when suffering pain caused by righteous obedience to a commandment to depart from the law? He does not. When Abraham was asked to make a sacrifice not justified under the law, his heart mourned and we do not think less of him for it—and neither did God. Indeed, we know God loved Abraham with great intensity. In truth, if God wept with Christ in Gethsemane and on Calvary, if he wept with Abraham on the road to Mount Moriah, did he not also weep when Abraham, Sarah, Hagar, and other righteous polygamous wives and husbands wept?[16] The Lord's own analogy leads us to believe that He did. Christ, Abraham, and many righteous polygamous wives and husbands felt both suffering and paradoxical joy in their chosen sacrifices.

As noted before, Abraham's sacrifice and the sacrifice of the polygamous wives and husbands are noble precisely because they typify the sacrifice of Christ. Christ was required to make a sacrifice that could not be justified in His own case because He was pure and innocent. Abraham's sacrifice was also given so that many (all of Abraham's worthy descendants) would be heirs to the great blessings of eternal life and exaltation given to Abraham. Likewise, the sacrifice of the righteous polygamous wives and husbands in the early days of the Church was willing but Christlike, and was made so that all their worthy descendants might be raised in righteousness and become heirs of eternal life. These sacrifices all point to the great sacrifice of the Atonement.[17]

The final aspect of the Lord's analogy between the Isaac situation and the Hagar situation must not be overlooked. Since, in a sense, the Lord is inviting us to reason about *two* Abrahamic sacrifices, we cannot fail to recognize the theme of eventual relief that pervades both. When Abraham raises his hand to slay his son Isaac:

The angel of the Lord called unto him out of heaven, and said, Abraham, Abraham: and he said: Here am I. And he said, Lay not thine hand upon the lad, neither do thou any thing unto him: for now I know that thou fearest God, seeing thou hast not withheld thy son, thine only son from me. And Abraham lifted up his eyes, and looked, and behold behind him a ram caught in a thicket by his horns: and Abraham went and took the ram, and offered him up for a burnt offering in the stead of his son (Genesis 22:11-13).

The first Abrahamic sacrifice is brought to an end by the Lord, who relieves Abraham from the exceptional commandment which has caused him suffering. The paradoxical joy is replaced by the fuller natural joy. By offering to sacrifice Isaac, Abraham regains Isaac forever. *This is a very important element of any Abrahamic sacrifice: it is always eventually brought to an end by God.* The lifting of the exceptional commandment comes as a tangible relief to the sacrificer, despite the fact that the sacrificer has not only felt suffering but also paradoxical joy in the sacrifice.

Why does the Lord bring this relief? We can only reiterate it is because God is not indifferent between a state of sacrifice and a state of relief, and that all other things being equal, He actively prefers eventual relief to perpetual sacrifice for His innocent children. Lest we mistake this natural Fatherly preference, Christ asks rhetorically, "Or what man is there of you, whom if his son ask bread, will he give him a stone? Or if he ask a fish, will he give him a serpent? If ye, then, being evil, know how to give good gifts unto your children, how much more shall your Father which is in heaven give good things to them that ask him?" (Matthew 7:9-11). The great sacrifice to which Abraham's sacrifices point, the Atonement of our Savior Jesus Christ, was also brought to an end by God. His sacrifice ended, we sing of Christ,

> *Once rejected by his own/Now their King he shall be known/Once forsaken, left alone/Now exalted to a throne/Once he groaned in blood and tears/Now in glory he appears/ Once he suffered grief and pain/Now he comes on earth to reign/Once upon the cross he bowed/Now his chariot is the cloud/Once all things he meekly bore/But he now will bear no more (Hymn no. 196, The Church of Jesus Christ of Latter-day Saints).*

This sacrificial assignment came to Christ because of His perfect righteousness, but we must understand that though Christ's sacrifice *merited* His reward, Christ's sacrifice did not *constitute* His reward.

If the Lord has chosen the Isaac-Hagar analogy with care, then we would expect to see an end to the exceptional commandment in this case as well, which end would bring relief. Obedience to God's exceptional commandment to practice polygamy merited a reward for Abraham, Sarah, and Hagar, but it did not constitute their reward. Implicit in God's sanctioning of Sarah's demand that Hagar and Ishmael be banished is God's recognition of the sacrifice and suffering from the point of view of the two mothers involved and His desire to provide relief to them. Interestingly, God does not condemn either woman for feeling the way she does. He seems to accept the negative emotional situation as a natural consequence and agrees to a change in the situation to relieve the tension and sorrow. The appearance of God's angel to Hagar in two situations and God's miraculous rescue of Hagar and Ishmael are very important components of this relief (Genesis 16; 21). As we shall see, we believe the separation of Hagar and Ishmael was not the only relief God was to extend.[18]

Before turning to that theme in a later section, we must pause to note the strength of this theme of eventual relief in connection with polygamy in D & C 132. God extends this analogy of sacrifice and sorrow and eventual relief in relation to polygamy to Joseph Smith's own personal situation in polygamy in verse 50. Speaking to Joseph Smith, the Lord says, "I have seen your sacrifices in obedience to that which I have told you. Go, therefore, and I make a way for your escape, as I accepted the offering of Abraham of his son Isaac."

Joseph Smith made many sacrifices in his lifetime. But these other sacrifices by Joseph—deprivation of property, of liberty, and so forth—are not in the same class as an Abrahamic sacrifice, because God did not command of Joseph a departure from the law in these cases. In our opinion, the only sacrifices required of Joseph at that time that met the characteristics present in the case of Abraham sacrificing Isaac were Joseph's sacrifices in connection with polygamy. Furthermore, all of the surrounding verses are speaking of polygamy and the only other mention of Isaac in the revelation is in the context of polygamy. The escape is not in reference to escape from enemies or poverty or other travails, because the last phrase about Isaac reiterates that it is an escape from a command the Lord gives that is being discussed. The whole of which verse 50 is a part begins with verse 36, because these are the only two verses in which Isaac is mentioned. In addition, remember that

D & C 132 is not a new revelation initiating the practice of plural marriage for the first time in this dispensation. That initial revelation has already been given, for Joseph had been practicing polygamy for some years already when the revelation of D & C 132 was given in 1843.

It seems reasonable to conclude, then, that God is speaking of polygamy in verse 50. The Lord is expressing sympathy for the hardships and sorrow imposed on Joseph by this exceptional commandment to depart from the law of marriage.[19] He is promising to count Joseph's obedience for righteousness as Abraham's sacrifice was counted. And, very significantly, He is promising that at some future point Joseph will have an escape from this exceptional commandment to depart from the law of marriage and that the sacrifice and suffering that attended His obedience would come to an end. This exceptional commandment was no doubt given to Joseph because of his great righteousness. But again, we must not fail to understand that Joseph's practice of the exceptional commandment of polygamy merited him a reward, but it could not conceivably constitute the reward under the conceptual framework that the Lord's argument lays out for us. Christ chose to sacrifice his life, but He regained it and felt the relief and natural joy that came from living once more. Abraham chose to sacrifice Isaac, but he regained his son and felt the relief and natural joy of embracing Isaac once again. If the Lord chose this Isaac-Hagar analogy with care, and we have every reason to believe He did, then verse 50 is telling us that one day there would be a ram in the thicket for Joseph Smith concerning polygamy, and he would feel the relief and natural joy that attends such an escape.

Implications for Sundry LDS Cultural Assumptions about Polygamy

If this interpretation of D & C 132 is correct, then some interesting things begin to happen to our casual acceptance of certain "folkways" in Latter-day Saint culture. A whole new vision begins to appear when we understand from God's own reasoning that monogamy is the rule, polygamy is the exception,

208 — *Women in Eternity, Women of Zion*

and He is not indifferent between the two because the second is an Abrahamic sacrifice in His eyes. Serious doubt is now cast on a variety of pervasive assumptions concerning polygamy in our culture.

Doubt is now cast on the uncritical assumption that polygamous marriage is ubiquitous in the celestial kingdom, and that even if we are not commanded to practice polygamy here, we may be required to practice polygamy there. As God's commandments are not temporal but spiritual in nature (D&C 29:34-35), God will continue to view polygamy as an Abrahamic sacrifice even in the context of the hereafter. A general law of God continues, but a departure from the law, involving as it does Christlike sacrifice, by its very nature is temporally bounded because of God's love for His children and His desire to see such Christlike sacrifices come to an eventual end, even if they have wrought great good in their time and place. It is unclear how God could be constrained for all eternity to command a departure from the law of marriage, which departure He Himself would desire to bring to an end. To disallow individuals a choice in this important matter, given that God Himself is not indifferent about the subject, would imply that heaven is not the best of all possible worlds from God's own perspective and does not represent perfection.

Furthermore, we must keep in mind the two-fold spiritual purpose of marriage in the new and everlasting covenant—to raise up a righteous seed unto God in mortality, and to prepare the marriage partners for their work as gods with their own eternal increase. Remember from Jacob 2 that the rationale the Lord gives for polygamy is related only to the first purpose, not to the second: "For if I will, saith the Lord of Hosts, raise up seed unto me, I will command my people; otherwise they shall hearken unto these things [the law of monogamy]" (Jacob 2:30). From what we have learned from D & C 132, we know why the Lord relates polygamy only to the first purpose and not to the second: polygamy is seen by the Lord as an Abrahamic sacrifice that merits eventual relief and thus does not continue in the hereafter. After this life, those who become gods will be engaged in their *own* work of eternal increase, whereas in this life we are engaged in the work of God's eternal increase. Since the exception of polygamy is related to God's servants assisting Him in His work "to raise up seed *unto me*," as part of a preparatory stage to godhood, what applicability can the departure from the law have to those who become gods after this life is over? Thus, though the principle of marriage in the new and everlasting covenant serves the dual spiritual purpose of marriage, and the law of monogamy serves the dual purpose as well, the lawful exception of polygamy is not in general commanded by God because its form serves only one of the two purposes of eternal marriage.

Some in Latter-day Saint culture assume polygamy is not merely a doctrinal necessity but a *circumstantial* necessity in the hereafter. Generally this assumption takes one of two forms. In the first form, some assert there will be more women who inherit the celestial fullness than men, and since everyone in the highest level of the celestial kingdom is married, polygamy then must follow as a natural consequence of the sex ratio there. This "folkways" is unsound both doctrinally and demographically. There is simply no basis for assuming a celestial sex ratio highly skewed in favor of women.

First, how could God be no respecter of persons and create a system where one spirit, *because of gender*, has a much better chance of reaching the celestial kingdom than the other gender? If God is the author of all fairness and if gender equality is a foundational principle of the gospel, He could not have authored such a system. Even if this system were somehow fair, for such an outcome to ensue would mean that the male gender was disproportionately assigned to or an attribute of weaker spirits. There is no doctrinal or scriptural basis for such a belief.

For those who feel polygamy is ubiquitous in the celestial kingdom, this belief demands that, at a minimum, twice as many women make it to the celestial kingdom as men. But human demographics argues against such a conclusion. Approximately 106 male babies are born on earth for every 100 female babies born.[20] More males have existed on earth than females. Yet by age five, the sex ratio is about 1:1, for male babies are more susceptible to genetic disorders. Therefore, a large number of males die before the age of accountability and are automatically saved in the celestial kingdom. Also, male deaths through such mechanisms as the wholesale killing of male children by an enemy power (e.g., in Moses' time and in Jesus' time), or males laying down their lives in righteous defense of family and homeland, also increases the pool of males eligible for the celestial kingdom. Using established demographic procedures, several BYU sociologists declare in perhaps only a partially tongue-in-cheek essay that they can demonstrate there will be more males in the celestial kingdom than females![21]

All the foregoing serves to make the point that it is by no means clear that females will outnumber males in the celestial kingdom. There is absolutely no scriptural or empirical basis upon which to assert the sex ratio of the celestial kingdom. If we cannot confidently assume there will be more exalted women than exalted men, then one cannot conclude polygamy must then follow.

The second form of the assumption that polygamy is a circumstantial necessity in the celestial kingdom is the notion that one Heavenly Mother is incapable of producing and nurturing the vast numbers of spirit children Heavenly Father appears to have fathered. After Christ comes, "time is no longer" (D&C 84:100; D&C 88:110). With God, past, present, and future are continually before His eyes (D&C 130:7). What this means, no one knows in this life. But clearly it means the same temporal constraints do not exist for Gods. What, then, does it mean to say that something "would take too long" for a God? Additionally, it does not appear that God is in some great hurry to do His work. It may have taken billions of years to produce the universe and, eventually, our solar system. Why does He need to rush the production of spirit children? Furthermore, we do not know anything about how spirit children are organized or how long it takes to organize them.

But how could one Heavenly Mother take care of so many children? This question takes on its true character if we change it to ask: How could one Heavenly Father take care of so many children? We believe Heavenly Father is capable of loving each one of us completely. If a single man has such abilities, why do we doubt that a single woman has the same?[22] In addition, Heavenly Father and Heavenly Mother do not exist as a typically modern nuclear family unit—they have an entire and very large eternal family organization to help them. Think of all that Christ accomplished in creating numberless worlds at a time when He did not yet possess a body and had not yet entered into the new and everlasting covenant of marriage. We must suppose our divine parents have plenty of help in bringing to pass the immortality and eternal life of man.

We see other things in a new light as well. In mortality, when God does command polygamy, He understands it is an exceptional sacrifice by the innocent of the joy that would be theirs if they could obey the law, despite the paradoxical joy given to the innocent sacrificer. This departure from the law can cause pain and sorrow, but it brings about a greater good that makes faithful endurance and obedience a source of paradoxical joy. Nevertheless, if His righteous daughters and sons weep because of polygamy—*even in times when he commands it*—He is not upset at them. Rather, He weeps when they weep because, like Abraham, they are willing to sacrifice and suffer for a time that God's work of love might be accomplished. And, like Christ, they willingly make a sacrifice the law itself cannot demand of them because that sacrifice provides the blessings of eternal life for the many.

Since God is not indifferent between monogamy and polygamy, His love dictates that at the earliest possible moment when the exceptional commandment to depart from the law can be lifted, *he will do so*. If no greater good can come from a Christlike sacrifice, it becomes meaningless and gratuitous suffering. Our understanding of God's love for His children would appear to preclude continuing to command sacrifice that has no meaning. Indeed, the sacrifices of the

Mosaic law had meaning up until the victory of Christ, and God scrupulously required them until that point (3 Nephi 1:24-25). But after Christ's victory, the sacrifices of the Mosaic law became meaningless and God no longer required them to be performed. This not only applied to the sacrifice of innocent animals, but also to a sacrifice on the part of innocent humans, such as circumcision (Moroni 8:8). Indeed, continuing Mosaic sacrifice was tantamount to a rejection of Christ or at least a profound misunderstanding of the Atonement, about which God was surely not indifferent.[23]

Though initially commanding Abrahamic sacrifices, God also strongly desires to eventually provide a ram in the thicket. He is not indifferent to whether the ram is there or not. He *wants* that ram to be there, and He will guarantee its presence. Though an Abrahamic sacrifice may merit a reward, it can never constitute such a reward. To think otherwise is incompatible with the idea of a loving God, who sees a distinction between pleasure and pain, happiness and sorrow. Indeed, Lehi teaches that if such distinctions cannot be made, then "there is no God" (2 Nephi 2:13). There will always be a ram in the thicket for those who are obedient to a commandment to depart from the law; somehow God will "make an escape" (D&C 132:50) for these innocent and obedient and righteous souls whom He must love even more intensely because of their willingness to make such a Christlike sacrifice. Sometimes this escape cannot be within the space of one's mortal lifetime. Christ's own escape came after His death. But no matter whether the escape be in this life or after this life, somehow righteous souls such as Abraham and Joseph Smith will have their "ram in the thicket."

The Ram in the Thicket

What will the ram be? Here we inevitably move beyond what the scriptures and modern revelation have told us. Though we can feel fairly assured our description of the situation in mortality is accurate, we do not know enough to feel so assured about our thoughts on the hereafter. Nevertheless, we venture into that territory for one good reason: no woman who has ever felt pain about polygamy is satisfied until her concerns about the hereafter are at least addressed. No woman who has felt pain about polygamy can honestly strive for a place in the celestial kingdom unless she feels that kingdom is a place in which she would actually want to live. Please be advised these thoughts on the hereafter are merely our own and of no authority.

What will the ram be? Perhaps those who honorably entered and kept their marriage covenants in a time of God-commanded polygamy will have the opportunity to "escape" that exceptional commandment in the next life, if they so desire. For God not to allow that escape would be tantamount to condemning certain persons, because of the time period in which they entered mortality, never to partake of the natural joy brought by the law of marriage ordained by God. Remember that whatever an individual's reaction to polygamy in this life—joy, sorrow, or the two intermixed—the most mature and fully understanding perspective must be that of the Lord, who appears to view polygamy as an Abrahamic sacrifice. If escape were not allowed at some future point, this sacrifice, and its accompanying suffering, would then be an eternal decree for persons who were born in periods when God commanded a departure from the law. Heaven, in a sense, would be a place of eternal sacrifice and eternal suffering for these individuals.

We feel strongly that God could not ask this of any person, especially given God's view that polygamy is an Abrahamic sacrifice. Even Christ's sacrifice and His suffering came to an end. God in his infinite mercy must provide an escape from all Abrahamic sacrifices He commands His children to make because of the greater good that comes to others from them. In the eternities, those who sacrificed and suffered like Abraham will have the opportunity to live under the law, not under the departure from the law, without this affecting their exalta-tion.[24] We do not say that no one will live polygamously in heaven. We do claim that, given the Lord's analogy as discussed above, it is plain that no one can be commanded to do so, and that the choice to opt out of polygamy cannot and will not affect an individual's exaltation.

Whatever escape the Lord has provided for these faithful souls, it will be consistent with the law of sealing and sealing transferability. The doctrine of sealing transferability is the means by which God's eternal family is to be organized after all the unworthy "links" in the great family chain have been dropped. When a link thus falls out, not only is a "child" dropping out, but a husband or a wife is dropping out as well. This circumstance does not leave the worthy spouse dangling—it merely leaves a place for another more worthy person to fill. We can see this transferability operation with reference to all sealings, not simply the marriage sealing. For example, if children are born under the covenant to parents who wind up unworthy of them, the children will not undergo a new sealing ordinance after this life. The fact that they worthily entered into the covenant and stayed worthy of being persons born under the covenant appears to be sufficient. Their sealing will simply be "transferred" to worthy parents in the next life. Church manuals of instruction teach us,

> When a man and a woman are married in the temple for time and all eternity and then separate, the chil - dren will go with the parent who is justified and who has kept the covenants. If neither of them has kept his covenants, the children may be taken away from both of them and given to somebody else and that would be by virtue of being born under the covenant. A child is not to be sealed the second time when born under the covenant, but by virtue of that birthright can be trans - ferred.[25]

Thus it appears that choosing to enter sacred covenants of sealing and remaining worthy of those covenants is *all that matters* from the standpoint of the individual's exaltation as a member of God's eternal family—the actual people to whom one is sealed might or might not change in the re-forging of the great family link of all God's exalted children. Even if you are sealed to an unworthy person, it is as if that person is a stand-in for one who is worthy—whom you may not even meet in this life. This explains why the Church does not cancel the sealing of a wife in a divorce situation unless another marriage sealing is to take place, because what matters is that the wife chose and presumably remains worthy to be sealed to a worthy Melchizedek Priesthood holder—even though she will most likely end up having that sealing transferred to someone else. Her first husband remains a "stand-in" until a transfer can take place.[26]

Such stand-in, or "proxy," marriages were common in the early Church, because in the first several decades of the restored Church, one could not be sealed to loved ones who had not been baptized into the Church before they died. Surviving family members were sealed to General Authorities to assure their exaltation. Widows whose husbands had died before hearing the Gospel were sealed to a general authority as the authority's wife in order to assure their exaltation, and then typically had their husbands sealed to the same General Authority as a child so as "to keep him in the family!"[27] This resulted in many women becoming plural wives because of the mistaken understanding that they could not be sealed to their dead husbands and could not gain their exaltation unless sealed to *someone* as a wife. For example, women who had never even met Joseph Smith while he was alive were sealed to him after his death. One woman had her aged mother sealed to her (the daughter's) husband shortly before the mother died so the mother could receive her exaltation. Wilford Woodruff had over 400 of his dead female ancestors sealed to him as wives. These practices seem to indicate that the parties involved understood the man in question was more a proxy so the woman could receive the marriage ordinance and thus her exaltation, rather than an understanding that these women were married in some meaningful sense to these particular men for all eternity. What can it mean to have a dead woman sealed to you, whom you have never met in this life, whose will on the matter you cannot possibly know, and who is in fact one of your great-great grandmothers? Or to have your own mother-in-law sealed to you as a wife? Or, in the case of a woman, to be sealed to a dead man whom you have never met and whose will on the matter you cannot possibly know? These marriages make sense best as proxy marriages. Indeed, when President Wilford Woodruff announced in 1894 that women could be sealed to their dead husbands (and children to their dead parents) even if the deceased had not been baptized before their deaths, many thousands of sealing transfers took place to rightfully reorganize family lines.[28]

This understanding of sealing transferability in the final welding together of all those who are worthy to become members of God's eternal family may help us envision an honorable "escape" for those faithful men and women who were commanded to depart from the law of marriage and the natural joy that derives from living that law. If God is truly no respecter of persons, then the time period in which one entered mortality should not determine one's opportunity for ending an Abrahamic sacrifice.

Ambiguous Verses and the "Reward" Interpretation

Three verses in D & C 132 have caused some to misinterpret the Lord's clear and strong message concerning his lack of indifference between monogamy and polygamy and his view that polygamy is an Abrahamic sacrifice. Though there are many variants of this alternative interpretation, generally speaking, this viewpoint suggests that polygamy is seen as restricted because it is the reward of especially righteous individuals. It is restricted because less righteous individuals should not have such a privilege. Indeed, in this interpretation the more righteous a man, the more wives he will be given in the hereafter. The three verses in question are verses 39, 44, and 55 of D & C 132.

In verse 39 the Lord explains that because of David's sin, "he shall not inherit them [his wives and concubines] out of the world, for I gave them unto another." In verse 44 the Lord says that if a woman is wronged by her husband, the prophet should "take her and give her unto him that hath not committed adultery but hath been faithful; for he shall be made ruler over many." In verse 55 the Lord promises Joseph "an hundredfold in this world, of fathers and mothers, brothers and sisters, houses and lands, wives and children, and crowns of eternal lives in the eternal worlds." Verse 55 echoes the Lord's statements to his disciples:

There is no man that hath left house, or brethren, or sisters, or father, or mother, or wife, or children, or lands, for my sake and the gospel's, but he shall receive an hundredfold now in this time, houses, and brethren, and sisters, and mothers, and children, and lands, with persecutions; and in the world to come eternal life" (Mark 10:29-30).

Some view these three verses as supporting an interpretation of celestial polygamy as a reward for righteousness. Verse 39 is interpreted as meaning that all of David's wives and concubines will be given to one exalted man. Verse 44 is interpreted as meaning that faithful men will be rulers over many wives. Verse 55 is interpreted to mean that righteous men will have many wives as a reward for service to the Lord.

The overarching reason for rejecting this interpretation is the Lord's own lengthy analogy between Isaac and Hagar. God is not restricting polygamy because it is a special reward or privilege reserved for the especially righteous. God is restricting polygamy because it is an Abrahamic sacrifice and he does not wish to prolong such sacrifice any longer than is necessary. One can not accept the "reward" interpretation without simultaneously rejecting the "sacrifice" interpretation the Lord himself gives. As we have seen, the test of Abrahamic sacrifice may indeed come to persons because of their special righteousness, and obedience in that sacrifice can merit one a reward, but the reward itself cannot be perpetual Abrahamic sacrifice. This would mean that Abraham's reward for obedience to the commandment to sacrifice Isaac is to be commanded to go back to Moriah or that Christ's reward for the Atonement is to be nailed once more to the cross. This interpretation reduces the Lord's strong reasoning in D & C 132 to incoherence, and thus it cannot be preferred to an interpretation that preserves coherence in the Lord's statements, as the "sacrifice" interpretation does.

Furthermore, the verses are ambiguous enough that no hard and fast interpretation of a "reward" of polygamy can be inferred. We do not know how David's wives and concubines will be reassigned in their sealings. They will clearly only be given to another with their consent, but if they choose to depart from the exceptional commandment of polygamy, which is their right under the Lord's designation of an "escape" from all Abrahamic sacrifices (D&C 132:50), then the manner of distribution might be one to one other righteous man, another to still another righteous man, and so forth. We must allow the Lord's own analogy to constrain our interpretation of verse 39.[29]

Pertaining to verse 44, from a broader scriptural context the Lord cannot be saying that a faithful man will be a ruler over many *wives*. First, God does not say "wives" in this verse. Second, we know that in other scriptures talking about "ruling over many," the Lord is referring to the exalted man and woman, side by side as equals, ruling *together* over many *things*: worlds and kingdoms and numberless posterity (see our discussion in Chapters Two and Three). *All* of the righteous, both men and women, are of the Church of the Firstborn (D&C 93:22) and thus inherit the fullness of the father (D&C 76:94), and stand as joint heirs and equals with Christ (D&C 76:95, 88:107). Joined in the new and everlasting covenant of marriage, they are gods, having all power (D&C 132:20; 76:58), and they rule over many *things* together as a result (D&C 52:13; 76:54-5, 59; 78:15). Interpreting verse 44 as indicating that a faithful man will rule with his wife over many things is more in harmony with the broader context of revealed scripture and is more in harmony with the Lord's view of polygamy as an Abrahamic sacrifice, not a reward.

Verse 55 is interesting but sufficiently ambiguous that it cannot be used to support the "reward" interpretation either. A careful reading of verse 55 and Mark 10:30 indicates the Lord is talking of a familial reward in reference to "this world" and "now in this time." Since this familial reward did not come to the disciples or to Joseph Smith in their mortal lives, perhaps the Lord could be referring to a righteous person "now in this time" *meriting* a place in the celestial kingdom, where all who are worthy of that kingdom will be welded together in the great family chain of heaven.

Be that as it may, how are we to understand the word "wives" in verse 55? Since the verse is ambiguous, let us try to understand one of the other terms in the string of family relations the righteous man will obtain. How is it that a man may have a hundred "mothers"? Will these many women all be able to claim the physical experience of having given birth to Joseph Smith, which is how we usually define the relationship of mother to child? That interpretation seems unreasonable. Some larger sense of the relation implied in the word "mother" must be at work here. The Lord Himself suggests that this is so. When told that his mother and brethren awaited him, Christ asked "Who is my mother? And who are my brethren? And He stretched forth His hand toward his disciples, and said, Behold my mother and my brethren! For whosoever shall do the will of my Father which is in heaven, the same is my brother, and sister, and mother" (Matthew 12:48-50).

We suggest that the tremendous vision of the final welded human family, where everyone is connected to everyone else through the generations, is being alluded to here. In this interpretation Joseph Smith may have thousands of mothers and thousands of all other relations, but these linkages may not be as direct and immediate as the linkage between Joseph Smith and his own mother, Lucy Mack Smith. Likewise, the linkage between Joseph Smith and the "wives" of verse 55 may also be in the context of the great human chain and may not be referencing a direct and immediate relationship. Verse 55 is still too ambiguous to permit a "reward" interpretation concerning polygamy, given the unambiguous nature of the Lord's own elaboration of the "sacrifice" interpretation. The reward spoken of here—that of eternal place in the righteous extended human family—is for both men and women (Mark 10:30) and as such may not be making a comment on polygamous marriage at all.

Last, nonscriptural statements by early Saints indicate that they believed polygamy to be the mode of married life in the celestial kingdom and that quantity of wives in the hereafter is a sign of a man's degree of righteousness, which statements seem to support the reward interpretation.[30] However, we must remember that these statements were made in that period of time where some confusion existed about the sealing order of heaven. It was thought that one could not be sealed to dead relatives who had passed away without being baptized. Remember that widows felt they had to be sealed to a general authority to assure their exaltation. Men thought they had to be sealed to General Authorities as their children, and that all must eventually be sealed directly or indirectly to the head of the dispensation (Joseph Smith). Thus, many early General Authorities had many wives and many children because of the confluence of these ideas about sealing and the God-given commandment to practice polygamy. In a sense, then, the actual practice of polygamy in the early Church was profoundly affected by some confusion over the sealing order. It is conceivable that this situation affected the understandings of these early Saints on the topic of husband-wife sealing in marriage, as well.[31]

We note that this confusion was cleared up by the same prophet in whose tenure God rescinded the exceptional commandment to practice polygamy: Wilford Woodruff. Indeed, we believe it is no coincidence this was the case. In rescinding polygamy in the context of the constrained views of the time about sealing, Wilford Woodruff, acting as the Lord's mouthpiece, was seemingly placing exaltation out of the reach of many persons whose immediate family had not received the Gospel before death. The sorrow of this situation could only have been rectified by removing the confusion over sealing. Thus, resolving the confusion over sealing in 1894 was a necessary appendage to the rescindment of the commandment to practice polygamy in 1890.

Joseph Smith, Brigham Young, John Taylor, and Wilford Woodruff led the Church with courage, inspiration, and nobility at a time when the Saints were commanded to make great sacrifices, including the Abrahamic sacrifice of polygamy. They, and all who willingly made the sacrifices required of them by the Lord, are due all our honor. They placed devotion to God above all else, and placed their reputations and even their very lives on the altar. In addition, Wilford Woodruff led the Church with inspiration and skill during the period when the Lord rescinded the commandment to practice polygamy, which rescindment must have seemed to many at the time as a great sacrifice, as well.[32] Our understanding of the commandment to practice polygamy as an Abrahamic sacrifice should cause us to deeply revere those early Saints of whom that sacrifice was required.

Conclusion

This new vision of the compatibility of Jacob 2 and D & C 132 is important for many reasons; however, the most comforting aspect is that those women and men who feel pain at the thought of polygamy are all right in God's eyes because He, too, views polygamy as an Abrahamic sacrifice which will cause suffering, but also (for the righteous) paradoxical joy and a closer relationship with Him. We envision God weeping when righteous polygamous wives and husbands wept. Just think of what that means! For those who weep at the mistaken thought they may be commanded to practice polygamy in Heaven, God does not condemn your feelings. On the contrary, God will not command you to practice polygamy in the next life, and if He commands you to practice it in this life, you can rest assured of two things: 1) he will make it up to you: you will have a ram in the thicket, even if it be in the next life; and 2) God will lift the exceptional commandment of polygamy just as soon as His loving purposes in commanding it have been fulfilled. Though an exceptional commandment may come to one because of special righteousness, and though obedience to an exceptional commandment to practice polygamy may merit one a great reward, the sacrifice itself cannot constitute that reward. God desires that all His children have the natural joy that comes from the law of marriage, which law is monogamy in the new and everlasting covenant of marriage.

If we as a culture have lost the capacity to see God-commanded polygamy as the Abrahamic sacrifice God tells us it is, if we have lost the capacity to see that God actively desires there be an escape for the righteous who have obeyed this exceptional commandment, then we have lost something profoundly precious. We have lost the vision of the greatness of God's love for his children. To lose that vision brings "the gall of bitterness," as Mormon remarked about others who similarly placed constraints on God's love of the innocent, for we "deny" the "mercies" of God (Moroni 8:14, 23). If cultural misinterpretations cause the women and men of the Church to mourn over polygamy, either because they mistakenly believe God is indifferent between sacrifice and nonsacrifice and so no escape from this sacrifice will be provided, or because they are led to feel they are selfish and not righteous if they feel pain at the thought of polygamy, then these cultural misinterpretations are actively harming our people. We have a duty to root out these cultural misinterpretations from our midst, lest they cause great spiritual mischief (Moroni 8:6).[33]

The balm to be had in Gilead on the issue of polygamy is great indeed. One can only hope that the encrusted scales of our cultural folkways will fall from our eyes as we understand that Jacob of the Book of Mormon and the Prophet Joseph Smith *received the very same revelation from the Lord.*

Notes

1   They may ask, how can woman be the equal of man if the number of
    women in an eternal marriage—the ordinance at the very heart of
    the plan of salvation and exaltation—is indeterminate, but the
    number of men is always one? They may note that two equals united
    in eternal marriage partnership squares more easily with gender
    equality than one man plus more than one woman.

2   Let us clarify the terms as we use them in this chapter. The Lord at
    times refers to marriage in the new and everlasting covenant as his
    "law" (D&C 132:3-5), sometimes refers to monogamy in the new and
    everlasting covenant as his "law" (D&C 49:16), and sometimes
    refers to God-commanded polygamy in the new and everlasting
    covenant as his "law" (D&C 132:34). Nevertheless, as we shall see,
    the Lord discriminates between all three in His discourses on the
    topic, and we would err in our understanding if we did not make the
    same discrimination he does. In order that we not bring confusion
    upon ourselves in this discussion, we refer to the principle of
    marriage in the new and everlasting covenant, subsumed under
    which we find the general law of monogamy and the lawful excep-
    tion of God-commanded polygamy.

3   While there were sometimes changes made to the revelations which
    now form the text of the Doctrine and Covenants, Robert J.
    Woodford, whose 1974 dissertation was based on a textual analysis
    of the Doctrine and Covenants, determined that there were no
    changes made to the text of the revelation now found in section 132.
    See Robert J. Woodford, *The Historical Development of the
    Doctrine and Covenants, Volume III* (Dissertation Presented to the
    Department of Ancient Scripture, Brigham Young University, 1974),
    1742. This is corroborated by a sworn statement by William Clayton,
    who wrote the revelation as the Prophet dictated it to him. William
    Clayton said: "Joseph and Hyrum then sat down and Joseph
    commenced to dictate the revelation on celestial marriage, and I
    wrote it, sentence by sentence as he dictated. After the whole was
    written, Joseph asked me to read it through slowly and carefully,
    which I did, and he pronounced it correct." The revelation was
    copied the next day by Joseph C. Kingsbury, and pronounced a true
    copy by William Clayton. It is this copy, without change to the orig-
    inal, which was later incorporated into the *Doctrine and Covenants*
    (Sidney B. Sperry, *Doctrine and Covenants Compendium* [Salt Lake
    City: Bookcraft, 1960], 716-717).

4   Words from President Gordon B. Hinckley at Salt Lake University
    Third Stake Conference, 3 November 1996, as cited in *Church
    News*, 1 March 1997, 2; emphasis added.

5   We are indebted to Professor Kathleen Bahr of Brigham Young
    University for this insight.

6   Joseph Fielding Smith, ed., *Teachings of the Prophet Joseph Smith* (Salt Lake City: Deseret Book, 1977), 323.

7   Bruce R. McConkie, *Mormon Doctrine*, 2d ed., rev. (Salt Lake City: Bookcraft, 1966), 577.

8   This is why polygamous investigators, even if residing in lands where polygamy is legal, cannot be baptized into the Church in this life. Even if the United States of America were to legalize polygamy, members of the Church could not practice it unless the Lord issued a commandment through the prophet sanctioning polygamy among His people.

9   Some take the words of Isaiah as meaning that God will once again sanction polygamy in the last days. Isaiah predicts a time when "Thy men shall fall by the sword, and thy mighty in the war. And her gates shall lament and mourn; and she being desolate shall sit upon the ground. And in that day seven women shall take hold of one man, saying, We will eat our own bread, and wear our own apparel: only let us be called by thy name, to take away our reproach" (Isaiah 3:25-26; 4:1). Because of a physical lack of men due to war casualties, women will seek to enter polygamous unions. Indeed, this is a common consequence of devastating war even today: for example, in the aftermath of the genocide in Rwanda, it is noted that "There is nothing but widows in this village. There are not too many men. Women share men among themselves to have children. The desire for children is so strong many do not care if the man is faithful. . . There are women here who lost children in the war and they just want to replace them." ("AIDS Brings Another Scourge to War-Devastated Rwanda," by James C. McKinley, Jr., *The New York Times*, 28 May 1998).

As noted in Isaiah, these post-war polygamous unions appear not to be God-sanctioned, because the women initiate the request (as versus the community receiving a commandment from God's mouthpiece, the prophet), and the marriage does not involve the God-ordained husbandly support and protection due to the wives in question (D&C 83:2). Furthermore, these circumstances are presented in a survey of the horrible consequences that are the reward of the iniquitous. These women will be smitten with "a scab" on the crown of their heads (Isaiah 3:17) and will be afflicted with "stink" and "baldness" and "burning" (Isaiah 3:24). The depiction in Isaiah 4:1 of seven women taking hold of one man is the final element in Isaiah's description of the punishment of the wicked. Nevertheless, in addition to such cases of polygamy not sanctioned by the Lord, it is possible that these calamities will affect the community of the Saints as well (or that for some other reason which God in his infinite wisdom determines), and that Bruce R. McConkie may be correct when he predicts a reinstitution of the "holy practice" of God-sanctioned polygamy around the time of the

Second Coming (*Mormon Doctrine*, 2nd ed., rev. [Salt Lake City: Bookcraft, 1966], 577). But we must remain clear that God is under no necessity to do so as part of the restoration of all things.

10 Hyrum M. Smith and Janne M. Sjodahl, *Doctrine and Covenants Containing Revelation* (Salt Lake City: Deseret Book Company, 1978), 821. This commentary was originally published in 1919.

11 Note that only monogamy outside of the new and everlasting covenant is recognized by the Lord; polygamy outside of the new and everlasting covenant is grievous sin and is condemned by the Lord in the harshest possible terms.

12 Hyrum M. Smith and Janne M. Sjodahl, *Doctrine and Covenants Containing Revelation* (Salt Lake City: Deseret Book Company, 1978), 821. This commentary was originally published in 1919.

13 Elder Harold Hillam suggests that Abraham's heart wept throughout this ordeal (Devotional given at BYU, June 25, 1996).

14 Hyrum M. Smith and Janne M. Sjodahl concur, explicitly stating that their analysis of Doctrine and Covenants 132 leads them to the conclusion that the scripture indicates plural marriage "is a sacrifice" (Hyrum M. Smith and Janne M. Sjodahl, *Doctrine and Covenants Containing Revelation* [Salt Lake City: Deseret Book Company, 1978], 821).

15 Note that Sarah and Hagar were also not changed into some sort of "new being" when God issued the exceptional commandment to depart from the law; they were normal women with normal passions and felt the loss of departing from the law of marriage. Likewise, the women of the early Church were not "changed" when God commanded polygamy be practiced. Because they were not changed, they made a righteous and exceptional sacrifice. Those who claim women will be "changed" in the hereafter to accept polygamy seem not to see the significance of this. The natural joy that would be brought by adherence to the law of God is lost even when it is God commanding the departure from the law. Nevertheless, as noted above, there is paradoxical joy in sacrifice and faithful obedience to God's exceptional commands.

16 Indeed, it is noteworthy that when Hagar is banished from camp the first time, the angel of the Lord appears to her, comforts her, and tells her that she should name her unborn son Ishmael, which means "God hears," because "the Lord hath heard thy affliction" (Genesis 16:11).

17 We are indebted to Ronald Hinckley for this insight.

18 Elsewhere in the scriptures we find other examples in which God attempts to make the Abrahamic sacrifice of polygamy less of a burden on the woman experiencing heartache. In Deuteronomy

21:15-17, for instance, the firstborn of a despised wife is to inherit twice that of the firstborn of a beloved wife in a polygamous marriage. And in Leviticus 18:18, the Lord commands that a man not marry the sister of his wife, as such a situation would "vex" the wife.

19   It is personally healing to think of Joseph feeling pain over practicing polygamy. He sacrificed the natural joy that would come from the law of marriage and which was lost in God-commanded departure from the law. Other General Authorities who practiced polygamy also felt initial reluctance upon hearing the commandment; for example, Brigham Young recounted that he envied the dead when he was first taught about it. Initial reluctance to depart from the law of marriage that brings natural joy is thus not only a hallmark of the first reaction of righteous women, it is a hallmark of the first reaction of righteous men, as well. From the perspective outlined in this chapter, we see that this reluctance is not based in some idiosyncratic cultural mores but in the deep law of happiness that pervades all human existence regardless of culture or time period. Of course, we expect Joseph Smith, Brigham Young, and others eventually felt the paradoxical joy that accompanies Abrahamic sacrifice.

20   Indeed, some estimate that up to 60 percent more male fetuses are conceived than female fetuses. However, most miscarriages and stillbirths involve male fetuses, so the ratio of males to females at birth is lower—though still favoring males—than the conception ratio would indicate. (See Stephan Klasen, "'Missing Women' Reconsidered," *World Development* 22, no. 7 [1994]: 1061-1071.)

21   See Tim Heaton, et al., "In the Heavens Are Parents Single?: Report No. 1," *Dialogue* 17, no. 1, (Spring 1984): 84-86.

22   Some in Latter-day Saint culture take this assumption even further. One interpretation of human male sexual anatomy holds that males are designed to be polygamous. Whatever the merits of that interpretation, we cannot then infer that celestial life is polygamous. To understand this point, consider the lion. The lion has been given an anatomy replete with large, sharp teeth and claws. In the fallen world this anatomical endowment is used to kill prey and tear flesh. However, we know that in the millennium "the wolf also shall dwell with the lamb, and the leopard shall lie down with the kid, and the calf and the young lion and fatling together" (2 Nephi 21:6), and "they shall not hurt nor destroy in all my holy mountain" (2 Nephi 21:9). Indeed, scripture tells us that "the lion shall eat straw like the ox" (2 Nephi 21:7). The function and purpose of the lion's teeth and claws in celestial life thus cannot be derived from their function and purpose in meeting the exigencies of the fallen world. Therefore we cannot infer from male sexual anatomy that males will practice polygamy in the celestial world because they have a presumed

proclivity and anatomical capability for practicing it in the fallen world. It may be more helpful to interpret the presumed proclivity and anatomical capability for polygamy on the part of males as arising from the exigencies of the fallen world, just as the proclivity and capability for killing prey and tearing flesh with teeth and claws has arisen for the lion from the conditions of the fallen world. Otherwise, we must either conclude that the lion will be unfulfilled and frustrated living in the celestial world because his anatomy is not being used for that which it was designed, or we must conclude that the manner of life in the celestial world is bounded by the manner of life in the fallen world and that God must permit violence in his holy kingdom for the sake of leonine anatomy. Neither conclusion is justified. That this case is parallel to that concerning human male anatomy should be clear. If God's law of marriage is monogamy in the new and everlasting covenant, as scripture unequivocally states, then God's law—not human male sexual proclivities or anatomical capabilities in the fallen world—is the determinant of sexual relations in the celestial world.

23 Indeed, those who desire to practice polygamy in times when God has not commanded it are in spiritual chaos. That desire would be analogous to Abraham, after hearing the message of the angel and seeing the ram, proceeding to sacrifice Isaac anyway as a testimony of his faithfulness to God. We can only surmise that from God's point of view, such an act would constitute anything but a testimony of faithfulness!

24 We also do not believe that the exercise of one's right to opt out of the exceptional commandment to practice polygamy could affect the ability of loved ones to enjoy one another's presence. If all within the celestial kingdom are entitled to dwell in the presence of our Father (D&C 76:62, 94), surely they are all entitled to dwell in each other's presence. Descendants of those who practiced polygamy with honor, then, need not fear that particular ancestors would be "lost" to them if these ancestors chose to make their escape. No one is lost and no one is unconnected in the final welding of the great chain of the human family.

25 Questions Frequently Asked About the Temple and the Endowment (Salt Lake City: The Church of Jesus Christ of Latter-day Saints, 1981), 10.

26 Much needless heartache can be prevented if this is understood. If her husband marries again in the temple after he has divorced her, a woman whose sealing is still intact may feel she is being forced into eternal polygamy against her will. This is not the case. As we have noted, her ex-husband is a "proxy" for he who will be her sealed companion if she remains worthy of this blessing. Similarly, a woman's children with a subsequent husband being automatically sealed to her former husband (unless a sealing cancellation takes

228 — Women in Eternity, Women of Zion

place) is similarly to be understood. The children are worthy to be born under the covenant and will be so. Given the principle of sealing transferability, to whom they are sealed is not as important to their exaltation as the children being involved in the sealing in the first place. Sealing transferability lends equity to sealing situations that cannot be understood as equitable to women in any other way. However, as Eugene England noted, this understanding still cannot explain why a woman who is dead may be sealed to more than one man, but a woman who is alive cannot. We have good reason, however, to believe that constraint will be removed by the Lord in the near future.

27 Gordon Irving, "The Law of Adoption: One Phase of the Development of the Mormon Concept of Salvation, 1830-1900," BYU Studies 14, no. 3 (1974): 306.

28 Over 13,000 such sealing transfers occurred. See Gordon Irving, "The Law of Adoption: One Phase of the Development of the Mormon Concept of Salvation, 1830-1900," BYU Studies 14, no. 3 (1974): 308-312.

29 Notice how this verse and also verse 44 point to the doctrine of sealing transferability as discussed in the previous section. Worthy wives of unworthy men (such as David) are transferred by right of their original marriage sealing. These wives are worthy to occupy a place as a wife in the grand genealogy of God's eternal family, but their marriage partner may or may not be he to whom they were married in mortality.

30 The quantity of wives a man takes in mortal life when commanded by God to practice polygamy could be a sign of his degree of right-eousness. We suppose this would depend on the motivation of the individual man in taking these additional wives.

31 Indeed, Irving contends that a proper interpretation of the state-ment by Joseph Smith (in the context of a vision given to Brigham Young following Joseph's death) concerning the "confused" state of the human family had specific reference to these erroneous sealing practices. If Irving's interpretation is correct, then it is indeed note-worthy that Joseph Smith, from the vantage point of the hereafter, was able to see the error he did not notice during his mortal proba-tion and that he desired to impart his new and clearer perspective to his successor on earth. (See Irving, op cit.).

32 Spiritual manifestations accompanied the rescindment of the commandment to practice polygamy. Here is but one example that could be cited in this context: "More than once I heard Father say before other members of the family that when he went to that Conference he and some of his friends who had suffered exile and imprisonment had determined to vote against the Manifesto. 'But,' said Father, 'some power not my own raised my arm, and I voted to

sustain President Woodruff in this matter. As soon as I had done it a sense of peace and contentment came over me.'" (Jensen, Juliaetta Bateman, *Little Gold Pieces* [Salt Lake City: Stanway Printing Company, 1948], 130. We are indebted to B. Kent Harrison, Juliaetta's grandson, for bringing this episode to our attention.)

33   Indeed, in the course of writing this chapter we discovered how great this spiritual mischief can be. The research assistant helping me with this chapter spoke about the issue of polygamy with another of my research assistants, a wonderful young woman from a family active in the Church. The young woman in question stated that she has strong reservations about marrying in the temple for fear that if she died, her husband might remarry and she would become a polygamous wife in heaven. She stated that polygamy sounded like hell, not heaven, to her and she did not want to wind up in such a place. I had no clue that my research assistant felt this way! Another young mother spoke to me of how she held her feelings of love for her husband in check, because she "knew" that if they were worthy to go to the celestial kingdom, he would be assigned many wives. To combat the feeling of anguish and despair this caused her, she tried to love her husband less! One young man, suffering from a life-shortening genetic disorder, was told by his roommates (all returned missionaries) that because of his physical difficulties here on earth, when he got to the celestial kingdom he would be given "hundreds" of "the most beautiful women imaginable" as his reward. The young man replied that he would prefer one not-so-beautiful but loving companion here and in the hereafter. These are but a few of many such cases that space does not permit us to mention. Indeed, these cases bring to mind a quotation by C.S. Lewis: "Not that I am (I think) in much danger of ceasing to believe in God. The real danger is of coming to believe such dreadful things about him. The conclusion I dread is not, 'So there's no God after all,' but 'So this is what God's really like. Deceive yourself no longer.'" We cannot allow this spiritual mischief to continue, given that the scriptures revealing the Lord's mind on the subject provide the needed balm to dispel it completely.

CHAPTER 8

The Pursuit of Zion: Wisdom from the Book of Mormon

by
Alma Don Sorensen

The Latter-day Saints have not yet become a people of Zion. We are not yet a people pure in heart who live by celestial law. But it is our destiny to become so, and we prepare even now for it. To better anticipate that future, we turn to the Book of Mormon, a record preeminently about Zion—about the pursuit of Zion, obstacles that hindered that pursuit, and the final tragic loss of it by an ancient people. It was a hope of Moroni, the last known prophet among those people, that the Saints in the last days might learn from the book to be more wise than his people had been (Mormon 9:31). We review the history of the pursuit of Zion in the Book of Mormon in search of some of that wisdom, and for insights concerning what the future of Zion may hold for Latter-day Saint women.

A Brief Overview of Past Dispensations
In every great dispensation of the gospel, prophets of God have labored to establish Zion among their people. They have sought to purify their people's hearts and motivate them to live by celestial law. We know the reasons why: the purpose of the gospel is always to prepare a people for eternal life, which requires them to live by celestial law and be purified—to live as a people of Zion—during their time of probation (D&C 97:21, 105:4-5; Alma 42:4, 10). Accordingly, Adam, who with Eve headed the first gospel dispensation as well as all dispensations since then, taught his posterity that they could be "born of the Spirit" and "sanctified from all sin" through Christ and,

consequently, could "enjoy the words of eternal life in this world, and eternal life in the world to come" (Moses 6:59-68). Persons who "enjoy the words of eternal life in this world," because they have been "born of the Spirit" and "sanctified from all sin," are persons whose hearts have been made pure and who abide by celestial law. They are they who enjoy "eternal life in the world to come" (see D&C 105:4-5, 32). Adam and, we must assume, Eve also were "born of the Spirit" and lived according to the eternal "order" in this world (Moses 6:64-68), as did many of their posterity (Moses 7:1).

The second great gospel dispensation saw the people of Enoch become a people of Zion. We read that the Lord called them "Zion" because "they were of one heart and one mind, and dwelt in righteousness; and there was no poor among them" (Moses 7:18). Enoch brought his people to Zion by teaching them the gospel given to Adam so that they could be "sanctified" and enjoy "the words of eternal life in this world" and "eternal life" itself in "the world to come" (Moses 6:32-68; 7:1).

Noah, head of the third great dispensation of the gospel, declared the "Gospel unto the children of men, even as it was given unto Enoch" (Moses 8:19). But the people "hearkened not unto his words" (Moses 8:20). We know the rest of the story as far as the people were concerned. However, Noah himself was "perfect in his generation; and he walked with God, as did his three sons" (Moses 8:27). This means that Noah and his family must have accepted the gospel as "it was given unto Enoch," meaning that they were also purified by being born of the Spirit and lived by celestial law, as did Enoch and his people.

Father Abraham, who stands at the head of the fourth gospel dispensation, received the keys to preside over it from the great high priest Melchizedek (D&C 84:14; 107:2). We read nothing from scripture about whether the people who followed Abraham became a pure-in-heart people. But from the prophet Alma we learn that "the people in the days of Melchizedek," whose time overlapped the days of Abraham, were "made pure" by being "sanctified by the Holy Ghost" and "entered into the rest of the Lord their God" (Alma 13:10-14; Moroni 7:3), which is to say that the people of Melchizedek enjoyed the words of eternal life in this world and inherited eternal life in the world to come. Because Melchizedek "was such a great high priest," the "Holy Priesthood" now has his name. We suppose it was partly because his people became a pure-in-heart people and entered God's rest that he was judged such a great high priest (Alma 13:12-19; D&C 107:2).

Moses initiated the fifth gospel dispensation, but without the success of Enoch or Melchizedek. Moses "sought diligently to sanctify his people" through the power and ordinances of the "priesthood," so that they might enter into God's "rest" and enjoy "the fullness of his glory." But as we know, the people "hardened their hearts," which seems to indicate they were able but unwilling to live according to the order of the higher priesthood (D&C 84:19-24; 88:21-22). As a consequence of their unwillingness, God took Moses out of their midst and the "Holy Priesthood" also, leaving them with only "the lesser priesthood" and "the preparatory gospel" (D&C 84:25-26).

The sixth dispensation of the gospel began with the apostles of Christ in the meridian of time (Matthew 16:18-19). They became, or at least tried to become, a people of Zion, for they received instructions in living the law of consecration, which requires the people of the Lord to live together as equals (1 Corinthians 10:24-26; 2 Corinthians 8:9-16), and for at least a short time they had "all things in common" among them (Acts 2:44; 4:32).

That brings us to the last great dispensation of the gospel—our own dispensation—established by God through the Prophet Joseph (D&C 27:13). The message of Zion in latter-day revelations is clear: the Saints in the last times must become a people of Zion if they want to realize the purpose of their dispensation and prepare for and receive eternal life (see, for example, D&C 6:6; 11:6; 12:6; 14:6; 88:74-75; 97:21; 105:4-5; 113:8; 133:62; Moses 7:62-67). Because we live during the final gospel dispensation we, even more than the peoples of past dispensations, must become a people of Zion. One primary reason the Book of Mormon was compiled and preserved for our time is so the latter-day people of God might learn the wisdom they need to establish Zion among them and fulfill the purpose of the final gospel dispensation. The prophets of the Book of Mormon, like prophets in all gospel dispensations, labored diligently to establish and preserve the ways of Zion among their people, and a record of their successes and failures was preserved for our time.

The Book of Mormon Story

We begin our review among the peoples of ancient America with those who lived under the leadership of the first Nephi and his brother Jacob. From the Book of Jacob we learn that he and his brother Joseph "labored diligently among the people" to persuade them to "come unto Christ" and "enter into his rest" (Jacob 1:7). Their immediate purpose was to preserve and restore purity of heart among their people, implying that prior to that time the people had become "pure in heart" (Jacob 1-2), probably under the leadership of Nephi. As prophets always do, Jacob and Joseph gave attention to how a people of God should "seek for riches." Before endeavoring to obtain riches, they admonished their people to first "seek ye the kingdom of God" (Jacob 2:18). A people successfully seek the kingdom of God by becoming or remaining a purified people who live by celestial law, for "Zion" thus defined "is in very deed the kingdom of our God" (D&C 105:4-5; 32: 88:21). Then they may pursue riches, but only "for the intent to do good" (Jacob 2:19), meaning among other things that riches must be used and distributed according to the law of consecration.

We say Jacob intended his people to live the law of consecration in seeking riches after obtaining the kingdom because one of the first requirements of the law of consecration among a pure-in-heart people is to "impart of your substance" unto "the poor" and "needy" (D&C 42:31-34), and a notable consequence of doing so is that there will soon be "no rich and poor" among them (Moses 7:18; 4 Nephi 1:3). So when Jacob a d m o nished his people to seek riches with "the intent to do good," he exhorted them to provide for the poor and needy—"clothe the naked," "feed the hungry," "administer relief to the sick and afflicted"—reminding them that "one being is as precious" in God's "sight as the other" (Jacob 2:19, 21). Indeed, he taught them that in the overall distribution of wealth they must "think of your brethren like unto yourselves" and be "free with your substance, that they may be rich like unto you"—in other words, so there would be no "rich and poor" among them (Jacob 2:17; 4 Nephi 1:3). That is how a people whose hearts have been made pure, or who want to remain pure in heart, always live together: they live as equals, the law of consecration governs their endeavors to obtain riches, and no rich and poor exist among them.

After Jacob's time, for a period well over two hundred years, no mention is made of a people becoming pure in heart and living by celestial law. Perhaps that is why the record is exceedingly brief, telling us precious little about God's dealings with His people, even though prophets continued to labor among them. For when we come to the Book of Mosiah, where the record becomes very detailed again, we learn that "the people of God" (Mosiah 25:24) in two separate places became pure in heart by being born of the Spirit and lived the law of consecration's requirement to raise up the poor and care for the needy. One group was the people of King Benjamin. They lived in the land of Zarahemla and began to live the law of consecration after being born of the Spirit, about 130 years before the coming of Christ (Mosiah 4:2, 26; 5:2, 7). But about 20 years earlier in the "land of Mormon," the first Alma, "having received authority from God," formed "the church of God" and taught his people the gospel of Christ. Alma's people also underwent a purification of heart by being born of the Spirit, and they began living the law of consecration (Mosiah 23:16-17; 21:30; 18:17).

We learn about the spiritual transformation of the first Alma and his people from his son Alma. He tells us that his father was first "spiritually born of God," experienced a "mighty change of heart," and then "preached the word" unto his people. Their "souls were illuminated by the light of the everlasting word," and "a mighty change was also wrought in their hearts." They, too, were spiritually "born of God" (Alma 5:1-14). Having had their hearts purified by the word, the "hearts" of the people of Alma were "knit together in unity and in love towards one another," and they were commanded to live the law of consecration (Mosiah 18:21, 27-29). If Zion means a people pure in heart who live by celestial law (D&C 97:21; 105:4-5), then those in "the church of God" (Mosiah 18:17), founded by the first Alma, were well on their way to becoming a people of Zion. "And behold, they were faithful unto the end; therefore they were saved" (Alma 5:13).

Alma led his people from the land of Mormon into the land of Zarahemla, where he received authority from Mosiah to establish "the church of God" among the people in that land (Mosiah 25:18-24; 26:8, 17). The people of Mosiah, under the leadership of his father King Benjamin, had themselves been born of Christ and lived the law of consecration about 10 years before Alma formed the Church among them (Mosiah 5:2; 4:2, 26). Except for Christ's personal ministry among the people of the Book of Mormon, nowhere in sacred text can we find a more detailed account of a people's purification under the leadership of a prophet of God than the one found in the book of Mosiah about King Benjamin's people.

As prophet, Benjamin, along with other servants of the Lord, labored many years in the hope that his people might undergo purification and become a people of Zion (Words of Mormon 1:12-18; Mosiah 1:1). Consequently, there was much about the gospel the people, as Benjamin himself said, had "been taught" and "knew" (Mosiah 2:34-36). His ministry was not without success, for just three years before he died, King Benjamin describes his people as "a diligent people in obeying the commandments" and a "highly favored people of the Lord" (Mosiah 1:11-13).

Yet, as Benjamin knew and his people needed to discover, they had not yet undergone the rebirth that marks the passage

from their carnal state to spiritual life as part of their probationary experience. They had not yet been "filled with love
towards God and all men," even though they had been taught
much about love and in their way had diligently obeyed the
commandments comprehended by love (Mosiah 2:4). Before
the word could transform them and fill them with divine love,
they had to reach a new healing awareness of it and be purified
by the power of the Spirit.

Their new awareness began when they discovered they
were still in a carnal state despite their knowledge of the
gospel, their diligence in obeying God's commandments, and
the prosperity that resulted from their obedience. As Mormon
tells us, King Benjamin's people "viewed themselves in their
own carnal state, even less than the dust of the earth" (Mosiah
4:2). Discovering that they were still in a "carnal state" despite
their diligent obedience, the people "cried aloud with one
voice" that their "hearts [would] be purified." The "Spirit of the
Lord" then "wrought a change" in their "hearts," so they had
"no more disposition to do evil, but to do good continually"
(Mosiah 4:2; 5:2).

Like all peoples whose hearts become pure by being
obedient to God and undergoing spiritual rebirth, King
Benjamin's people were required to begin living the law of
consecration. In the first days of any Zion society, a major
requirement of that law is that members lift up the poor and
care for the needy among them. In the words of modern revelation, they "impart" of their "substance," according to that
which they have, to "the poor" so that "every man who has need
may be amply supplied and receive according to his wants"
(D&C 42:30-33). As a result of providing for the poor, the time
soon arrives when there are no "rich and poor" among God's
people (4 Nephi 1:3; Moses 7:18; D&C 104:11-17). In terms
much the same as those found in modern revelation, King
Benjamin instructed his people, after their hearts were made
pure, that they "should impart of [their] substance to the poor,
every man according to that which he hath," so their needs
could be fulfilled and they could "receive according to their

wants" (Mosiah 4:26). Decades later, church members were living and being admonished to live this requirement of the law of consecration (Alma 1:27-31; 4:13; 5:54-55; 34:28).

When a people become pure in heart, every person esteems and respects others as her or his equal, and one does not "possess that which is above another" as a result of living the law of consecration (D&C 38:16, 24-27; 49:20; 51:9; 70:14). Accordingly, Jacob taught the people that persons are equally precious in God's sight and that among his people there should be no rich and poor (Jacob 2:17-21). King Benjamin taught his people that they were equally nothing before the power and goodness of God and yet equally everything in the eyes of His love (Mosiah 4:11-13, 26). When Mosiah became king, he also taught the people "that every man should esteem his brother as himself" and that "there should be an equality among all men" (Mosiah 27:3-4). Under Mosiah's reign, the people of God continued to live the law of consecration (Alma 1:27; 4:13; 5:54-55; D&C 42:30-33). The prophet Alma, who founded the church among the Nephites, taught his people "that every man should love his neighbor as himself" (Mosiah 23:15) and commanded them to keep the law of consecration (Mosiah 18:27-29; D&C 42:30-33).

What especially impresses us is how these three great leaders held themselves strictly to the requirement that there should be equality among the people of God. All were men of great talent and high calling, but they held no illusions that they were better than others. What is more, they were particularly anxious that the people should hold themselves and their leaders in equal esteem.

Accordingly, in his final address to his people, King Benjamin insisted that they were his equals, saying to them, "And I, even I, whom ye call your king, am no better than ye yourselves are; for I also am of the dust" (Mosiah 2:26). For reasons we can appreciate, Alma was "beloved of his people," and they were "desirous that Alma should be their king" (Mosiah 23:6). Alma refused them, citing as his primary reason the Lord's will that the people consider one another as equals:

"Behold, it is not expedient that we should have a king; for thus saith the Lord: Ye shall not esteem one flesh above another, or one man shall not think himself above another; therefore I say unto you it is not expedient that ye should have a king" (Mosiah 23:7).

This brings us to King Mosiah. Because of his strong belief in equality, he brought to an end kingship among his people, telling them "that this inequality should be no more in this land, especially among this my people" (Mosiah 29:32; 27:3-4). Could it be that these three righteous men, who themselves had undergone spiritual birth and who presided over a people many of whose hearts had been purified, understood that they and their people were preparing themselves to be joint heirs with Christ and as gods to share all power as equals in the world to come (D&C 76:94-95; 50:27-29)? We think they did.

It was about fifty years after King Benjamin's people began embracing the ways of Zion, and over sixty years since Alma the elder's people also had done so, that the younger Alma, having received authority from his father to be prophet and head of the Church (Alma 5:3), began to labor in earnest to uphold the ways of Zion among his people. He composed one of the great sermons in all scripture about being spiritually born of God and becoming pure in heart. Flowing as they do from the mind and heart of one who himself was born of God (Alma 36:5), his words are truly memorable and beautifully expressed so they might transform the hearts of all who hear or read them. He first reminded his people of the spiritual birth and purification of an earlier generation in the land of Mormon. He rehearsed how God "changed their hearts"; how "their souls were illuminated by the light of the everlasting word"; and how "their souls did expand, and they did sing redeeming love" (Alma 5:7, 9). Furthermore, he said they "were faithful unto the end" and "were saved" (Alma 5:13). He then asked the present generation of his people: Have "ye been spiritually born of God"? Has "the image of God" been engraven "upon your countenances"? "Have ye experienced a mighty change of heart?" Can "ye look up to God" with "a pure heart and clean hands"? Have ye felt to sing the "song of redeeming love" (Alma 5:14, 19, 26)? Mormon informs us that "these are the words" Alma delivered "throughout all the land" as prophet and head of the Church (Alma 5:1-3).

In another equally remarkable sermon, Alma beautifully and simply described the experience of being born of God and becoming pure in heart by likening "the word" found "in the Son of God" to the "seed" that grows into "the tree" of "everlasting life" when "planted in the heart" through "faith" and given proper "nourishment" (Alma 32:27-39). The tree of life represents the fullness without end that only those who have the image of God engraven upon their countenance through spiritual birth and have been filled with his redeeming love can enjoy (Alma 32:40-41). "The word" found in Christ alone contains the "seed" that grows into "the tree of life"; it alone can give fullness to our lives by awakening us to the goodness of God and filling us with his love. When we finally embrace the word through faith, it will, says Alma, "swell within your breast," "enlarge [your] souls," and "expand your mind" with that fullness until "ye hunger not, neither shall ye thirst" any more for that which gives purpose or brings happiness (Alma 32:28-42).

As we have said, both of Alma's great sermons are about becoming and remaining a people pure in heart, in other words, a people of Zion. For they are they whose souls have been illuminated by the light of the everlasting word, who have experienced a mighty change of heart and felt to sing the song of redeeming love, whose souls have been enlarged and minds expanded with the fullness promised by the word, and who are partakers of the tree of life in this world and in the world to come.

Alma and others called to assist him in the works of the ministry traveled "throughout all the land" among the Nephites, laboring to establish or secure the ways of Zion among the people (Alma 5:1 (1-62)). They taught the people that they must be "born again" if they wished to "inherit the kingdom of heaven" (Alma 7:14; 5:49) and (among other things) that they must live the law of consecration introduced by Benjamin and the elder Alma (Mosiah 4:26; 18:27; Alma 1:27; 4:13; 5:55; 34:28). All in all, Alma and those who traveled with him enjoyed much success, for Alma confided in his son Helaman that "many" had been "born of God" and "tasted" as he had "tasted" because of "the word," which had been "imparted" unto him (Alma 36:26).

Meanwhile, the sons of Mosiah proselytized among the Lamanites with much success. Lamoni, the Lamanite king, received "the marvelous light" of God's "goodness" into his "soul," and the "light of everlasting life," and he saw his "Redeemer" (Alma 19:6). His heart and "the hearts" of many of his people were "changed" so that, like King Benjamin's people, "they had no more disposition to do evil" (Alma 19:33, 35; Mosiah 5:2). Lamoni's father, also a Lamanite king, and his household were "born of God," as were many of his people (Alma 22:1, 15-26; 23:9). In all, the Lamanites in seven lands and cities (Alma 23:7-15) were "brought to sing redeeming love" because of "the power of God" (Alma 26:13, 33), and they, like Alma the Elder's people, remained "firm in the faith of Christ, even unto the end" (Alma 27:27; 5:13).

The ministry of Alma the Younger ended with his somewhat mysterious disappearance around 73 B.C. (Alma 45:18-19). His departure marked the end of an era in which many came unto God through Christ and became pure in heart. From that time until Christ manifested himself to the Nephites and Lamanites shortly after his resurrection, the work to bring people to Zion continued with great devotion, but apparently with much less success. However, during the time of Helaman, the grandson of Alma the Younger, some members grew "firmer and firmer in the faith of Christ," unto "the purifying and the sanctification of their hearts" (Helaman 3:35). Also, through the devoted preaching of Helaman's sons, Nephi and Lehi, thousands of Lamanites came into the church (Helaman 5:19), and on one occasion "the Holy Spirit" entered into "the hearts" of 300 Lamanites, filling them "as if with fire," and angels "ministered unto them" (Helaman 5:45-48). The record of their ministry ends with Nephi's disappearance near the time of Christ's birth (3 Nephi 1:2; 2:9).

That brings us to the high point in the pursuit of Zion by the people of the Book of Mormon—or by any people, for that matter—which is the establishment of Zion among them through the personal ministry of the Savior himself. We cannot begin to describe here the wonderful ministry of Jesus Christ among the Nephites and Lamanites when He visited them after His resurrection. It was an event unequalled in all sacred history as measured by the manner in which souls were brought unto God and the spiritual blessings poured out upon them. The great purpose in the Savior's ministry among that ancient people was to establish Zion among them, which He did indeed accomplish. Through a great outpouring of the Holy Spirit, their hearts were purified, and they lived by celestial law (3 Nephi 11-28). When Jesus beheld the people's hearts after their purification, He exclaimed, "And now my joy is great, even unto fullness," and "even the Father rejoiceth, and also his holy angels, because of you and this generation; for none of them is lost" (3 Nephi 27:30-31). For almost 170 years the people of the Book of Mormon remained a people of Zion and lived by celestial law (4 Nephi 1:24-25).We read that the "love of God" did "dwell in the hearts of the people," "they had all things common among them," and "there could not be a happier people among all the people who had been created by the hand of God" (4 Nephi 1:1-17).

We know that a fuller account was made of Christ's ministry among that ancient people and His founding of Zion among them, and we suppose a detailed history exists of life in Zion during its duration. Marvelous will be the day when these sacred records come forth among the Latter-day Saints! But they have been held back until after a trial of faith (3 Nephi 26:11, 18)—presumably a trial of our willingness to become a people of Zion.

We conclude our brief overview of the pursuit of Zion among the peoples of the *Book of Mormon* by underscoring the fact that God always brings His people to Zion through the inspired leadership of the prophet called by Him to preside over his work. For example, that is how the pursuit of Zion was undertaken among Enoch's people, the people of Melchizedek, Alma the Elder's people, the people of King Benjamin, even the people visited and converted by Christ himself (3 Nephi 20:23). There is no other way.

Obstacles to the Pursuit of Zion: Lessons from the Book of Mormon

Though many things about Zion have been held back from us, the sacred record makes plain that becoming a people of Zion and living by celestial law is within our reach. Even so, if we are to be wiser than those ancient people of America (Mormon 9-11), then we must study the obstacles they faced in establishing and preserving Zion among them, especially within the Church membership itself, for the obstacles that stood in the way of Zion existed for the most part in their own midst and not solely in the world around them.

When the people of God failed to attain or even pursue Zion, it was because they chose the way of death over the way of life. This does not mean they were unrepentant liars, thieves, adulterers, or murderers. The way of death they typically lived, or at least the one most often described in the Book of Mormon for our learning, seemed right and good to many of them and would seem so to many honorable persons today. We must bear in mind that the way of spiritual death has many paths, and most of them in their earlier stages do not seem grossly wicked or reprehensible to most decent people. Recall that King Benjamin's people were, according to him, "a diligent people in keeping the commandments of the Lord" (Mosiah 1:11), and yet upon hearing his last address to them concerning the principles of Zion they discovered they were still in a "carnal state" (Mosiah 4:2). As Jacob tells us, "to be carnally minded is death" (2 Nephi 9:39), even when it is accompanied by or issues in a certain kind of diligent obedience (Mosiah 1:11; 4:2: 5:2,5). The carnal state the people found in themselves was one that plagued the Church throughout most of its history, as we shall see, and when it fully realized itself it did indeed bring destruction to the Nephites as a people.

We want to identify the carnal state of King Benjamin's people, bring out its nature, and trace its path as it hindered and undermined the pursuit of Zion. As should become clear, the way of death characteristic of people of the Church in that ancient time is deeply rooted in our own times. Because all humankind have become fallen in nature, all are carnal (Alma 22:13), and all seek happiness in ways that eventually bring death (Helaman 13:38; Alma 41:10; 2 Nephi 9:39; Mormon 2:13). Essentially, the carnal mind is one that seeks its own life according to its own will and desires and, consequently, loses its life (JST Matthew 10:34; Mosiah 16:11-12). It is opposite the spiritual mind that loses its life in following God's will and receives life as one alive to his goodness (Mosiah 5:2; 27:25; Alma 19:6; JST Luke 9:24-25).

The "carnal state" of King Benjamin's people infected how they lived their whole lives. For until a people are "born of God," thereby becoming "new creatures," their "carnal and fallen state" continues to affect their overall way of being, and King Benjamin's people had not yet been born of God despite their diligent obedience (Mosiah 4:2; 1:11). Accordingly, when any person or people are in a carnal state, it gives form to how they produce and distribute wealth. How they think about power and the forms it takes spring from their carnal minded-ness, as does the esteem in which they actually hold one another as persons and as members of society. It even shapes how they obey God, for nothing escapes the influence of their desire to seek their own lives and live according to their own wills. Of course, not all carnal states are equal in their degree of wickedness, although all involve seeking one's own life. To a considerable degree, King Benjamin's people sought their own lives in how they lived, but they did not do so by lying, robbing, committing adultery, or the like. Bear in mind they were in their way a diligent people in keeping the commandments of the Lord, and King Benjamin acknowledged them for that (Mosiah 1:11).

Certain precepts organized the carnal mind of King Benjamin's people, including how they obeyed God, and functioned as major obstacles in their becoming a people of Zion. Indeed, these precepts worked as major obstacles in the pursuit of Zion throughout the Book of Mormon times. They can be found in King Benjamin's address when he brings out the principles of Zion in his successful effort to open the hearts of his people to the goodness of God, the mission of Christ, and to the purifying power of the Spirit. But one of the most explicit and articulate defenses of these carnal precepts recorded in the Book of Mormon can be found in the teachings of Korihor, a devoted opponent of Zion. Apparently he had a copy of King Benjamin's address (Mosiah 2:8), for he counters point by point the principles of Zion found in it by advocating opposing carnal precepts that the Nephites so often found reasonable and appealing.

The first precept concerns the status and power of the human agent himself. Human agency is the power to choose and act in making a difference in the world, and no normative concept is more basic to how a people live. Indeed, we may say that any way to live, carnal or spiritual, is primarily a formula for defining and organizing human agency so that life might turn out well rather than poorly. Recall that King Benjamin taught his people that all they possess, all they are, all they can become that is good depends on the goodness and power of God. The dust out of which their bodies are made, the air they breathe, their riches of every kind, their very lives—all come from God (Mosiah 2:20-25; 4:19-22). Without God's power in their lives, the human being is "nothing"; he could not exist or continue to exist (Mosiah 4:5, 11). This is not to say that persons have no power and can make no difference in the world. Rather it means that their power to do good and help make life turn out well come from the gifts and power of God (Moroni 7:16; 10:24-25). As King Benjamin's grandson Ammon later explained, "Yea, I know that I am nothing; as to my strength I am weak; therefore I will not boast of myself, but I will boast of my God, for in his strength I can do all things"

(Alma 26:12; see Moroni 7:16; 10:24-35). To have faith in God—the faith that purifies a people and enables them to live by celestial law, including having all things common and living the law of consecration—a people must believe that all they are issues from God's power and goodness.

Korihor attacked this view of the human agent by offering a contrary view, one deeply rooted in much of Nephite history. It is a view of individualism and self-reliance, which teaches a people to have a mistaken faith in their own abilities to make things happen in their personal and collective lives. It makes much of human efficacy in the larger cause-and-effect world, promoting the belief that whether life turns out well for anyone depends primarily on his or her own efforts. In words notable for their fluency, Korihor said that "every man fared in this life according to the management of the creature; therefore every man prospered according to his genius, and that every man conquered according to his strength" (Alma 30:17). Such a view seems very attractive, and we can appreciate why even the people of God might accept it. It fits well with the carnal mind's desire to seek its own life and live according to its own will. But again, it is deeply at odds with true faith, wherein God's power and goodness ground and permeate a people's whole understanding of individual and collective agency.

The second precept has to do with how a people own their lives and define the right to possess and control material and immaterial goods on which they rely to satisfy various needs and wants. King Benjamin found it necessary to convert his people to the fact that all good things they may possess—the fact of their existence, their food and shelter, their substance and riches of every kind, even the dust from which their bodies were made, and their very lives—belong not to them but to God (Mosiah 2:20, 25; 4:19, 21-22). Believing that all good things belong to God is also essential to having a saving faith in Him, and that belief provides the basis for having all things common and living the law of consecration.

Korihor defended a contrary belief concerning ownership, one familiar to the Nephite people before as well as after his time. Korihor reminded and assured the Nephite people that they were "a free people" who possessed "rights and privileges" that justified them in enjoying the fruits of their labors—to "make use of that which is their own" (Alma 30:27-28). He upheld a version of private ownership that fits well with the belief in individual efficacy—that "every man" fares and prospers in this life "according to the management of the creature" (Alma 30:17)—considered just a moment ago.

A key idea in the view of economic freedom and rights expounded by Korihor is that those who privately own and control the factors of production have a right to possess and enjoy individually the income generated by their use of those factors. This idea is contrary to the principles of Zion, which require a people to have all things in common. According to these celestial precepts, all good things belong to God, He bestows all things upon all His followers in common, they define control over factors and income of production strictly in stewardship terms, and they separate control over these factors by a steward from control over income generated by the steward's employment (see, for example, D&C 104:55-56, 67-71; 42:33-34; 82:17-19).[1]

When a people live by the carnal precepts upheld by Korihor—when they seek their own lives, having a belief in their own individual efficacy and their rights of personal ownership—inequalities of power, wealth, and status seem justified and desirable, and they inevitably occur. Many come to believe that the good life includes being a successful person as measured by these inequalities. Consequently, those who gain more of these vain things of the world become "puffed up in the pride of their hearts," esteeming themselves above others because they have riches or power, or think themselves wise or learned (see, for example, Jacob 2:12-13; Alma 4:6-12; 3 Nephi 6:15). Among the Nephites the source of pride resided in the carnal precepts defended by Korihor. They believed they fared well according to their own management or strength and deserved what they gained, and some possessed more and esteemed themselves better than others.

Fundamental to Korihor's attack on Zion and its promise of eternal life was his desire to persuade people that there is no need for an atonement and, indeed, that there is no Christ and no God (Alma 30:12, 17, 36-37). Eventually belief in God and Christ conflict with the carnal mind and stand in the way of its full expression (Alma 30:26-28). Indeed, even though it may not know or admit it, the carnal mind is "an enemy of God" and in rebellion against Him from its inception (Mosiah 3:19). If it persists in its wickedness, it comes out in "willful" and "open rebellion against God" in the pursuit of happiness through iniquity (Mosiah 2:34-37; 3 Nephi 6:18; Mormon 1:16; Moses 4:3). Denying God's existence is the form that rebellion eventually will take. Having debunked the existence of God and mission of Christ, Korihor opened the way for the carnal mind to fully realize itself by declaring that "whatever a man did was no crime" and "that when a man was dead, that was the end thereof" (Alma 30:17-18).

So we see that Korihor took to their natural conclusion the carnal principles he defended, and it takes no genius to anticipate the misery and destruction that await any people who live by them. We can find in Korihor's teachings the formula for the final decline and destruction of the Nephite people.

Though still in a carnal state (Mosiah 4:2), King Benjamin's people did not deny the existence of God and did not believe that whatever a person does is no sin. Their carnal mindedness had not reached this extreme. But they did believe that persons fare in the world according to the management of the creature and their own strength, and because they saw themselves as a free people with certain rights and privileges, they believed they deserved to enjoy individually the economic fruits of their labors. Consider the reason they gave themselves for not imparting their substance to the poor, a reason that stood in the way of their living the law of consecration. In the words of King Benjamin: "Perhaps thou shalt say: The man has brought upon himself his misery; therefore I shall stay my hand, and will not give unto him of my food, not impart unto him of my substance that he may not suffer, for his punishments are just"

(Mosiah 4:17). If punishments thus understood are just, then so are rewards. If a person works hard and is a wise manager of his affairs, then most likely he will prosper, and if he is not industrious or wise, then he will reap accordingly. So however life turns out, persons usually get what they deserve. This is vintage Korihor, and to disabuse them of these beliefs, King Benjamin made clear to them that all they are or may become that is good are blessings from God and that all they now possess or will yet possess that is of value belongs to Him (Mosiah 2:23-24; 4:19, 21-22).

It seems that the people also obeyed God under the influence of carnal precepts. They sought their own lives through their obedience while presuming too much that they would fare in eternity according to their strength and management, deserving whatever reward they earned. To discourage them of this false belief, King Benjamin informed them that however diligent they were in keeping the commandments of God, they could not save themselves and, as measured by works alone, would be forever unworthy of salvation (Mosiah 4:11). He said to them that even if they served God "with all your own souls" and "render all the thanks which your whole soul has power to possess," they would remain "unprofitable servants" and be "indebted" to Him "forever and ever" (Mosiah 2:20-21).

After they were "spiritually begotten of Christ,", King Benjamin warned his people that as they had "tasted of [God's] love" and "known of his goodness," they must now "remember, and always retain in remembrance, the greatness of God, and your own nothingness, and his goodness and long-suffering towards you, unworthy creatures, and humble yourselves even in the depths of humility" and stand "steadfastly in the faith" (Mosiah 4:11). By always remembering these things, the people would not turn back to seeking their own lives according to those carnal precepts. By remembering these things, they would "always rejoice, and be filled with the love of God" (Mosiah 4:2, 6, 12; 5:2, 5, 7).

Just over a half century after Lehi brought his family to the American continent, the carnal precepts later promoted by

Korihor were already at work undermining Zion among the people of the Lord. In an effort to preserve purity of heart among the people (Jacob 2:10; 3:1-3), Jacob preached against the growing disposition among them to obtain riches "more abundantly than that of your brethren" and to "suppose that ye are better than they" (Jacob 2:13). He reminded those who would become rich that "one being is as precious in [God's] sight as the other" and that they must impart of their riches so all "may be rich like unto you" (Jacob 2:17-21). Unlike King Benjamin's people, some men among Jacob's people were also guilty of a "grosser crime" because they desired "concubines" and more than "one wife," using as scriptural justification the practices of David and Solomon (Jacob 2:21-33). These men had become carnal minded, as indicated by their desire for riches and love of inequality, and it is the nature of the carnal mind to increase in iniquity unless checked by the precepts of righteousness.

It was about 60 years after the first Alma founded "the church of God" in the land of Mormon (Mosiah 18:15-17) and about forty years after he established it in the land of Zarahemla (Mosiah 25:19) that great inequality began to grow up in the Church (Alma 4:12, 15). Bear in mind that the church was first established among a people whose hearts had been made pure and lived the law of consecration (Alma 5:3-13; Mosiah 4:2, 26; 5:2; 18:27). Alma tells us that those who had been "spiritually born of God" in the land of Mormon "were faithful unto the end; therefore they were saved" (Alma 5:13, Mosiah 18). So when Mormon tells us that a "great inequality" began to grow up in "the church," he presumes that for about sixty years many members for the most part lived by the principle of equality as a pure-in-heart people. In fact, "the people" of the church were still living the law of consecration at the time inequality appeared once more among them. Indeed, in part because they lived that law they had become "prosperous" and "far more wealthy than those who did not belong to their church" (Alma 1:30-31).

But then some among the second and third generations began keeping for themselves the "riches" that "they had obtained by their industry," thinking themselves above others and turning "their backs upon the needy" (Alma 4:6, 12). This was the cause of the "great inequality" that began to appear among the Church members that troubled Alma the younger so much (Alma 4:12, 15). It seems that the industrious rich made a concerted effort to justify personal ownership and inequality of riches to other members—presumably by evoking the same carnal precepts of earlier generations, precepts Korihor would promote a decade later partly in defense of those with riches—for "they began to persecute those that did not believe according to their own will and pleasure" (Alma 4:8). The "contentions among the people of the church" over matters concerning riches and inequality became "a great stumbling block to those that did not belong to the church, and thus the church began to fail in its progress" (Alma 4:10). It was at this time that Alma the Younger, "seeing all this inequality" and being "very sorrowful" because of it, resigned his office as "chief judge" and devoted himself fully to his calling as "high priest over the church" (Alma 4:15-18). As we observed earlier, he dedicated himself to preserving and renewing among his people the ways of Zion, ways established during the ministry of his father and King Benjamin (Alma 5:1-14).

Compared to the time between the beginning of the ministry of the first Alma and the end of the ministry of his son Alma, a period of about seventy-five years, the next hundred years the work of Zion is noticeably less successful. There were those in the Church whose hearts were sanctified and purified, who remained humble and penitent before God, and who died firmly believing that their souls were redeemed (Alma 46:39; Helaman 3:35; 15:4-8; 3 Nephi 6:13).

But others turn away from the pursuit of Zion, pursuing their own lives according to their own wills, seeking power and riches, lifting themselves one above another, and withholding their substance from the poor (see Alma 45:23-24; Helaman 3:33-35; 4:11-13; 13:27-28; 3 Nephi 6:12-14). As is always the case when a people of the Church live by these carnal precepts, they became "distinguished by ranks" according to their "riches" and "chances for learning" made possible by their "riches," which caused divisions and dissensions among them. This "inequality" reached the point where the "church" itself "was broken up in all the land save it were among a few of the Lamanites who were converted unto the true faith, and they would not depart from it," and were "willing with all diligence to keep the commandments of the Lord" (3 Nephi 6:14). Apparently, at least some Lamanite church members did not distinguish themselves according to ranks and inequality had not grown up among them as it had among Nephite members. As Mormon tells us, "the cause of this iniquity of the people was this—Satan had great power, unto the stirring up of the people to do all manner of iniquity, and to puffing them up with pride, tempting them to seek for power, and authority, and riches, and the vain things of the world" (3 Nephi 6:15).

The last time Zion existed among the people of the Book of Mormon, it endured about 170 years. It was established by Jesus himself, and it is written that "surely there could not be a happier people among all the people who had been created by the hand of God" (4 Nephi 1:16). The end of Zion came when the people "began to deny the true church of Christ," held "their goods and substance no more common among them," and "began to be divided into classes" (4 Nephi 1:25-26). But unlike times before, the growth of carnal mindedness could not be reversed or contained by the precepts of righteousness and the labors of the prophets of God. It developed until it reached its full natural growth, inherent in it from the beginning, and the people pursued evil for evil's sake despite the suffering and destruction it brought upon them. We read that the people were "without order and without mercy," "without principle and past feeling," and did "delight in everything save that which is good" (Moroni 9:18-20). They did not "dwindle in unbelief" but "did wilfully rebel against the gospel of Christ" or did come out in "open rebellion against God" (4 Nephi 1:38; Mormon 1:16; 2:15). They became one with "the devil and his angels," who "abideth not by law" and "willeth to abide in sin, and altogether abideth in sin" (3 Nephi 27:32; D&C 88:35).

Mormon tells us "it is impossible for the tongue to describe, or for a man to write a perfect description of the horrible scene of the blood and carnage which was among the people" (Mormon 4:11). Their overriding aim, the aim of the fully ripened carnal mind, is to destroy life itself—as Mormon says, "They delighted in the shedding of blood continually" (Mormon 4:11)—and in the cruelest manner possible. Despite the revulsion he felt in reporting the terrible evils he saw all around him, Mormon singled out what he judged to be the greatest abomination. First he describes how Lamanite men fed the Nephite "women upon the flesh of their husbands and the children upon the flesh of their fathers" (Moroni 9:8). But "notwithstanding this great abomination of the Lamanites," he went on to write that it "does not exceed that of our own people." For they took prisoner "many of the daughters of the Lamanites," and after "depriving them of that which was most dear and precious above all things, which is chastity and virtue," they "did murder them in the most cruel manner, torturing their bodies even unto death"; and having done this, "they devour their flesh like unto wild beasts" as "a token of their bravery" (Moroni 9:8-10).

The violent nature of the carnal mind is deeply rooted within it and present from its inception. Its less extreme forms can be observed, for example, when persons compete for gain and glory, when they divide into classes and distinguish themselves by ranks, when the rich turn their backs on the poor, and when the poor envy the rich. It exists among church members when divisions and dissensions occur among them because of inequalities of power, wealth, and status.

Notably, violence is covert as well as overt in the inequalities between men and women that characterize most carnal societies and cultures and enable men to exercise dominion over women. How men treat women in the carnal world represents a prominent part of that world's rebellion against the gospel of Christ and God himself. It is a principal barometer in measuring the spiritual health of the church itself.² For the purpose of the gospel of Christ is above all else to prepare women and men to be joint heirs and equals with one another in Christ by purifying their hearts and enabling them to live by celestial law. That is why Satan's work to destroy the work of God consists above much else in turning the man against the woman—a turning against that can finally result, if left unchecked, in the rape, torture, and murder of women, and even in the eating of their flesh, as a token of male superiority and bravery.

Zion in the Last Days: Warnings from the Book of Mormon

The time will come in the last gospel dispensation when the people of the Church will become pure in heart and live by celestial law; they will become a people of Zion. About this there can be no question (see, for example, 3 Nephi 16:18; Moses 7:62-64). The question is, what path will take them to Zion? Will the latter-day people of God learn from the mistakes as well as the successes of the peoples of the Book of Mormon and follow the easier path under the leadership of their prophets, as did King Benjamin's people, or will they repeat their mistakes and go down the harder path, as did the people of the Church immediately preceding Christ's personal ministry among them? Which path they take depends on how they overcome the obstacles in their own midst and face the opposition around them to becoming a people of Zion.

In the world around them, people will be hostile to the building up of Zion, for Satan will "rage in the hearts of the children of men" and "stir them up to anger against that which is good," leading them to say "that it is of no worth" (2 Nephi 28:16, 20-21). Some among the people of the Church may themselves believe that in light of the "wisdom of the world," the precepts of Zion are unworkable. In the face of the world's "scoffing" and "mocking," some may even become "ashamed" of the gospel and its promise of Zion and fall "away into forbidden paths," after tasting the fruit of the tree of life

(1 Nephi 8:25-28; 11:35-36). Hopefully, the latter-day people of God will avoid the divisions that sometimes plagued the Nephite church between those who embraced the precepts of Zion and those that would not (see, for example, Alma 4; 3 Nephi 6:10-16). The Lord warns that those who "fighteth against Zion" in the last days "shall perish" or "be cut off" (1 Nephi 22:14, 19; 2 Nephi 10:13).

What the people of the Church in the latter days should fear more than opposition to Zion is an apathy that comes from believing all is well in Zion while they are still in a carnal state. Nephi forewarns members of the latter-day church that Satan will "pacify and lull them away into carnal security" by persuading them that "all is well in Zion; yea, Zion prospereth, all is well—and thus the devil cheateth their souls, and leadeth them away carefully down to hell" (2 Nephi 28:21, 24). From the lessons of the Book of Mormon, we can anticipate the carnal security and kind of prosperity that would lull away members of the Church in the latter days, hindering them from becoming pure in heart and living by celestial law. It is a carnal security informed by the carnal precepts that so often hampered the pursuit of Zion among the Nephites, the very precepts defended by Korihor "because they were pleasing to the carnal mind" (Alma 30:53)—precepts that can lead to material prosperity, though not for all, at least for a time.

As we have observed earlier, these precepts justify and motivate a people to live as a "free people" with "rights and privileges"[3] to pursue their own lives according to their own wills, while believing that they prosper according to their own "strength" and "management" and that they deserve to possess and enjoy individually "that which is their own" (Alma 30:17, 24, 27-28). While living by these precepts can result in material prosperity for a majority for a time, it also inevitably creates and sanctions inequalities of power, wealth, and status among the people of the Church. These inequalities stand entrenched against being equal in the bonds of earthly and heavenly things as required by celestial law and the pure love of Christ. When this is so, all is not well in Zion, even for those who prosper because of their freedom and industry.

Nephi warns that in the world of the latter days, when people will "wear stiff necks and high heads," presumably because of inequalities among them, even "the humble followers of Christ" in "many instances" do "err because they are taught by the precepts of men" (2 Nephi 28:14). What are these "precepts of men" that may cause even "the humble followers of Christ" to "err" in "many instances"? We should not be surprised to learn, in view of what so often hampered the attainment of Zion by the Nephites, that among these precepts are those who "put trust in man" and "make flesh [their] arm," and those who "deny the power of God, and the gift of the Holy Ghost" (2 Nephi 28:26, 31).

Recall how King Benjamin's people, despite their diligent obedience, put their "trust in man" by behaving as though they prospered according to their own strength and deserved to make use of that which they thought was their own. They denied the "power of God" by failing to live the truth that all a people have and are and all they may become and possess that is good comes from and belongs to God. They made "flesh" their "arm" by acting as though they make themselves "profitable servants" of God who are "worthy" of salvation through their "diligent obedience" while still in a "carnal state." And for a time they denied "the power of the Holy Ghost" by not turning to him through Christ with their whole souls so He could purify their hearts (Mosiah 1-5). As Nephi said, Satan "cheateth the souls" of all who live by the precepts of men, including the "humble followers of Christ" who do "err," because those precepts promise happiness but eventually bring sorrow and suffering (2 Nephi 28:21-24; 26:31).

The only way latter-day church members can be "changed" from their "carnal state" to a "state of righteousness" is to be "born of God" and be spiritually obedient to His commandments (Mosiah 27:25-26; 5:2, 5-7). They cannot save themselves from their carnal state through carnal obedience, however diligent. To be born of God, a people must recognize their carnal state; be brought down to the depths of humility; undergo a mighty change of heart through faith in Christ and the power of the Holy Spirit; and be spiritually obedient to God's commandments in all things, including living by celestial law (Mosiah 3:19; 4:2, 11; 5:2, 5, 7; D&C 105:4-5). All episodes of spiritual birth and purification recorded by Mormon involve these things.

Refusing to Know

When King Benjamin gave his final address to his people and converted them to the principles of Zion, he told them that "there are not any among you, except it be our little children that have not been taught these things before" (Mosiah 2:34). Even so, the principles of Zion had not yet changed their hearts and replaced the carnal precepts that ordered their lives.

In asking how it can be that a people who diligently obeyed God and who had been taught the principles of Zion still failed to exercise true faith in Him and embrace those principles, we are reminded of Amulek's confession in which he explains why he just recently in his life had not lived those principles even though he knew them. To understand his explanation we must first place it in its proper context. Recall that Amulek joined Alma in the work of the ministry about one year after Alma resigned his position as chief judge to devote himself as prophet of the Church to upholding the ways of Zion that had been successfully taught by his father and King Benjamin, doing so because "he saw great inequality among the people" and thus became "very sorrowful" (Alma 4:12-20). As we indicated earlier, Alma began laboring full-time among the people to uphold the principles of Zion "throughout all the land" (Alma 5:1-14). Amulek became Alma's companion when Alma began preaching "unto the people in the land of Ammonihah" (Alma 9:1). In administering the word to these people, he taught them how "many, exceedingly great many," had been "made pure and entered into the rest of the Lord their God" through His "holy order" (Alma 13; see Alma 5:1-14).

Amulek's first sermon as Alma's companion was to the people of Ammonihah, where he lived. He began his address by telling them that he was "a man of no small reputation" and had "acquired much riches by the hand of my industry" (Alma 10:4). Also, he said he had "known much of the ways of the Lord" (Alma 10:5), but even so, he confessed, he "harden[ed] his heart" and "was called many times" and "would not hear" (Alma 10:5-6). What he was "called" to do but would not "hear" was to live the very principles he and Alma came among the people of Ammonihah to teach: the principles of Zion. He wanted to help prepare the minds of the people to accept these principles by using himself as an example of one who did not live that which he knew. As he said, "I knew concerning these things" (he knew concerning "the ways of the Lord" and "his marvelous power") and "yet I would not know; therefore I went on rebelling against God" (Alma 10:6). But as we know, Amulek ceased "rebelling against God" and pretending "not" to "know." For he forsook "all his gold, and silver, and his precious things" for "the word of God" (Alma 10:4-6; 15:16). Having done this, he could more convincingly teach others to live one of the law of consecration's first requirements—in his words, to "impart of your substance, if ye have, to those who stand in need" (Alma 34:28).

He knew but he would not know—this we think was the state of mind that initially kept King Benjamin's people from becoming pure in heart despite their knowledge of the gospel and diligent obedience in keeping God's commandments. Unless we learn wisdom from the Book of Mormon, this state of mind could hinder even the "humble followers of Christ" among the latter-day people of God from becoming a people of Zion (2 Nephi 28:14).

To know and yet not to know seems to be an instance of self-deception. In the case of King Benjamin's people, the false beliefs with which they deceived themselves had to do with the justifications they adopted for living according to carnal precepts in the face of the principles of Zion they had been taught. Perhaps they misconstrued the nature of Zion; told themselves they presently were not yet able or prepared to live its lofty principles; or were actually on their way to living them through their diligent obedience while in a carnal state, or in fact were already living them. Whatever their false beliefs may have been, those beliefs could have served to disguise or excuse their desires to pursue carnal ends according to carnal precepts, permitting them, as they supposed, to seek for riches, power, and honor, and to accept worldly inequalities even among themselves. Perhaps their diligent obedience itself helped them not know what they knew. All seems "well" when a people are a "diligent people" in keeping the commandments and "prosper" because of their industry (Mosiah 1:7, 11-12; 2 Nephi 28:21) while at the same time they know and yet will not know the call from God through his prophet to become a people of Zion.

The central truth a people of the Church refuse to know so they can continue in their carnal ways while trying to be good members—members who may even diligently obey the commandments while in their carnal state (Mosiah 1:11;; 4:2)— is the truth about the power and goodness of God (Mosiah 4:5-6, 11). Before an angel appeared to him, it seems that Amulek was a good man, as measured by most standards. He confessed that he had "seen" much of "the marvelous power of God," and yet he "would not know," which apparently permitted him to enjoy living as a person of "no small reputation" and "much riches" (Alma 10:1-6) while refusing to embrace the ways of Zion that he, as Alma's companion, would be called on to teach (Alma 5; 10:4-6; 15:16; 34:28). It seems that by refusing to acknowledge God's power and goodness, members of the church can justify themselves in not becoming a people of Zion by both affirming and denying their own powers; by, on the one hand, telling themselves that they fare in this world according to their own strength and, on the other hand, by believing they are yet unable to become a people of Zion and live by celestial law. Like King Benjamin's people, they rationalize, for example, some possessing that which is above others and esteeming themselves superior to others by claiming that those who prosper do so according to their own management and deserve to enjoy as their own the fruits of their industry (Mosiah 4:17-22). At the same time, they can rationalize not living by celestial principles by saying that they must first become a people pure in heart, a transformation which they believe will certainly occur in the indefinite future, but which seems to be perpetually beyond their present capacity.

By affirming and denying their own powers in these and other ways, members of the Church can refuse to open their hearts to the marvelous powers of God. For if they truly believed in that power, they could no longer believe in their own efficacy the way they do and in possessing more and esteeming themselves better than others. If they truly believe in that power, they would accept with glad hearts that God can do what they by themselves cannot do—that He can and will transform their hearts and enable them to live by celestial law as soon as they stop refusing to know and become willing for him to do so. Recall that Melchizedek's people "waxed strong in iniquity" and "were full of all manner of wickedness" before he preached repentance unto them and they were "made pure" and entered into God's rest (Alma 13:10-19). Though King Benjamin's people were in a "carnal state, even less than the dust of the earth," once they acknowledged fully God's "power and goodness" and "cried with one voice" that their "hearts" might be "purified," the "Lord Omnipotent . . . wrought a mighty change" in their hearts, and they began to live by celestial law (Mosiah 4:2, 11, 26; 5:2, 5). God through His Son and the Holy Spirit made it possible for them to do what they could not do left to themselves however diligent their obedience.

It was through the power of the word preached by King Benjamin that his people forsook their carnal state and opened their hearts to the healing power of God. But preaching the word does not have, by itself, the power to change the hearts of a people who persist in refusing to know the things of God. Consequently, God may withdraw the Holy Priesthood from among them and with it their opportunity to enter His rest by becoming a people of Zion, as He did in the days of Moses (D&C 84:23-26). But when His plan requires that Zion be established among His people and they persist in withholding their hearts from Him, God may manifest His marvelous power in a physically forceful manner to prepare them for Zion.

This was the situation of the Book of Mormon people just before Christ visited them soon after His resurrection. The people of that time, including many Church members, were doing "all manner of iniquity," such as "puffing [themselves] up with pride," seeking for "power," "authority," and "riches," "distinguishing themselves according to ranks" and "their chances for learning," and pursuing "the vain things of the world" (3 Nephi 6:12-15). Mormon tells us that the people "did not sin ignorantly, for they knew the will of God concerning them, for it had been taught unto them; therefore they did willfully rebel against God" (3 Nephi 6:18). They knew but would not know Him.

After giving the people ample opportunity to be healed by Him and become a people of Zion, the Lord finally caused a great destruction to fall upon them in the form of all manner of physical destruction. The whole infrastructure that supported their carnal world collapsed around them, and much suffering resulted, so that the "howlings of the people" were "great and terrible" (3 Nephi 8:25). The purpose of the Lord was to separate "the more righteous"—those "who received the prophets"—from the wicked and to prepare them to receive Him and His Zion (3 Nephi 9:13; 10:12). So that the more righteous would understand the reasons for their suffering, the Lord reminded them of how "oft" he "gathered" some of them and "would have gathered" others to Himself to be healed and to become a people of Zion, but they "would not" (3 Nephi 8:1-12). So that they would know the source of their destruction, He proclaimed to the more righteous that He, the Lord, "caused" the "great city Moroni" to sink into "the depths of the sea"; that He "caused" the "great city of Moronihah" to be "covered with earth"; that He "caused" the "waters" to cover the cities of "Onihah" and "Mocum"; and much more did He "cause" so that the "whole earth became deformed" (3 Nephi 8:17; 9:4-12). Then the Lord asked the more righteous who had "received the prophets" if they would now finally let Him heal them and pour out upon them the great blessings He had been holding in store for them. "O all ye that are spared because ye were more righteous than they, will ye not now return unto me, and repent of your sins, and be converted, that I may heal you? Yea, verily I say unto you, if ye will come unto me ye shall have eternal life. Behold, mine arm of mercy is extended towards you, and whosoever will come, him will I receive; and blessed are those who come unto me" (3 Nephi 9:13-14).

After all the destructions they had suffered and after being administered to by Christ himself, how could the more righteous refuse to be healed and to receive the great blessings that await all who become a people of Zion? How could they now refuse to know the marvelous power and goodness of God and to receive the wonderful blessings he desired to give them? The record says they did indeed become a pure in heart people, the love of God dwelled in their midst, they had all things in common, there were no rich and poor among them, and "there could not be a happier people among all the people who had been created by the hand of God" (3 Nephi 26:17-19; 4 Nephi 1:3, 15-16). The happiness they now enjoyed was far greater than any happiness they might have imagined they could achieve by continuing in their carnal ways and refusing to know him.

The plan of God also requires that Zion be established in the last gospel dispensation among the Latter-day Saints. As a warning voice out of the dust (2 Nephi 26:16; Moroni 10:27), the Book of Mormon asks us whether we will learn wisdom from it and become a people of Zion by hearkening to the words of our prophets, or will we refuse to know so that we might continue in our carnal state and bring down upon us the testimony of calamity in order to fulfill the will of the Lord and to establish Zion in the last days. As modern revelation reminds us, the people of the Church in the latter days can "escape" the "scourge" that will inflict the "ungodly" and enjoy a "multiplicity of blessings" if they will "do all things" commanded them, which include the commandment to establish Zion. But if they fail to do as commanded, they also will

262 — Women in Eternity, Women of Zion

suffer "sore affliction" (D&C 97:21-27). One way or the other, whether we choose the hard path or the easy one, the Latter-day Saints are destined to become a people of Zion and to receive the great blessings God holds in store for us. Once we become a people of Zion in this the last gospel dispensation, we will remain so for a millennium, and beyond.

Women and the Future of Zion

First among the lessons the Book of Mormon offers us are warnings concerning worldly inequalities, particularly among the people of the church. The carnal world is always deeply infected by inequalities of status, power, and wealth, whereas in a Zion society the people of God esteem and respect each other as equals, share as equals all power, possess all things common, and have no poor among them. The central contrast between Zion and the carnal world involves the relations between women and men. This contrast is central because the first purpose of earth existence is to prepare a people for eternal life, and eternal life centers on the relationships between exalted men and women, who live and serve together as gods and are joined together into an eternal family by ever-lasting covenants of marriage. Becoming a people of Zion is how a people prepare for godhood and eternal life, so Zion also centers on the relations between purified women and men who possess all things, including all power, as if they were joint heirs. More than any other inequalities between persons in the carnal world, those between men and women prevent the coming forth of Zion. This is notably true when the inequalities of the world become entrenched in the lives of the people of God.

Because women typically are subordinate to men and treated as inferior in the carnal world, women have much to gain from the coming forth of Zion as measured by the stan-dard of equality alone, not to mention that degree of fullness of life which comes from being filled with God's love and being alive to good. In the carnal world women generally are unequal to men in wealth, in Zion they have all things common with men. In the world women typically are unequal to men in power; in Zion they share all power as equals. And inasmuch as women enjoy less value or less respect and esteem than men in the carnal world, women and men esteem and respect each other as equals in Zion. Consequently, in Zion women will have greater opportunity to develop and exercise their gifts and talents than they typically do in the carnal world. Their opportunities as agents of the light and the word to make and execute decisions will also be greater than in the carnal world.[4] Unlike in much of the world, in Zion women will not be under the economic domination of men, women and their children will not constitute so much of the poor (for there will be no rich and poor) and one woman's child will not have less opportunity than the child of another woman because of inequality of power and wealth.

Men also have much to gain from the establishment of Zion, perhaps more than women do. So long as men exercise dominion over women in an order of unequal power, however benevolent, so long as men receive greater esteem and respect than women, and so long as men enjoy greater wealth than women, men will suffer darkness in their lives and their lives will be impoverished. Indeed, it seems that often those who dominate suffer more spiritually than those dominated.

We do not mean to say that the only inequalities the members of the church must put aside to become a people of Zion are those between men and women. Obviously, this is not so. Inequalities exist among women of the church themselves, some women enjoying more esteem, wealth, and power than their sisters in Christ. And of course, the same is true among the men of the church. These inequalities, too, will melt away when the people of the church experience that healing awareness of God's love for all His children which causes them to live and serve together as equals. But still, because the relations between men and women are absolutely central in the celestial world and in Zion as it prepares us for that world, carnal inequalities between women and men may prove to be the most critical ones we must overcome on the path to Zion.

Worldly inequalities are not without their rationalizations that help shape the mind and heart so that those inequalities seem right and natural to women as well as men. As we have seen, such false beliefs can constitute a serious obstacle to the establishment of Zion, and only when freed from them can men and women come into full awareness of God's purifying love and live in Zion as equals. Because the inequalities of the carnal world favor men over women, women may be initially in a better position than men to recognize the possibility of Zion and to embrace its precepts. As the Book of Mormon indicates, those most successful in gaining power, wealth, and status are often the least likely to welcome the establishment of Zion and the most likely to turn from it once it has been established. It does seem that women today, especially women of God, are more disposed to the ways of Zion than many men. For example, they experience social life more in terms of love than rights, they are less likely to let some worldly view of justice stand in the way of compassion, they pursue ends more in the spirit of cooperation than competition, they seem less inclined to war and the destruction of life. These traits go with their natures and roles as caretakers of the light in the tradition of Eve; indeed, they are traits all agents of the light should possess regardless of gender, but occupying a less favored position in the carnal world may help preserve and perpetuate those traits, making women more Zion disposed than men.

Of course, the women and men of God must bring forth Zion together. The one cannot move forward without the other. They must undergo rebirth and live by celestial law as one. But whether serving as helpmeets in the works of the word or laboring in other ways as stewards of the light, the women of God can and should exercise initiative and leadership in preparing the way for Zion and making it a reality in the last gospel dispensation. They have a divine calling to help establish Zion, for they are stewards of the light, and the purpose of the light is that persons lay hold upon that which is good by becoming pure in heart and living by celestial law. So the women of God can and should be anxiously engaged in the cause of Zion, doing many things of their own free will and bringing forth much righteousness in making Zion possible. It is not necessary that they always be set apart or receive specific callings from the priesthood. They already are called and have the gifts and powers, by virtue of being women of God and agents of the light, to help establish Zion.[5]

However, because we live in the times we do, when people in many places seek to remedy the inequalities from which women suffer, some among the Saints may promote the pursuit of carnal ends and uphold carnal precepts as they try to help achieve equality for women. We applaud many of the advances women have made, most notably in recent years, in overcoming the inequalities between men and women. Latter-day scripture clearly affirms that certain "rights" are "inherent and inalienable," belonging as they do to all humankind. Without trying to be exhaustive, these rights include the right to "life," the "free exercise of conscience" and "religious belief," the right to "control property," and the right to be free from "personal abuse" (D&C 98:4-5; 101:76-80; 134). The inherent and inalienable freedoms belong to women as well as men.[6]

But in any debate over fundamental freedoms, the people of the church should bear in mind two things. One is that such freedoms were established in particular by "the power of the Father" so that he might "gather in" a people of God and establish "among them" His "Zion" (3 Nephi 21:1, 4). Another is that, as the Book of Mormon makes plain, these same freedoms can justify and motivate people of the church to seek carnal ends and uphold carnal precepts, thereby hindering the establishment of Zion among them—which is to say that the enjoyment of rights and freedoms can become an obstacle to Zion rather than a means to Zion. In demanding equal "rights and privileges," people in the Church may feel further justified and motivated to seek their own lives and live according to their own wills, behaving as through they fare in this world according to their own "strengths" and "management," believing they should individually "make use of that which is their own," possessing that which is above another, or esteeming themselves above others (see again Alma 30:17-18, 23-24, 27-28).

The Saints should not ignore the fact that the pursuit of equality in the carnal world, whether by men or women, typically means seeking equal access to a world deeply infected by inequalities of power, wealth, and status—a world deeply at odds with the ways of Zion. Unless a people undergo that mighty change of heart caused by spiritual birth, worldly inequalities will continue to infect them, including probably the inequalities that enable men to exercise dominion over women.

Needless to say, to pursue the equality of Zion itself by means of carnal precepts can only be self-defeating and set back the cause of Zion. Whenever there were some among the people of God in ancient America who lived by these precepts, they caused dissension and persecution, which hindered their progress as a people. To promote Zion and the equality it promises, a people must not be lifted up in the pride of their eyes, must not return railing for railing, and must not cause contention or persecute those who do not believe as they do. Rather they must humble themselves exceedingly before God, be submissive and gentle, be easy to be entreated, be full of patience and long-suffering, be diligent in keeping the commandments of God, always returning thanks unto Him for whatever blessing they receive, succoring those who stand in need of succoring, and living so the light of God's goodness can manifest itself through the work of the ministry. Only such can be a voice in bringing forth Zion. Let us stress that these virtues give that voice its authentic and effective expression; they should not be construed so as to silence that voice.

We would do well to recall here the "command" that was given to the people of the church during the reign of King Mosiah which concerned the equality that should exist among them—a command given incidentally at a time when the church was being "inflicted" with great "persecutions" by "unbelievers" (Mosiah 27:2): "And there was a strict command throughout all the churches that there should be no persecutions among them, that there should be an equality among all men; that they should let no pride nor haughtiness disturb their peace; that every man should esteem his neighbour as himself, laboring with their own hands for their support" (Mosiah 27:3-4).

Conclusion

What we set out to do was to search latter-day scripture for further understanding concerning the status and power of women, and therefore of men, in eternal life and among the people of God as they prepare for eternal life. Having the growing debate over so-called women's issues in mind, we wanted to offer scriptural answers to some of those issues to members of the Church who simply might have an interest in such matters; or who might be troubled by the questions being raised by that debate or by the variety of conflicting, largely secular voices that can be heard addressing those questions; or who might be suffering from the inequalities or abuses that infect the carnal world, of which we remain a part. Hopefully, what we have written will help further elevate the relations between men and women of the church and help move us along the path toward being a people of Zion.

We recognize that there are alternative viewpoints in the church on these matters, all of which claim scriptural support. We hope our thoughts on this subject may contribute to the work of reconciling these apparently divergent views. However, we reaffirm our thesis—that alternative visions inconsistent with the equality of men and women before God are inconsistent with the gospel of Jesus Christ.

The Saints have learned through the revelation giving the priesthood to worthy African-American members that the Church is not a whites-are-first church. We have learned through the exhilarating internationalization of the Church and its leadership that it is not an Americans-are-first church. These steps of loving change, guided by our leaders, have only increased our prospects of successfully building a Zion community. The next transformation preceding Zion may be to learn with our whole beings and to an extent we currently cannot conceive that the Church is not a males-are-first church.

If we are near that transformation, a period of great introspection and some pain and some change is before us. We should not shrink from it, but should rather embrace it as a refiner's fire. If we have faith in God and really want to be like Him, we must listen to the voices of the women. As with male voices, not all that is said or recommended by female voices will be right, but without hearing those voices, without speaking and listening in righteousness, there will be inadequate emotional impetus for the Saints to become Zion.

Why should women be hopeful or joyful? Why should women feel they are truly equal in God's eyes and His plan, when current practice and language can be interpreted by some as suggesting that they are not? Why should women look forward to heavenly life with great expectation? Why should women have faith that the things they now suffer as women will finally be overcome? Why should women be as happy to bring daughters into the world as sons? In a time when women appear to be coming into their own, unless questions such as these are answered in a gospel context many of our women may turn to the "world and the wisdom thereof" to learn what to think and to feel about who and what they are, can be, and should be.

If we have the fullness of the gospel, then we, as a people, have the means to obtain the fullness of the answers to such questions and to confound the hope-destroying wisdom of the world. Every man and woman in the Church should actively yearn for the greater light and knowledge God promises to all who seek for the same without doubting his goodness and fairness.

Notes

1   Of course, being a "free people" and enjoying fundamental "rights and privileges" are not in themselves carnal precepts. Indeed, such is "just and holy" and belongs to "all mankind" (see, for example, D&C 98:4-5; 101:76-80; 134; Mosiah 29:32, 38; Alma 30:11; 46:10). But the very same rights and freedoms that help make possible the works of God (see 3 Nephi 21:1, 4) can also be construed so that they hinder that work, as the history of the Nephite church shows. As defended by Korihor and others like him, rights and freedoms become carnal precepts that function as especially powerful obstacles to the establishment and preservation of Zion among a people.

2   "[In the *Book of Mormon*], the behavior and treatment of women were seen as an index of social and spiritual health" (Daniel H. Ludlow, ed. *The Encyclopedia of Mormonism*, ed., [New York: Macmillan Publishers, 1992], s.v. "Women in the Book of Mormon," by Donna Lee Bowen and Camille S. Williams).

3   See footnote 1 this chapter.

4   Righteous women of Zion can have a great impact on their families and on society in general. As President Spencer W. Kimball taught: "The righteous woman's strength and influence today can be tenfold what it might be in more tranquil times. She has been placed here to help to enrich, to protect, and to guard the home—which is society's basic and most noble institution. Other institutions in society may falter and even fail, but the righteous woman can help save the home, which may be the last and only sanctuary some mortals know in the midst of storm and strife" (*My Beloved Sisters* [Salt Lake City: Deseret Book, 1979], 17).

5   The leaders of the Church of Jesus Christ of Latter-day Saints have taught that women can and should do much to build up Zion: Joseph Smith, the first prophet of the Church, organized the women's organization known as Relief Society and told the sisters that their work was "not only to relieve the poor, but to save souls" (Joseph Smith, *Teachings of the Prophet Joseph Smith*, ed. Joseph Fielding Smith [Salt Lake City: Deseret Book Press] Section 5 1842-43, 242); the prophet Brigham Young taught that women should "develop the powers with which they are endowed," "that they should stand behind the counter, study law or physic, or become good bookkeepers and be able to do the business in any counting house, and all this to enlarge their sphere of usefulness for the benefit of society at large" (*Discourses of Brigham Young*, comp. John A. Widtsoe [Salt Lake City: Deseret Book], 216); modern Church authorities such as President Howard W. Hunter entreated women "to minister with your powerful influence for good in strengthening our families, our church, and our communities" ("Stand Firm in the Faith," *Ensign* 24 [November 1994]: 97);

President James E. Faust told the women of the Church that their work included "building faith by testimony and example," "teaching the doctrines of salvation," "following the Savior's example of love for all mankind," and "ministering to others" ("The Grand Key-Words For the Relief Society," *Ensign* 26 [November 1996]: 94-96); and President Gordon B. Hinckley singled out the women of the Church, telling them to "become anxiously engaged in other activities," to "reach out," and "to serve, to help," because the Lord had given them "capabilities to round out this great and marvelous organization, which is the Church and kingdom of God" ("Women of the Church," *Ensign* 26 [November 1996]: 67-70).

6   President Gordon B. Hinckley has emphasized the need to move beyond discussions of rights for women and focus more on women's, and men's, responsibilities to build up Zion: "Legislation should provide equality of opportunity, equality of compensation, equality of political privilege. But any legislation which is designed to create neuter gender of that which God created male and female will bring more problems than benefits. Of that I am convinced. I wish with all my heart we would spend less of our time talking about rights and more talking about responsibilities. God has given the women of this church a work to do in building his kingdom" (*Teachings of Gordon B. Hinckley* [Salt Lake City: Deseret Book, 1997], 690).

The Situation of Women in the Fallen World

by
Valerie Hudson Cassler

Here we aim to examine the situation of women in the fallen world today. Since approximately eighty percent of the women of the world live in what are termed "less developed countries" (LDCs), let us focus on the situation there.[1] In these traditional cultures, women are as much agents as they are victims of the traditions of their forefathers. We must acknowledge that women, in traditional cultures may wield great power, though only within the family context. Networks of women have provided support and shelter for women in their cultures.[2] Nevertheless, women's agency is confined to the sphere their culture allows, which sphere is dramatically smaller than the sphere of their brothers in the same culture.[3] Their agency is like that of the bonsai tree; it flourishes within the most confining circumstances. Let us examine some of the ways in which their agency is confined.

Women hold very little formal power in the world. Only a tiny percentage of the world's leaders, whether in business or in politics or in religion, are women.[4] Most of the women who do achieve such high positions do so as the surviving female relative of a powerful male leader.[5] Only about eleven percent of the world's legislators are women.[6] The low representation of women in politics is traced to traditions asserting that only males are truly citizens of the nation. "Women may create babies, but only men can create nations" is an aphorism reflecting this perspective. Thus it seemed unreasonable that women should have any say in the governance of the *polis* when they did not protect it through force of arms. It was not until this century that women's voting rights became common. Indeed, Switzerland did not extend the vote to women until 1971, again on the grounds that since women did not serve in the military, they were not fully citizens. This view of the noncitizenship of women is reflected in laws that plague women's lives to this day. For example, in many parts of the world if a woman marries a foreigner, she loses her citizenship rights; her citizenship rights are contingent upon those of the man who is her guardian. Likewise, in most legal systems a woman holds the status of a minor.[7]

Women are not full members of the group, and yet because the group can only be perpetuated if women bear new members for the group's men, women are often viewed as *fitna*, an Arabic term connoting a dangerous source of chaos and decay that must be strictly controlled. Since women bear the young and are the main socializers of the young, women must be controlled, and so they must be placed in a subordinate position to the real members of the group (the men). A woman's behavior has to be scrupulous; if not, her guardian males are shamed and perhaps punished by the group. This need for control of women has led to a variety of customs that limit the options available to women and thus limit the degree to which women can be "dangerous." Sometimes these customs dictate dress and in some cultures, women must be covered literally from head to foot. In many customs, women have no say in who their spouse is to be. In some countries women are married as children, many times purposefully before the onset of menarche.[8] *Purdah*, which is a custom not confined to India, dictates that a woman may not leave the confines of her household for any reason.[9] In several cultures, widows (who are plentiful because of their youth at marriage) cannot remarry, for they become wards of the dead men's family. "Loose" women, whether or not they have actually had sexual relations with anyone, are killed by family members in many traditional societies.[10] In some cultures, girl brides who are declared not to be virgins because their marriage night did not bring the obligatory blood-stained sheet, are killed (this despite the fact that gynecologists tell us that for purely physiological reasons about thirty percent of women will not bleed upon first intercourse).[11] Women with deviant ideas are often killed, as well, many times on the grounds of "witchcraft."[12] Short of murder, probably the most extreme form of control can be seen in infibulation, a form of what is euphemistically termed female circumcision. In addition to cutting off the clitoris and the inner labia of the vulva, a woman's outer labia are then cut and sewn together, leaving a hole the size of a Q-tip through which to pass urine and menstrual flow. A low-tech form of chastity belt, infibulation ensures that a woman will not have unauthorized sexual intercourse and that she will feel no sexual desire that would render her *fitna*.[13]

Because a woman functions as the symbol of man's honor and control, rape in traditional societies is a particularly heinous crime. In addition to all the suffering that naturally comes from rape, a woman must also worry if she will be literally cast out from her family, whether she will be imprisoned, or whether she will be killed by her own family or even the state.[14] Why? Because the rape has sullied the honor of the man and shown he was not in control of his woman. Rather than suffer such shame, the woman is made to bear the guilt of the crime. Thus rape is accepted grounds for divorce in most traditional societies. Of course a girl who has been raped has no hope of marriage in such cultures. In Pakistan, Islamic law at one time was interpreted to mean that women who cannot identify their rapists are automatically guilty of adultery or fornication. Adultery is punishable by execution, fornication by flogging.[15] In northern Nigeria in 2002, a mother of three awaited execution by stoning because she was raped. She was able to identify her attacker, however, since there were no witnesses, the man was acquitted. She became pregnant because of the rape and the very fact of her pregnancy meant she could be convicted of adultery.[16]

Control may also involve physical coercion by male guardians. In some societies it is a civic duty to publicly beat one's wife at least once a week to show that the men of the society are still in control of the women. Battery and assault of wives by husbands is considered a normal part of married life in many cultures.[17] Indeed, among the Aborigines of Australia, battering is a woman's proof that her husband loves her.[18] The right to batter often derives from the brideprice a groom may have paid for his wife.[19] She is literally his possession and the law cannot come between a man and his possession. In "crimes of passion," such as when a woman is killed by a jealous husband, the perpetrators are almost never prosecuted in many areas of the world. Lest we think all is well outside of the LDCs, domestic violence is the leading cause of physical injury to U.S. women ages fifteen to forty-four, surpassing even auto accidents, rapes, and muggings combined.[20]

The need for women to be subordinate to men, the need for men to control women's lives, starts the deep alienation between men and women. That great division begins to ripen beyond the more visible forms of control enumerated above the other, equally controlling customs that are less well seen. Women begin to be viewed as natural resources that can become commodities. This can be seen in various phrases and proverbs from around the world: woman is "the ground," "the soil"; "the poorest man is he who does not have a wife to work for him and make his children." Treatment of women begins to resemble the treatment one would accord, for example, one's livestock. If women are on a par with livestock, then they can be culled. The horrifying practice of female infanticide does just that. The United Nations reports a list of over a dozen countries where the female/male sex ratio is less than 95/100.[21] The practice of pouring boiling water or poisonous berries down a newborn baby daughter's throat and burying her in the field is being replaced by more high-tech methods: the ultrasound machine and the abortionist's tools. Over a six-month period in 1992 in just one clinic in Bombay, India, 8,000 abortions were performed—7,999 of the aborted fetuses were female.[22] In a report by the Indian government on the status of women in 1992, its Department of Women and Child Development concedes, "In a culture that idolizes sons and dreads the birth of a daughter, to be born female comes perilously close to being born less than human."[23]

If a woman is less than human, then other practices become understandable. Women eat less and eat last in many traditional cultures, even when they are pregnant.[24] Over two-thirds of the most severely malnourished children are daughters.[25] Of those daughters who survive the newborn period in India, a quarter will die before their 15th birthday simply because attention to their health is less important than attention to the health of sons. The comparable mortality rate for Indian sons is six percent.[26] In one study in India, if immunizations were given free, boys and girls were immunized in approximately equal proportions. If the slightest fee were charged for those immunizations, the number of girls brought in for vaccination would plummet.[27] If precious money is to be spent, it must be spent on those who have the greatest value, and that simply is not one's daughters. Though women on average around the world have a slightly higher life expectancy than men,[28] increased mortality in youth plus the rigors of childbearing while still a child oneself are a chief contributing factor to untimely death.

Women are also less likely to be literate. Slightly less than two-thirds of the world's illiterate are women.[29] Not only can education of daughters be seen as a waste of money because of patrilocality (see below), but education may once again shake the degree of control a woman's male guardians may have over her.

With woman occupying a lower status in the human hierarchy, marriage becomes more of a commodity exchange between two men (the husband and the bridegroom) than a union of hearts and minds. Marriage is perverted to mean how men trade women and their labor and reproductive power. This view of marriage has its epitome in China, where the selling of women as "wives" has reached a new high. Women are kidnapped or sold by their families and bought by men for an average of \$250 to \$500.[30] However, even "normal" marriage arrangements in LDCs can be an occasion for sorrow. Aside from having no choice over her husband, the prevalent custom of patrilocality undermines the woman's position to an astonishing degree. Patrilocality means that when a woman marries, she goes to live with her husband's family, often far away from the home of her birth. Within the new household, she of course occupies the very lowest rung on the status ladder. She is seen by her husband's family as a burden and as a source of dangerous new practices and beliefs. She is often given the greatest amount of work to do in the household, yet she invariably has the least rights and privileges.

If this new bride lives in a culture where her own family has paid her husband's family a dowry to offset the burden she is to them, she may be beaten, otherwise maltreated, or even killed if the two families quarrel over the dowry.[31] Patrilocality has an even more insidious face within her own family. Because she will become the member of another household within about thirteen to fifteen years, her birth family views her care as "watering a plant in another man's garden." A daughter is not really a family member, explained one mother in Ethiopia—she is but a guest. All the natural ties of affection and love that should flow from parent to daughter are undermined, and ultimately the girl has no refuge. She is a transient in her birth family and she is a dangerous burden in her new family.

Because a woman is more of a commodity than a full human being, several prevalent customs insure her familial rights are less than those of males. For example, in most traditional societies it is almost impossible for a woman to divorce her husband. Yet in these same societies, divorce of a wife may be as simple as a husband saying to her three times, "I divorce you." Likewise, the children of their union belong to the husband. If the wife leaves or is divorced, she is forced to leave her children behind. Fidelity in marriage is a one way street in most cultures; a wife may be killed if she is unfaithful, but a man is actually encouraged to be unfaithful to his wife as a positive means of demonstrating his manhood. In polygamous cultures, wives live in perpetual fear lest their husbands be displeased with them and take another wife. Last, rights of inheritance for females are profoundly circumscribed. Usually when a man dies, his property (including his house and all his household goods) goes to his nearest paternal kin, usually a brother. The widow then becomes a ward of the brother and must live off the charity of that man. In most traditional cultures a woman may not inherit land at all. This inability to support oneself leads to female dependence on males for the key resource with which to sustain life: land.[32]

Management of women as a commodity of men can take an even more debased turn, by which the management of women is but a necessity to the treatment of sex as a commodity. Sex tourism is becoming widespread in Asia, attracting male "tourists" from Asia, the Middle East, and Europe. Girls are duped, kidnapped, or sold into the fleshpots of Bangkok, Tokyo, and other cities, where they are forced into prostitution, sometimes chained to their beds.[33] Many governments are actively involved in promoting sex tourism because the government receives a "tax," or a "cut," on all these activities. The most sickening turn in the sex tourism trade has been sparked by the AIDS epidemic, where rich customers can afford sex services by "bodies" that are certifiably free of the virus. This is done by procuring virgins as young as six or seven years of age for the very rich to deflower.[34] Pedophile tours, needless to say, are a growing business.

Women have also been prostituted in other ways: as mail order "brides" and as "comfort women" for various militaries. The U.S. government even ran clinics for Filipino prostitutes where they were required to get a card proving they were free of VD. The military ordered its soldiers to demand to see the card before having sex with prostitutes. Of course, U.S. soldiers did not need to show such a card when buying the services of the women.[35]

Though sex is a prized commodity, women's bodies in most cultures are viewed in very negative terms. The very reproductive system that has given life to every person on the planet is viewed as "unclean," "defiling," "unholy," and "contaminating." Menstruating women must be segregated from others in many traditional societies, where they are not allowed to touch anyone, not even their own children. Food is left for them by the door. The afterbirth and placenta are also viewed as disgusting and sickening. In some parts of the world, women give birth in the barn so as not to defile the household.[36] The perceived subordination of women to their bodily rhythms has given support to beliefs that women are not rational, are incapable of higher thought, and are rightfully subject those who are not ruled by their bodies (i.e., men).[37] "The height of a woman's thoughts are the height of a kitchen spoon," according to one African proverb.

The irony of the debased status of women is that when we make women "visible," life on the earth would be unlivable without women. Obviously, life would cease to exist without a woman reproducing the species. Yet women's reproductive labor is not confined to childbearing; women are the habitat makers of the world. Women in all cultures are given the responsibility to make a habitat suitable for human existence. They gather wood, tote water, cook, clean, and take care of children. They work significantly more hours in the day than men simply because they must maintain everyone's life.[38] Women also feed the world. For instance, in Sub-Saharan Africa women produce eighty percent of the food, and worldwide they produce fifty percent.[39]

Women in traditional societies are paid less than men for equivalent work on the rationale that men have to support their families, whereas women do not. But in a world where at least one-third of all households are headed by women, and in a world where ninety-five percent of a woman's earnings go to her household but only sixty percent of a man's earnings go to the household, [40] that rationale has less and less support. It is women's unpaid labor in the home and women's lesser earnings outside the home that make economies tick. If women were paid equally with men and if women were paid for their unpaid labor, it is estimated that eleven trillion dollars would be needed annually to cover the bill.[41]

Even in Utah, though the situation of women is far, far better than the situation of most women in the world, we can still identify a few areas of deep concern to those who value women. In Utah, approximately 41 percent of all murders in the year 2001 were caused by domestic violence.[42] Though Utah's murder, robbery, aggravated assault, and burglary rates are lower than the national average, Utah's rape rate is significantly higher than the national average, ranking 13th in the nation.[43] The percentage of mothers receiving late or no prenatal care in Utah was also significantly higher than the national average in 1999.[44]

How did the fallen world come to such an awful asymmetry between the power and status of the daughters of God and the power and status of the sons of God? The life creators, the life sustainers, are at the bottom of the hierarchy of the fallen world. Their lives are hemmed and controlled in a manner that cannot be pleasing to their Father. They are denied their full agency in a systematic way because of their gender. When Mother Earth groans because of the wickedness of man, is not a large part of her sorrow on behalf of the human mothers, who are on the receiving end of much of that wickedness?

Notes

1   All of the statistics in this section are from *The World's Women 1995* (New York: United Nations, 1995), or *The World's Women 2000* (New York: United Nations, 2000), unless otherwise noted.

2   See, for example, Clarice Auluck-Wilson, "When All the Women Lift," *Signs: Journal of Women in Culture and Society, 20,* no. 4 (Summer 1995): 1029-1038, for a stirring example of Third World women uniting to promote positive change for themselves and their sisters.

3   As an introduction to the complex web of inequalities most women in less developed countries face, we recommend to our readers two eloquent and heart-wrenching books of personal stories: *Fatima Mernissi, Doing Daily Battle: Interviews with Moroccan Women* (New Brunswick, NJ: Rutgers University Press, 1989); and Jean P. Sasson, Princess (New York: Avon Books, 1992). There are many other such books, as well, but space does not permit us to mention them all.

4   Less than ten women head their nation's government (out of a total of over almost 190 nations), and in the world of business, women hold less than two percent of senior management positions worldwide (*The World's Women 2000* [New York: United Nations, 2000], 168).

5   Such as Corazon Aquino, Indira Gandhi, Benazir Bhutto, and others.

6   The figures are lower for Asia and Oceania. In Oceania, only about three percent of the legislators are women (*The World's Women 2000*[New York: United Nations, 2000], 164).

7   An excellent overview of the legal status of women can be found in Katarina Tomasevski's *Women and Human Rights* (London: Zed Books, 1993).

8   See, for example, "Om Gad," Chapter One in *Nayra Atiya, Khul Khaal: Five Egyptian Women Tell Their Stories* (Syracuse: Syracuse University Press, 1982).

9   See Patricia Jeffrey, Frogs *In a Well: Indian Women in Purdah* (London: Zed Books, 1991).

10 Kanan Makiya, "State Rape: Violation of Iraqi Women," *New Statesman and Society* 6, no. 251 (7 May 1993): 16-17.

11 "Turkey: Forced and Fatal Virginity Testing," Ms 3, no. 1: 12.

12 Eschel M. Rhoodie, "The Status of Women: A Global View," in *Discrimination Against Women: A Global Survey of the Economic, Educational, Social, and Political Status of Women* (Jefferson, NC: McFarland and Co. Publishers, 1989).

13 Patricia Smyke, *Women and Health* (London: Zed Books, 1993), 73f.

14 Elaine Lutz, "When the Women Cry, Who Will Listen?" *The International Relations Journal XIV*, no. 2 (Spring 1993).

15 Eschel M. Rhoodie, "The Status of Women: A Global View," in *Discrimination Against Women: A Global Survey of the Economic, Educational, Social, and Political Status of Women* (Jefferson, NC: McFarland and Co. Publishers, 1989).

16 See Dowden, Richard, "Death by Stoning," *New York Times Magazine*, January 27, 2002, pp. 28-31.

17 See, for example, James Brooke, "Brazil Tries to Curb Crimes Against Women," *New York Times*, 17 November 1991.

18 Gay Alcron, "The Agony Within," *The Australian,* 15 March 1993.

19 See, for example, Rebecca Morley, "Wife Beating and Modernization: The Case of Papua New Guinea," *Journal of*

Comparative Family Studies 25, no. 1 (1994): 25-52, for an interesting treatment of how such a practice has evolved in the wake of modernization.

20 Statistics from *The Daily Universe*, 18 October 1995.

21 Most of these countries are in Asia and Oceania (*The World's Women 2000*[New York: United Nations, 2000], 19-20).

22 World Health Organization, *Women's Health: Across Age and Frontier* (Geneva: WHO Publications, 1992).

23 John Wood Anderson and Molly Moore, "Third World Women: A Lifetime of Oppression," *The International Herald Tribune*, 15 February 1993.

24 See Patricia Smyke, *Women and Health* (London: Zed Books, 1993).

25 *Gender and Poverty in India: A World Bank Country Study* (Washington, D.C.: The World Bank, 1991). The following story demonstrates this custom is not limited to India: " . . . I flew to Kapoeta in southern Sudan. The region was in the midst of famine; 250,000 people had already starved to death. As is common in Africa, when we landed on the dusty runway families came from miles around to see who had arrived. They knew we were from an aid organization, so mothers held up their emaciated children to show us how much they needed our help. It didn't take me long to notice the children's distended stomachs—a sure sign of malnutrition. But it was several minutes before I realized that in this sea of humanity, the mothers were only holding up sons; there were no daughters. In the familial hierarchy, girls were the last to be fed and the first to die. By the time we arrived, they were dead." (In "Female He Created Them," *World Vision Today*, Spring 1998, p. 2.)

26 "25% of Girls Die in India by Age 15, UNICEF Says," *New York Times*, 5 October 1990.

27 *Gender and Poverty in India: A World Bank Country Study* (Washington, D.C.: The World Bank, 1991).

28 Almost 600,000 women die each year in childbirth. In much of sub-Saharan Africa, a woman's life expectancy is forty-five to fifty years of age (*The World's Women 2000* [New York: United Nations, 2000], 60, 55).

29 *The World's Women 2000* (New York: United Nations, 2000), 87ff.

30 Seth Faison, "Women as Chattel: In China, Slavery Rises," *New York Times*, 6 September 1995.

31 Linda Stone and Caroline James, "Dowry, Bride Burning, and Female Power in India," *Women's Studies International Forum* 18, no. 2 (March-April, 1995): 125-134.

32 For exposition of these and many other examples, see Katarina Tomasevski, *Women and Human Rights* (London: Zed Books, 1993).

33 See Douglas Hodgson, "Sex Tourism and Child Prostitution in Asia: Legal Responses and Strategies," *Melbourne University Law Review* 19 (June 1994): 512-544.

34 M. Simons, "Child Prostitution Spreads, Partly Because of AIDS Fears," *The International Herald Tribune,* 10-11 April 1993.

35 See Farah Godrej, "Women and Post Cold War US Foreign Policy: Filipina Prostitutes as Participants in the Cold War," paper presented at the International Studies Association conference, Chicago, IL, 21-25 February 1995.

36 Maureen Minden, "Miss, We Cannot Read or Write," *World Health* (September-October, 1992): 10-11.

37 See Katarina Tomasevski, *Women and Human Rights* (London: Zed Books, 1994).

38 See Elder Alexander B. Morrison, "Let Your Light So Shine," presentation at Women's Conference, Provo, Utah, April 1993.

39 Annabel Rodda, *Women and the Environment* (London: Zed Books, 1993).

40 Gender and Poverty in India (Washington, D.C.: World Bank, 1991).

41 Figures from a 1995 report by UNIFEM, as reported in *USA Today,* 31 July 1995.

42 Pat Reavy, "Deadly year," *Deseret News,* 1 January 2002, http://deseretnews.com/dn/print/1,442,355016239,00.html?

43 World Almanac 2001, Mahwah, New Jersey: *World Almanac Books,* p. 889.

44 James Thalman, "Utah last in percentage of babies born to unwed," *Deseret News,* 6 February 2002.

The Teachings of Paul and Gender Equality

by
Alma Don Sorensen

Some who believe woman should be ruled over by man cite the teachings of Paul to justify their beliefs. He did write that wives should be "subject unto" their husbands "in every thing" (Ephesians 5:24). His teachings on men and women seem to bolster the view that when God told Eve that Adam should rule over her, he intended a wife to subject herself to her husband in all things, giving him the final say in their life together and in effect making her his subordinate and inferior. But we think a careful reading of Paul's words shows that his teachings about the eternal destiny of man and woman and how they prepare for it are, in their fundamentals, much the same as the teachings from other latter-day scriptures.

Let us consider what principles Paul actually did teach about relations between men and women. First, he tells us that persons faithful to Christ in this life can become "joint heirs" with him in eternal life and receive "all things" from the Father (Romans 8:16-17). Further, he taught that "neither is the man without the woman, neither is the woman without the man, in the Lord" (1 Corinthians 11:11). When joined together, these two teachings seem to say that the woman and man joined together become joint heirs with Christ in eternity—that the one cannot be a joint heir without the other. Also, according to Paul, joint heirs possess all the Father hath, or "all things," as their inheritance (1 Corinthians 3:21-23). Just as Christ himself has been "appointed heir of all things" by God (Hebrews 1:2), so God blesses those perfected through Christ with "all things" (Romans 8:32-33; 1 Corinthians 3:21-23). To possess all things as joint heirs indicates that perfected persons possess them as equals. The teaching seems to be that each and every exalted person, whether man or woman, receives all things as a joint heir; one does not possess that which is above another. In the language of Zion, they have all things common as equals.

To say that exalted persons possess all things implies that all things are subject unto them. As Luke, Paul's friend and fellow traveller (Acts 16:10; 2 Timothy 4:11), tells us, the exalted person is made "ruler over all [Christ] hath" (Luke 12:44; see D&C 50:27; 52:13). The idea that the exalted woman and man are rulers over all things as joint heirs and hence as equals suggests that in eternity they are as gods and have power over all things as equals as the Lord revealed to the Prophet Joseph (see Chapters 2 and 3). It seems reasonable to think that Paul, like Luke, understood that among eternal beings there is equality of power as well as possession and that the one involves the other. Certainly he taught that Christ himself is made "equal with God" (Philippians 2:6,9) as well as that perfected persons are "heir[s] of God through Christ" with whom they are "joint heirs" (Galatians 4:7; Romans 8:16-17, 32; Ephesians 3:19, 4:13).

Paul thought that the highest purpose of God in mortal life is to prepare and qualify persons for eternal life through the word in Christ (1 Timothy 6:12; Romans 2:6-7; 5:21). Since the exalted woman and man possess and rule over all things as joint heirs with Christ, the purpose of mortal existence includes making mortal men and women capable and eligible for those great blessings (Ephesians 4:12-13). Basically, what this means is that they must learn to live together here equal in the bonds of love much as heavenly persons do. According to Paul, persons prepare and qualify to be joint heirs with Christ in eternity through "faith" in Him and by loving others as He "hath loved us" (Ephesians 3:17-19; 5:2). The love of Christ comprehends all good in relations between persons (Galatians 5:13-14), and the faith in Him that justifies and sanctifies expresses itself in a life of love (Galatians 5:6; Ephesians 3:17; Romans 5).

When persons in this world join together in a single community through their faith in Christ and love as He loves, they live together as "one" (Philippians 1:27; 2:2; Galatians 3:28). Presumably, becoming one in Christ in this life schools a people and helps makes them eligible to be joint heirs with Him in the next life. Among a people of God who live as one, the woman is not inferior to the man nor the man to the woman. Paul indicates this by saying that among those who "put on Christ," there is, for example, "neither male nor female: for ye are all one in Christ Jesus" (Galatians 3:27-28). Paul does not mean that male and female have no place in our fellowship with Christ, for as we know, he taught that woman and man are not without each other in Christ (1 Corinthians 11:11). Also, he is not saying that the chances of persons to come unto Christ do not vary according to whether they are female or male, although that is true and Paul taught it (Romans 2:11, 10:12-13). Rather, his teaching is that when persons have "put on Christ" and become "one" in Him, one person's "stature" in that "unity" is not less than another's because one is male and the other is female. Both can receive equally of His "fullness" (Galatians 3:27-28; Ephesians 4:12-13). The "fullness of Christ" includes possessing "all things" as "joint heirs" with Him (Romans 8:17, 32).

We know that, according to Paul's friend and fellow traveler Luke (Acts 20:6; 2 Timothy 4:11), among the early saints being one meant having "all things common" (Acts 2:44; 4:32), just as in eternity perfected beings possess all things as joint heirs and share power over those things (Luke 12:44). Knowing this, Paul exhorted the Corinthian saints to impart of their substance to the poor, a requirement of the law of consecration, so "that there may be equality" among them (2 Corinthians 8:10-14), presumably in preparation for eternal life (Romans 8:17, 32).

According to Paul, husbands and wives in particular should live together as one in Christ. The woman and the man are not without each other "in the Lord," both on earth and in heaven (1 Corinthians 11:11), and so "a man" should "leave his father and mother" and "be joined unto his wife" as if "one flesh" (Ephesians 5:28, 31). Of course, this same is true of the woman: she should leave her parents and become united to her husband as one. Like all oneness in Christ, the oneness between wife and husband is grounded in the love of Christ and requires them to live together as equals, there being "neither male nor female" in their oneness (Galatians 3:28-29). Paul seems particularly concerned that men understand the equal esteem husbands and wives should have for each other, for he singles men out by admonishing every husband to be "one" with his wife and hence "lov[ing] his wife as himself" or as Christ loves her—to love her as his equal in Christ (Ephesians 5:28, 33; 3:17-19).

The scriptural context is now in place to interpret Paul's view that women should "submit" to their husbands in "every thing" (Ephesians 5:24). Clearly, he cannot mean literally *every thing*, for there are understood bounds and limits set by their oneness in Christ. Inasmuch as women and men in general and husbands and wives in particular have equal standing in the bonds of love when they are one in Christ, apparently wives should submit to their husbands in every thing within that relationship of equality. Let us see what Paul has to teach us about wives submitting to their husbands when they live as one in Christ.

Paul tells us that the "husband is the head of the wife as Christ is head of the church," and "as the church is subject unto Christ, so let wives be to their husbands" (Ephesians 5:23-24). How should husbands be heads of their wives as Christ is head of the church? Paul says Christ "loved the church" and "took upon himself the form of servant," ultimately by dying on the cross, so that "he might sanctify and cleanse it" by "the word" (Ephesians 5:25-26; Philippians 2:7). It is through the purifying power of the word that the church realizes its primary reason for being, which is "the perfecting of the saints" until they "all come into the unity of the faith," or oneness in Christ, and partake of "the fullness of Christ" (Ephesians 4:11-13). As we learned earlier, when members of the Church become one in Christ and enjoy His fullness they possess and rule over all things as joint heirs with Him (Romans 8:17, 32-33; 1 Corinthians 3:21-23; see D&C 50:27-28; 76:54-55, 94-95; 84:38; 88:107). Presumably this is true of how Church members should live together in this life when they become one as well as how exalted beings live together in eternity as one (Galatians 3:27-29; Romans 8:17, 32; Acts 2:44; 4:32).

Husbands should follow Christ's example in their relationship with their wives. They should, Paul says, "love [their] wives, even as Christ also loved the church, and gave himself for it, so that all might be sanctified and cleansed" (Ephesians 5:2, 25-26). They too should act as their wives' servants in presiding over the Word so that they and their wives might be cleansed and sanctified by it. As servants, husbands should give themselves to their wives as Christ gave himself to the Church, being willing to sacrifice their personal desires and perhaps all they have for the sake of their wives. The foremost purpose in all that husbands do in presiding over the Word in their homes should be to help prepare and qualify themselves and their wives to become one in Christ, possessing and ruling over all things as joint heirs with him. Husbands cannot do this by ruling over their wives, thereby treating them as subordinates or inferiors. That would be inconsistent with the Word over which they preside which requires that they be one and hence live in Christ's love as equals (Galatians 3:28-29). The Word should be administered only in ways consistent with itself. We are reminded of Christ's words to his apostles about how they should preside over the work of the ministry. He said to them that "whosoever will be chief among you, let him be your servant: Even as the Son of Man came not to be ministered unto, but to minister, and to give his life a ransom for many" (Matthew 20:27-28). To paraphrase Paul, the husband should be the servant of the wife, even as Christ is the servant of the church, and gave himself for it (Ephesians 5:22-25). In Christ, husbands can never be justified in "exercising

288 — Women in Eternity, Women of Zion

dominion" or "exercising authority" over their wives like many men in the carnal world do (Matthew 20:25-26).

We should take notice that the power of the Word to sanctify and purify cannot be separated from the love of God and Christ, from whom we receive the word. Love comprehends all that is good and right found in the word (Romans 13:8, 10), and the Word can transform the heart only as an expression of that love (Romans 5:5; Ephesians 3:17, 19). To purify and sanctify, the message of love requires a messenger of love, so if the man is to be the "head" of the wife as one who presides over the Word, then he must serve her, having Christ's love for her (Ephesians 5:2, 25). And if the woman is to be purified by yielding to the Word over which her husband presides, then she must recognize and embrace it as a manifestation of Christ's love for her.

We can find no better description of how true love conducts itself as the messenger of the Word when a wife and husband strive to be one or have become one in Christ than an oft-quoted passage found in Paul. True love seeks not its own; it suffers long and is kind; it does not vaunt itself and is not puffed up; it is not easily provoked; it thinks no evil and rejoices not in iniquity; it is not envious and does not behave unseemly; it never fails you (1 Corinthians 13). This indicates that (among other things) true love between husband and wife is not controlling; it does not manipulate; it does not feign or deceive; it does not force or coerce. When a wife and husband live as one in Christ, their love for one another leaves no room or need for a hierarchy in which the woman is subservient to the power of the man.

We are persuaded, then, that what Paul means when he instructs wives to "submit" to their husbands "in every thing" (Ephesians 5:24) is that wives should submit to all things required by the Word presided over by their husbands, acting as helpmeets to their wives within a relationship of oneness or equality in Christ. The Word contains all that is good and the love that comprehends it, and so in submitting to all things the wife submits to the things of love or all things that are good

(Ephesians 4:12-13; Romans 12:9; Philippians 4:8; Hebrews 13:21). She does not submit to her husband himself as one authorized to exercise dominion over her as his subordinate or inferior.

This may be put differently by saying that through Christ and the Word in Him, persons "die to sin" and become "alive to God" (Romans 6:11 (1-23)). When the Word transforms the wife, she becomes alive to God, and her aliveness to Him is as immediate and direct as her husband's aliveness to Him. Her aliveness to God does not include a relationship of dominion in which her husband stands as a mediator between herself and God and rules over her in that position. There is only "one mediator" between any person and God, and that is Christ (1 Timothy 2:5). In Christ the husband and wife are "one" and equal and joint "heirs" (Galatians 3:28-29; Romans 8:17, 32-33).

Of course, in presiding over the Word the man, too, must submit to the sanctifying and purifying power of the Word found in Christ, and therefore his submission is not less nor of a different kind than his wife's submission. In addition to submitting to the word of God, God does not require the woman to also submit to her husband as his servitor—fetching his slippers, filling his pipe, retrieving the remote at his command. In the end, the submission of husband and wife joined together as one in Christ is a mutual submission, a shared experience of yielding together to the purifying and sanctifying power of the word in Christ. To use Paul's words, they "walk" together in "love" and "in the newness of life" because of the Word in their lives and their mutual submission to it (Romans 6:4; Ephesians 4:2-3; 5:28, 33). Indeed, unless their "walk" together brings them "newness of life," something remains amiss in their "love" for one another or in their submitting themselves to the word. For "the word," when planted in their hearts and nourished by love, always "enlarges the soul" and "expands the mind" with its "fullness." It is the "tree of life" growing up in them (see Alma 32:28-42; Galatians 6:7-10; Ephesians 3:19; 4:13). Paul's vision contrasts with that of the carnal world, where men typically rule and women are subservient to them. In the carnal world, the message of love contained in the Word lacks a messenger of love in the man as one called to preside over the Word as the woman's helpmeet and equal.

We should observe that Paul's views of the relationship between wife and husband found in scripture as we now have it is not as complete and does not have the same level of detail found in other teachings of Latter-day Saint scriptures.[1] For example, he does not bring out in the same detail how exalted women and men live as gods, having all power as equals, nor how purified men and women live by celestial law as equals in power on earth in preparation for eternal life. This lack of detail may invite misinterpretation. Nevertheless, in light of other revealed scripture, though incomplete, what Paul does teach seems fundamentally consistent with this larger and deeper view.

Notes

1   Let us briefly consider here those passages in Paul where he writes that "it is a shame for women to speak in the Church"; that they should be "submissive" and "keep silent in the churches"—and that "if they will learn any thing, let them ask their husbands at home" (1 Corinthians 14:34-35). On their face, these verses are inconsistent with our interpretation of Paul just given and apparently with what Paul says in still other places as well about speaking in church (see, for example, 1 Corinthians 11:5, 13; Galatians 3:27-28). Gordon D. Fee reviews the current postulations that this is a non-Pauline interpolation by approaching it from three arguments: 1) that the material is inconsistent with the other views of Paul on women (see Philippians 4:3, 1 Corinthians 11:5, Gal 3:28); 2) these two verses appear after verse 40 (the end of the chapter) in many of the early Greek manuscripts (the fact that they are found in two different locations does not make it central to the development of the argument being addressed in 1 Corinthians 14); 3) the issue concerning women does not fit in the context of the argument here—it reads better without the women material. (See Gordon D. Fee, *1st Epistle to the Corinthians*, Grand Rapids, MI: Eerdmans, 1987). In the JST of 1 Corinthians 14:34, the verse says women are not to be permitted to "rule," rather than "speak," in the churches, suggesting perhaps that men and not women should preside over church meetings.

The claim of no more male or female found in Gal 3:28 is viewed by F. F. Bruce as meaning that it is "not their distinctiveness but their inequality of religious role that is abolished in Christ Jesus" (Epistle of Paul to the Galatians, [Paternoster Press, 1982, 1982]). This can be seen in Paul's allowing women to labor side by side with him in the ministry (Philippians 4:3) and his recognition of women's right to pray and prophesy in church—with the veil covering being the symbol of their authority to do so (the Greek *exousia* means authority and is used in relation to women wearing the veil in 1 Corinthians 11:5). Fee states that the material found in 1 Corinthians 11 concerning the veiling of women is really dealing with women who are trying to disregard the male/female relationships by breaking down the distinctions. The statement that a women who prophesies with uncovered head brings shame on herself may actually refer to the tradition that *uncovered* can better be translated *loosed hair*, which was associated with a shamed adulteress (Fee, 1st Corinthians, 508).

Another issue concerning Paul's understanding of women's role in the early church infrastructure can be seen in Romans 16, where Paul recommends that the saints in Ephesus assist Phoebe in her ministry. She apparently held office in the congregation at Cenchreae and Paul was requesting that her position of authority be recognized even outside of her own unit.

Lastly, 1 Corinthians 7 shows the chain of command, an administrative flow chart of the kingdom of God on the earth, not a paradigm of domination. In response to the Ephesians relationship between men and women, the analogy states that a man cannot violate his gospel covenant with Christ just as he cannot his marriage covenant with his wife. The Greek term translated in Ephesians 5:24 as "subject" comes from the Greek word *hypotasso*, which can mean to be arranged, to post or place (Liddell and Scott, *An Intermediate Greek-English Lexicon* taken from the seventh edition of Liddell and Scott's Greek English Lexicon, [Oxford: Oxford University Press, 1975], pg 848). Whatever Paul thought about women participating in church meetings, we stand by our claim that God made known to him the basic teachings concerning the equality of women and men found in other Latter-day Saint scripture.

Mary, Mother of Jesus

by
Valerie Hudson Cassler

It is Church doctrine that Jesus Christ was born to a virgin mother named Mary. We also believe that God works by natural laws. Since we further believe that Heavenly Father has a body of flesh and bone, some have put two and two together and come to the conclusion that God had sexual intercourse with Mary. Going even further, since extra-marital intercourse is against God's laws, it is then inferred that God married Mary, and then lent her to Joseph to be his wife for mortality. A third wave of inference then leads such authors to the conclusion that Heavenly Father practices polygamy. (For an example of this genre, see Bruce E. Dana, *Mary, Mother of Jesus*, Springville, UT: Cedar Fort, 2001).

However, we are told plainly by President Harold B. Lee that we are not to speculate on the manner of Christ's birth:

> *We are very much concerned that some of our Church teachers seem to be obsessed of the idea of teaching doctrine which cannot be substantiated and making comments beyond what the Lord has actually said. You asked about . . . the birth of the Savior. Never have I talked about sexual intercourse between Deity and the mother of the Savior. If teachers were wise in speaking of this matter about which the Lord has said but very little, they would rest their discussion on this subject with merely the words which are recorded on this subject in Luke 1:34-35: "Then said Mary unto the angel, How shall this be, seeing I know not a man? And the angel answered and said unto her, The Holy*

*Ghost shall come upon thee, and the power of the
Highest shall overshadow thee: therefore also that
holy things which shall be born of thee shall be called
the Son of God." Remember that the being who was
brought about by [Mary's] conception was a divine
personage. We need not question His methods to
accomplish His purposes. Perhaps we would do well to
remember the words of Isaiah 55:8-9: "For my
thoughts are not your thoughts, neither are your ways
my ways, saith the Lord. For as the heavens are higher
than the earth, so are my ways higher than your ways,
and my thoughts than your thoughts." Let the Lord
rest His case with this declaration and wait until He
sees fit to tell us more.*[1]

Let us take what we know to be fact, and then see if those
facts necessarily lead us to the same conclusions as authors like
Dana. Mary, a virgin, gave birth to Christ: fact. God works by
natural laws: fact. God has a body of flesh and bones: fact.
Jesus Christ was the Only Begotten of the Father in the flesh:
fact. Starting from these four facts, what do we know?

Is is fair to infer the conception of Jesus took place by using
natural laws. On that point, I think everyone would agree. But
from that point, we need not be locked into the scenario offered
by Dana and others. Though early prophets could not envision
any other form of conception other than sexual intercourse,
since the 1970s we have known that virgin conception is
entirely possible without sexual intercourse. Furthermore, a
virgin who conceives by use of these natural laws also gives
birth as a virgin. We can now envision God using natural laws
to bring about the conception of Jesus while maintaining the
virginity of Mary. In this scenario, it is not necessary for
Heavenly Father to marry Mary and then lend her to Joseph.
Mary is still a virgin, and Joseph is her husband — and Jesus is
the Only Begotten of the Father in the flesh.

Until further revelation clarifies the issue, orthodox Latter-
day Saint women are perfectly entitled to believe that Jesus

was conceived by natural law, but that Mary was a true virgin at both conception and birth. Orthodox Latter-day Saint women have every right to believe Heavenly Father has the utmost respect for His daughters and their emotional well-being—especially that daughter, Mary, who became the mother of the Savior of all His other children.

(By the way, my co-author Don Sorensen thinks this addendum is completely unnecessary because he cannot believe that anyone in the Church is being taught this as doctrine. However, he lives in California, and I live in Utah. My own son was taught this in Sunday School in 2000.)

Notes

1. Spoken January 2, 1969; recorded in Clyde J. Williams (ed.), *The Teachings of Harold B. Lee*, Salt Lake City: Bookcraft, 1996, pp. 13-14. I am indebted to Richard Holzapfel for this reference.

About the Authors

Alma Don Sorensen was born in Hyrum, Utah. After serving a mission to the New England states, he earned his B.A. at Utah State University and his Ph.D. at the University of Illinois in political science. His field of study is moral and political philosophy. Sorensen taught at Indiana for six years, and then came to BYU in 1970, where he taught ethics and political philosophy, garnering several teaching awards, including an Alcuin Award. He retired in 1998, but still teaches an occasional class at BYU. Sorensen is married to Necia Lee, and is the father of six children and has twelve grandchildren. He has served as a bishop, branch president at BYU, and has served on a high council, and as a priesthood teacher. He and Necia make their home in Indio, California.

Valerie Hudson Cassler was born in Washington, D.C., and joined the Church in 1971. She attended BYU where she received her B.A. in political science, with minors in International Relations and Russian. One of her BYU professors was Don Sorensen, who greatly influenced her life. She obtained her Ph.D. in political science from Ohio State University. She taught at Northwestern University and at Rutgers University before joining the political science faculty at BYU in 1987, becoming a colleague and neighbor of Sorensen's until his retirement. She served for eight years as director of graduate studies at the David M. Kennedy

Center for International and Area Studies, and is the recipient of several teaching awards, including the Karl G. Maeser Excellence in Teaching Award. She is the author, co-author, or editor of many scholarly books and articles on international relations, national security, and foreign policy. She is married to David Cassler, and they are the parents of six children. They reside in Orem, Utah.